NEOPLATONISM

CLASSICAL LIFE AND LETTERS

General Editor: HUGH LLOYD-JONES

Regius Professor of Greek in the University of Oxford

Cicero   *D. R. Shackleton Bailey*

Homer   *C. M. Bowra*

The Presocratics   *Edward Hussey*

NEO-
PLATONISM

R. T. Wallis

CHARLES SCRIBNER'S SONS
NEW YORK

Contents

To GLYN DAVIES

Foreword

Few of the movements that have shaped Western culture and thought have remained as little known as Neoplatonism. Some reasons for this neglect, and for my belief that it is unjustified, will be found in the final chapter of this book. But two of the basic reasons are simply the difficulty of the Neoplatonic writings and the absence of a satisfactory popular account, the last general study by a single hand being Whittaker's *Neoplatonists* (second edition 1918), which has been largely outdated by recent research. (The more recent *Cambridge History of Later Greek and Early Medieval Philosophy*, a product of several authors, is in many sections too difficult and compressed for the general reader). In such a situation, misconceptions and half-truths remain widespread, on the part of both admirers and critics of the school. To refute these would take a book in itself and, though some of them are dealt with at appropriate points, I have for the most part simply ignored them and concentrated on producing as accurate a picture of the movement as I could.

The defects of my own account others are more likely to notice than myself. One which I particularly regret is the absence of extended quotations from the Neoplatonists' works. But their inclusion would have converted the already difficult problem of summarising Neoplatonic doctrine in a book of reasonably short compass into a quite impossible one. It is hoped that this omission may in future years be remedied by an anthology of relevant texts. It should also be possible in future editions of the present work to include more extended discussions of topics, like the thought of Damascius, whose importance is unquestionable, but whose detailed treatment is hindered by insufficient progress of scholarly research.

My aim has been above all to afford readers some fundamental principles to assist them in penetrating the labyrinth of the Neoplatonists' works. Reference may be made in this connection to the first chapter's discussion of the school's three main aims and to the list on pp. 90–3 of the problems bequeathed by Plotinus to his successors. Here I have tried to show how most of the movement's later philosophical developments follow naturally from points made in the *Enneads*. Inevitably such a procedure runs the risk of over-simplification; that Neoplatonism is not as simple as I have made it appear a perusal of any of its metaphysical writings will show. In the present case, however, over-simplification seemed clearly the lesser of two opposing evils. Similarly the need for brevity has prevented my doing justice to the Neoplatonists' arguments, which generally go far beyond the brief hints I have been able to present. Here again recourse to their actual works is the only remedy. If as a result I have sometimes made them appear superficial—certainly the last defect with which those who know their writings would charge them—I can only claim their posthumous indulgence.

Even so, an account of Neoplatonism is necessarily more difficult than some other books in the present series. A special problem is posed by the school's liberal use of technical terms, generally derived from Classical philosophy, whose English equivalents, such as 'matter' or 'intelligence', tend to be misleading. Here again only the briefest of explanations have been possible. Study of Neoplatonism presupposes some acquaintance with earlier Greek thought and, if time were spent explaining matters whose proper place is a book on Plato or Aristotle, we should never reach the Neoplatonists at all.

Finally, there is the question of my debt to earlier scholars. If I have not always been able to warn the reader where my views differ from those generally accepted, neither have I been able to acknowledge the far more numerous occasions where my account is little more than a summary of my predecessors' work. None the less it seems worthwhile to present a summary of material for the most part available only in specialist studies in French or German, even though the progress of research will rapidly render much of it, especially its post-Plotinian sections, out of date. That the book is not even worse is due to Professors A. H. Armstrong, A. C. Lloyd and J. M. Dillon, Mr. David Esterly, Mr. Andrew Smith and Dr. Yahia Raef, who have read and commented on it, or parts of it, in typescript. I am particularly grateful to Professor Dillon for allowing me to use his unpublished work on Iamblichus. Needless to say none of the above scholars should be taken as endorsing all my views, and for such imperfections as remain I alone am responsible.

Thanks are also due to my typists and to the Faculty Research Council of the University of Oklahoma for undertaking and paying for the typing of the final version of this book; and to the Clarendon Press for permission to reproduce the diagram on p. 152, adapted from E. R. Dodds' edition of Proclus' *Elements*.

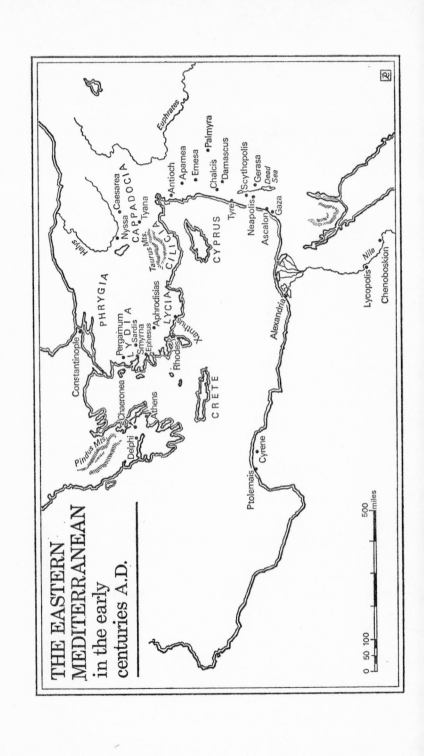

THE EASTERN
MEDITERRANEAN
in the early
centuries A.D.

CHAPTER ONE

The Aims of Neoplatonism

'NEOPLATONISM' is a term coined in modern times to distinguish the form of the Platonic tradition inaugurated by Plotinus (A.D. 204–70) and lasting in its pagan form down to the sixth century A.D. from the teaching of Plato's immediate disciples (the 'Old Academy') and from the Platonism of the earlier Roman Empire ('Middle Platonism'). Among the movement's post-Plotinian developments three periods may be distinguished: first, the teaching of Plotinus' pupils Porphyry (c. 232–c. 305) and Amelius; secondly, the Syrian and Pergamene schools deriving from the teaching of Iamblichus (died c. 326), and finally, the fifth- and sixth-century schools of Athens and Alexandria. The latter school, important mainly for its commentaries on Aristotle, passed in the sixth century into the hands of Christian teachers and was still active when the city was captured by the Moslems in 641; its dominant themes were subsequently incorporated into Islamic philosophy. The Athenian School, on the other hand, being more determinedly pagan, had been closed by the emperor Justinian in 529; its leading members were Plutarch of Athens (died 432),[1] Syrianus (died c. 437), Proclus (412–85), Damascius, head of the Academy at the time of its closure, and Damascius' younger contemporary Simplicius, the Athenian School's most important Aristotelian commentator. Contemporary Christian thinkers, such as the Cappadocians, Augustine and pseudo-Dionysius, were strongly influenced by the school, and the term 'Neoplatonism' is frequently applied both to their teaching and to later attempts to revive the school's leading ideas, such as those of Ficino and Pico at the Renaissance and Thomas Taylor in the nineteenth century. Some account of the school's later influence will be given in the final chapter, but the bulk of the book will be confined to the ancient Neoplatonists and, among these, to the pagans. This restriction is due to limitations both of space and of my own

---

[1] Not to be confused with the more famous Plutarch of Chaeronea, the second-century amateur Platonist philosopher and author of the *Moralia* and the *Parallel Lives*.

competence; it is the less serious since positive Christian influence on Neoplatonism was minimal, though reaction against the professedly Christian Gnostics helped to mould Plotinus' thought, just as his successors felt the need to construct a religious system to counter the growing appeal of Christianity. We shall thus have to provide a brief comparison of the Neoplatonic and Christian world-views (cf. pp. 100–5). It will also be necessary to prefix our account of the Neoplatonists themselves with a discussion of their treatment of Plato and Aristotle and to deal with the more important of their Middle Platonic predecessors.

The aims of Neoplatonism, as thus defined, can best be seen from Plotinus' treatise *On the Three Hypostases* (*Enn.* v. 1). The first part of that work (chapters 2–7) proceeds from an analysis of the world's constituent elements to the postulation of three successively more unified levels of true or divine reality (the three Plotinian 'Hypostases'), those of Soul (*psychē*), Intelligence (*nous*) and the One. Chapters 8 and 9 then endeavour to show that these principles are presupposed by the teaching of the Classical Greek philosophers, though they become fully articulate only in Plato, while chapters 10–12 demonstrate the existence of the Hypostases not just in external nature, but within the human mind (cf. v. 1. 10. 5–6). Corresponding to the three sections into which we have divided the treatise we may distinguish three aspects of Neoplatonism, which we may term respectively its metaphysical, exegetic and religious or experiential aspects. The last of these will need special explanation, since, as we shall see, different Neoplatonists understood it to mean different things; they were, however, unanimous that the theoretical knowledge afforded by the first two approaches was greatly inferior to the direct experience of Reality within one's own mind.

The metaphysical principles on which Neoplatonism rests are most conveniently set out in Proclus' *Elements of Theology*, where the whole Neoplatonic scale of being is systematically deduced from them. Fundamental among them were that the order, and indeed the very existence, of anything depends on its unity (props. 1–6; cf. Plotinus vi. 9. 1. 1–17) and that the cause is always more perfect than its effect (prop. 7). Others we shall discover in due course. These principles were for the most part derived from earlier Greek thought; for instance the axioms concerning unity had been fundamental to Pythagoreanism and Platonism, as later to Stoicism. Hence the school's metaphysics is intimately linked to its exegesis of the earlier philosophers. Indeed, as we shall see, the Neoplatonists regarded themselves as Platonists pure and simple, in the sense of expounding nothing not already present, at least by implication, in Plato's own teaching. The later Neoplatonists tried further to show the presence of the same truths not merely in Aristotle and the earlier Greek philosophers, but in Homer, Hesiod and Greek mythology in general. Two sources were here of outstanding importance, the poems ascribed to Orpheus and the *Chaldaean Oracles*, an alleged divine revelation containing both a theology and a way of salvation. And this brings us to the school's religious aims.

Even those who know nothing else of Neoplatonism are aware that Plotinus was a mystic. 'Mystic', it must be stressed, is here used not in the sense of 'irrationalist', 'occultist' or 'teacher of esoteric doctrine', but in its strict sense of one who believes himself to have experienced union with God or Ultimate Reality. Plotinus' experience of union with the One corresponds to the experience which W. T. Stace[1] calls the 'undifferentiated unity', a state in which sensuous imagery and conceptual thought are transcended, the mind becomes perfectly unified and individual limitations are felt to be abolished. Porphyry states that Plotinus experienced this state four times during the six years of their acquaintance and that he himself had in his old age once attained it (*V. Pl.* 23. 12–18), while Plotinus, in a work written before he met Porphyry, describes himself as having often experienced it (IV. 8. 1. 1 ff.). Where Plotinus differs from most mystics is that for him, as for Plato, the soul's purification is accomplished primarily through philosophy (cf. *Enn.* 1. 3 passim), though like other mystics he regards moral self-discipline as essential (*Enn.* 1. 3. 6. 16 ff., II. 9. 15 etc.) and regards abstract reasoning as of limited value unless it culminates in intuitive vision and finally in mystical union (cf. e.g. VI. 7. 36). Porphyry, however, though still regarding philosophy as necessary for the soul's final salvation, took the not unreasonable view that it was too difficult for the average man; as an easier first step he recommended the practice of theurgy, a system of ritual purification based on a magical view of the universe and derived from the *Chaldaean Oracles* (Augustine *CD* x. 9). And for Iamblichus and the Athenian School it was theurgy which assumed the higher value and which alone could afford full salvation[2] (though the final goal remained, at least in theory,

---

[1] Cf. his *Mysticism and Philosophy* (London 1961) and *The Teachings of the Mystics* (New York 1960) passim.
[2] Iamblichus *Myst.* II. 11, Proclus *PT* I. 25. p. 113. 6–10, Olympiodorus *In Phd.* 123. 3–6.

the mystical union). Hence the later Neoplatonists' stress on the justification of traditional ritual and the explanation of traditional mythology, culminating in the attempt of Julian the Apostate (sole emperor 361–3) to replace Christianity by a revived paganism with Neoplatonism as its philosophical basis.

That Neoplatonism should thus combine aims that appear divergent, if not incompatible, should not surprise us, since the same has been true of several of the greatest philosophies, not least those of the Greek world. Plato's theory of Forms, for instance, is an answer both to the logical problem of universals and to the ethical search for standards of ultimate value, while Aristotle's doctrine of substance has its roots both in logical analysis of the subject-predicate relation and in biological study of the structure of living organisms. But to construct a fully consistent philosophy on this basis is evidently far from easy. Doctrinal disputes among the Neoplatonists were in fact the result either of a different approach to a single one of the three aims we have distinguished or of divergent opinions as to which of them should be given preference where they conflicted. Not infrequently several issues were simultaneously involved; take for instance the complex sources, metaphysical, exegetic and experiential, of Plotinus' account of the Intelligible world, one of the major points of dispute within Neoplatonism (cf. pp. 54–6). If it seems surprising that the Neoplatonists never came to feel the incompatibility of their aims, two points should be remembered. First, as we have noted, most of the school's philosophical principles had already been at least implicit in Plato and Aristotle; hence, despite the perversity of Neoplatonic textual exegesis, Neoplatonic metaphysics could fairly claim at least to provide a logical development and systematisation of some of their fundamental ideas. Secondly, harmonisation of the school's metaphysical and religious aims was facilitated by the association, both in Pythagorean-Platonic tradition and in mystical discipline, of degrees of unity with degrees of perfection. Hence the One of Greek philosophical tradition could be identified with the mystics' 'undifferentiated unity' and the philosopher's ascent, whether through contemplation of the external world or by turning his attention within, could be seen as traversing the same stages.

Yet the result of Plotinus' approach to religious experience was the transposition of Greek philosophy into a new key. This was due not so much to the introduction of the mystical experience itself, which, if not certainly to be found in the Classical Greek thinkers, is present in

religious writings of the pre-Neoplatonic period, notably some of the
Hermetica (e.g. *CH* x. 4–6) and perhaps (though this is disputed) in the
Hellenising Jewish philosopher Philo of Alexandria. The decisive step
was rather Plotinus' identification of metaphysical realities with states
of consciousness. From a psychological point of view, his account of
consciousness forms a remarkable contrast both with Classical Greek
philosophy, which, except for a few passages in Aristotle (*De An.* III. 2.
425b 12 ff., III. 4. 429b 26 ff., *Met.* Λ. 9. 1074b 33 ff.), had barely recognised the concept, and with the Cartesian identification of 'consciousness' with 'thought' or 'mental activity' (cf. pp. 172–3). For Plotinus,
as we shall see, not all thought is conscious; more precisely, our surface
consciousness is only one of several levels of awareness and many
elements in our mental life normally escape our notice. In fact Plotinus'
observations on unconscious mental states form some of the most
fascinating and modern-sounding passages of his works. But what
concerns us here is that in his view it is states of consciousness that
constitute the primary realities, of which material objects are a very poor
imitation. In consequence his three Hypostases may be treated either
statically, as objectively existing realities, or dynamically, from the
point of view of the individual's inner life. The former tendency,
termed 'gegenständlich' by German scholars, corresponds to what we
have called the metaphysical approach to reality; the latter, experiential,
tendency, on the other hand (German 'aktuell'), is most pronounced in
Plotinus' vivid accounts of contemplation of the Ideal world and of
mystical union.[1] Even in Plotinus, however, the two approaches
cannot be sharply separated and in his successors the 'aktuell' element
in its Plotinian form largely disappears; in particular, descriptions of
mystical union become stereotyped and lack Plotinus' immediacy. But
the equation of mental states with metaphysical entities remains basic
for them and generates Neoplatonism's profoundest dilemma. Viewed
as a metaphysical reality each level is real in its own right; viewed as
states of consciousness, on the other hand, the lower levels become
imperfect ways of viewing the true realities contemplated by the higher
ones. This 'illusionist' view of the lower principles could claim further
support from the Platonic tradition's description of them as 'images' of
their priors. And here the question of their reality linked up with that
of their value. As an image of its prior, and therefore imitating that

---

[1] The terms in question were coined in P. O. Kristeller's *Der Begriff der Seele in
der Ethik des Plotin* (Tübingen 1929); cf. also H.-R. Schwyzer, 'Die Zweifache
Sicht in der Philosophie Plotins', *Museum Helveticum I* (1944) 87–99.

prior as well as it can, each level is good and valuable; on the other hand, being merely an image, it is decidedly inferior to that prior and so must be finally transcended. The problem had been posed by Plato's equivocal attitude to the sensible world; it was left for the Neoplatonists to extend it to the whole hierarchy of Hypostases.

Neoplatonism thus stands not as an abandonment of Greek rationalism, but as an adaptation of the categories of Greek thought to the world of inner experience. It was inevitable, however, that such an adaptation should result in the modification, on some points, of the traditional Hellenic conceptual scheme, the most obvious example concerning the status of infinity (cf. pp. 56-7, 148-9). Here the problem arises for the Neoplatonists of reconciling the mystical desire to transcend form and limit with the Classical Greek view of these as the essence of perfection. It is conflicting tendencies of this kind that explain such paradoxes as that a movement that substantially shaped the Renaissance notion of Classicism should have impressed modern scholars with its affinities to the utterly non-classical thought of India.

So far we have presented the conflicts in Neoplatonic thought as arising out of its historical situation and therefore perhaps removable by more careful thought on the part of its proponents. But here we touch on a deeper problem, that the realities with which Neoplatonism dealt were very imperfectly expressible, if expressible at all, in conceptual terms and that in consequence alternative, seemingly contradictory, formulae might appear equally good, and in the last resort equally inadequate. Reality, in short, is impossible to confine within rigid formulae; yet it was just the Greek stress on conceptual precision that the Neoplatonists were unwilling to sacrifice. A further difficulty arose from the necessity for any analysis of mental states to employ language drawn from, and originally intended to apply to, the world of physical objects. Hence, while the problem was most conspicuous on the higher levels of the Neoplatonic universe, especially that of the One, it is also visible, for instance, in Plotinus' alternative attempts to divide Soul into 'levels' (cf. pp. 73-4). The need, in short, was for formulae which were precise and yet not so rigid as to be untrue to living experience. Here Neoplatonism touches on a problem which is finally insoluble and yet which no metaphysical system can ignore. Since the Neoplatonists' historical situation posed this dilemma for them in an exceptionally acute form, their results deserve our special attention.

In its stress on finding reality by turning within, away from the sensible world, Neoplatonism exhibits, in its own distinctive form, the growing otherworldliness that affected all contemporary philosophies and religious movements. It would certainly be wrong to ascribe an otherworldly attitude to the population in general; as always, the hopes, fears and pleasures of both the masses and the aristocracy will have been firmly centred in the material sphere. The period has been more aptly characterised as an 'age of anxiety' or of insecurity, whose fruits manifested on the one hand in the proliferation of saviour cults, like those of Isis and Mithras, and of alleged divine revelations containing the knowledge needed for salvation (for instance the Gnostic systems and the writings ascribed to Hermes Trismegistus), and on the other in the growth of belief in and practice of magic, much of it directed to decidedly this-worldly ends. Both these forces, as we shall see, were to affect Neoplatonism, but in appraising their effect it is vital both to distinguish the Neoplatonic attitude as a whole from that of other movements and to appreciate the divergent views existing within the school itself. Another symptom of the times, reflected in the Neoplatonists' attitude to their philosophical and religious sources, was a greatly increased reverence for the sages of the East and of antiquity. But to treat the period as merely a time of intellectual decline is too simple a view; while science and literature were all but dead, art and architecture certainly were not, and both the Neoplatonists and the best of their Christian contemporaries show that the power to think had not been lost. It is safer to regard it as a time when men's energies were directed to new ends; whether these were better or worse than what had gone before, or merely different, the reader's own preconceptions may be left to decide.

Nor can we speculate here about the new attitude's sociological causes. Some are obvious enough; for instance Neoplatonism's lack of interest in political thought clearly stems from the lack of free discussion imposed by the imperial structure. Other supposed causes should be viewed with more caution; thus to ascribe the new otherworldliness simply to the unsettled political and social conditions prevailing from the third century onwards ignores the fact that the most otherworldly of the Gnostic systems had appeared in the preceding, relatively tranquil century.[1] It must none the less be noted that Plotinus' life fell within the most disturbed period of the pagan empire's history, that between the death of Marcus Aurelius in 180 and the accession of Diocletian in 284, and that the later Neoplatonic systems,

[1] Cf. E. R. Dodds, *The Greeks and the Irrational*, pp. 250–1, and *Pagan and Christian in an Age of Anxiety*, p. 4.

with their rigidly hierarchical structure, coincided with the development, from Diocletian onwards, of a correspondingly rigid hierarchy
among the empire's citizens. For the rest, the Neoplatonists were
relatively well-off by contemporary standards and external events, the
conflict with Christianity apart, have left virtually no trace on their
writings and may therefore be ignored here.

Yet, while the Neoplatonists' otherworldliness was more thorough-
going than that of their predecessors, the notion of philosophy as a way
of life involving the whole man had been basic to Greek thought from
the earliest times. The Neoplatonists' conception of the ideal philosophical life can be ascertained both from their ethical writings (for
instance some of those making up Plotinus' first Ennead or Porphyry's
letter to his wife Marcella) and from their disciples' accounts of their
lives. Our surviving biographical sources number four. The best
known are Porphyry's *Life of Plotinus* and the biography of Proclus by
his pupil and successor Marinus. The *Lives of the Sophists* by the
rhetorician Eunapius of Sardis deals with Porphyry, Iamblichus and
the latter's disciples, while Damascius' biography of his teacher Isidorus
(regrettably extant only in fragments) digresses at incredible length to
deal with most of the leading personalities of the Athenian and
Alexandrian schools. All these sources stood close in time to their
subjects (even Eunapius having had contact with Iamblichus' disciples)
and there seems little reason to doubt their accuracy on most matters of
fact. Unfortunately they all suffer to a greater or less extent from three
defects. First, as any reader of Porphyry's *Life of Plotinus* is aware (cf.
p. 37), they display irritating silences on crucial points; secondly, they
exhibit a predilection for the marvellous and miraculous; thirdly, they
aim less at a historical picture of their subject than at depicting him as a
model of all the philosophical virtues. This hagiographical tendency is
especially pronounced, and quite openly avowed, in Marinus (*V. Pr.* 2,
etc.), whose description of his master shamelessly pillages phrases from
the *Enneads* and from Porphyry's *Life of Plotinus*, while Damascius'
eulogy of Isidorus contrasts amusingly with his vivid depiction of the
foibles and failings of other late Neoplatonists.[1] At times, however,
their subjects' idiosyncrasies emerge against their will; Marinus, for
instance, has to acknowledge Proclus' quick temper (*V. Pr.* 16). The

---

[1] Cf. his epigrammatic comments on Hypatia (quoted below p. 141) and
Hierocles (cf. p. 143); also *V. Is.* 62 and fr. 115 (on Theon), 74 (on Hermeias),
144 (on Marinus), 221 (on Hegias), fr. 227 (on Domninus), fr. 316 (on Ammonius).

miraculous element is most pronounced in Eunapius' work, where it entirely obscures his subjects' role as theoretical philosophers; one should remember that he is the only one of the four who was not a philosopher himself. By contrast Porphyry's *Life of Plotinus* is much more restrained and affords a powerful, if somewhat idealised, picture of the impression made by a great philosopher on his contemporaries. But here we are concerned with the general picture of the Neoplatonic philosophical life these sources provide.

The theoretical basis of that life was laid down by Plotinus and will be discussed in connection with his philosophy. Here we need merely correct mistaken impressions that might arise from a careless reading of our sources; we can be the briefer since the task has recently been admirably performed by P. Hadot, who observes, for instance, that Porphyry's statement that Plotinus 'abstained from the bath' (*V. Pl.* 2. 5–6) means not that he never washed, but that he avoided the distractions of the public bathing establishments.[1] What should be stressed for those disconcerted by Porphyry's remark that his master 'seemed ashamed of being in the body' (*V. Pl.* 1. 1–2) is the mildness, by Manichaean and even some contemporary Christian standards, of Neoplatonic asceticism. Why this was so our account of Plotinus will show (cf. pp. 82 ff.); to its underlying cause we have already alluded, namely the Platonic view of the material world as an image of its ideal archetype. Hence the body is not seen as an enemy, the keynote remains Hellenic moderation and self-discipline rarely turns into self-torture. Excesses of course occurred; it is more than doubtful whether the school can be blamed for Julian's notorious indifference to hygiene (*Misopogon* 338c), but Damascius provides a number of examples, for instance the extremely unladylike shock-tactics used by the Alexandrian philosopher-martyr Hypatia to discourage a would-be suitor (*V. Is.* fr. 102). But while the general Neoplatonic attitude to sex was, to say the least, very different from that of our own day, it was none the less equally opposed to that of Manichaeism. That sexual relations have value only for procreation had been implicit in Plato and was common ground for most moralists of late Antiquity. And the *Symposium*'s doctrine that the sexual energy is more profitably directed towards the Ideal world provided a strong incentive to total celibacy. Plotinus himself never married, though his circle included married men and widows. Porphyry married the widow of a friend late in life and

[1] *Plotin*, pp. 105–16. On contemporary asceticism in general cf. E. R. Dodds, *Pagan and Christian in an Age of Anxiety*, pp. 29–36.

then only to care for her and her children (*Ad Marc.* III, Eunapius *VS* 457). In the later school, on the other hand, marriage became more common, with Proclus a notable exception (*V. Pr.* 17). Also remarkable was the school's rejection of the homosexuality of Classical Greece; Plotinus was shocked by a defence of the Platonic Alcibiades (*V. Pl.* 15. 6–17) and tacitly drops even Plato's conception of a sublimated non-physical relationship between philosophers (cf. p. 86), while Proclus' interpretation of Socrates' love for Alcibiades has more in common with Christian *agapē* than with Platonic *erōs* (cf. p. 154).

A similar attitude was taken to the question of vegetarianism. Plotinus himself abstained from meat (*V. Pl.* 2. 1–5), but the *Enneads* never mention the point, though Porphyry composed a treatise on the subject (the *De Abstinentia*). Later Neoplatonists had more difficulty, since animal sacrifice, involving consumption of part of the victim, was a feature of many of the traditional rites they wished to defend. Here again Proclus' attitude was stricter than that of most of his contemporaries and caused concern on his teachers' part for his health (*V. Pr.* 12); at sacrifices, however, he consented to taste a little meat for the sake of the ritual (ibid. 19). The Neoplatonic attitude to such points thus remained flexible and far removed from extreme asceticism.

Closer attention to our sources is apt indeed to raise doubts of an opposite kind. When we learn that Plotinus had full use of the large mansion of a wealthy widow (*V. Pl.* 9) or reflect on the revenues on which the Athenian Academy could draw in its last years (*V. Is.* 158, fr. 265, Olympiodorus *In Alc.* 141. 1–3), we may wonder whether the Neoplatonists' otherworldly protestations do not contain a tinge of hypocrisy. Against this we should recall that Plotinus' most determined affirmations of the philosopher's serenity come in the treatises written in his last two years, when his pupils had left him and he was dying of a painful disease. Nor, with persecution by the Christians an ever-present threat, was life without its problems for his later followers. And while the school had of course no doctrine of social service, the philosopher was expected to perform such tasks as came his way and show kindness to those he met. Once again Plotinus provides the best-known example, in his kindness (often involving very practical advice) to his friends and in particular his care for the welfare of the children bequeathed to his charge by senators on the point of death and impressed by his rectitude (*V. Pl.* 9. 5 ff.). From the later period we may quote such cases as the Alexandrian Hermeias' insistence on paying a fair price to booksellers ignorant of the value of their wares (*V. Is.* 74, fr. 122). But perhaps the best evidence is the fact that in an age when men were apt to seize on any scandalous charge to hurl at their opponents, the Neoplatonists' Christian adversaries could generally find nothing worse than 'impiety' and 'arrogance' with which to charge them.[1] There are exceptions; for instance Maximus of Ephesus, Julian's spiritual director, became notorious for his ambition and luxury (Eunapius *VS* 476–80). On the whole, however, we may conclude that, like most ancient philosophers, the Neoplatonists were concerned to practise what they preached and succeeded as well as most both in using resources well and in facing adversity with fortitude.

The effects of the new otherworldliness on theology were likewise profound. Its aim was now first and foremost to afford man security through knowledge of his true nature and destiny, a destiny no longer confined, as in Stoicism and Epicureanism, within the sensible cosmos. Hence the revival in the new systems of Plato's body-soul dualism and their stress on the remoteness of the supreme God from this world, with which many of them, however, sought to combine the cosmic piety of Stoicism. But it was in knowledge of the supreme God that salvation was now regarded as consisting, a knowledge expressible only inadequately, if at all, in conceptual terms. The result was the rise of negative theology, the doctrine—common to mystical systems the world over—that words can tell us only what God is not, never what he is. A further result was the introduction of subordinate intermediary powers to bridge the vast gulf between God and the cosmos. In the Alexandrian Jew Philo this function is fulfilled by the Logos and the divine powers, in Platonists by the World-soul of Plato's *Timaeus* and in popular writers by the daemons, semi-divine spirits, who might be either good or evil, and whom Plato had described as mediators between gods and men (*Symp.* 202E, *Epin.* 984E). The multiplication of intermediate hypostases was carried to its greatest extent in some of the Gnostic systems and, as we shall see, in post-Iamblichean Neoplatonism.

The effects of these trends on the Neoplatonists' philosophical predecessors will be briefly discussed in our next chapter. Here we need merely issue a warning against blanket terms characterising the above developments that ignore the important divergences between the theological schools of late Antiquity. A term of this kind popular during the nineteenth century was the 'School of Alexandria', a label

---

[1] Porphyry, however, had to face the charge that his marriage was prompted by mercenary motives (*Ad. Marc.* 1).

grouping the Neoplatonists with Jewish and Christian thinkers resident at Alexandria and exhibiting similar tendencies, notably Philo, Clement and Origen. Use of this term obscures the facts, first that the thinkers in question were never members of a single common school and second that the only Neoplatonists based at Alexandria after Plotinus himself were the fifth- and sixth-century scholars to whom we have referred, who were of all Neoplatonists the least influenced by such other-worldly religious tendencies. For these reasons the term is now generally and rightly abandoned.

A more dangerous term, and one still commonly used, is 'Gnosticism'. The trouble with this term is that it has two senses, one broader and the other narrower and more precise. The former application is very similar to, though rather wider than, that of the term 'School of Alexandria', embracing, as it does, all the religious systems of the early centuries A.D. which sought salvation through knowledge or 'gnosis'. In its strict sense, however, the term denotes a group of systems, the majority of those known to us maintained by Christian heretics, and all of them opposed to Neoplatonism in that the 'knowledge' they sought was the product, not of philosophical reasoning, but of revelation by a divine saviour. And while on the doctrinal side it may be the resemblances between Gnosticism and Neoplatonism that impress a modern reader, matters appeared very differently to Plotinus, as we can see from the polemic composed by him against some Gnostics who had infiltrated his school (*Enn.* II. 9; cf. *V. Pl.* 16). Most important was their view of the material world as the work of an evil, or at best ignorant, creator, himself the result of a fall within the spiritual hierarchy (II. 9. chs. 4, 10–12). Their refusal to reverence the material world as a divine creation and their excessive complaints against the body were bad enough (cf. ibid. chs. 8, 16–18); far worse were their abuse of its creator and their denial of divinity to the World-soul and the heavenly bodies (ibid. ch. 5. 1–16, etc.). Hardly less objectionable were the Gnostics' disparagement of Plato, from whom, in Plotinus' view, they had derived everything of value in their doctrine, and their refusal to put forward their own views by reasoned argument instead of in the form of anthropomorphic and melodramatic myths (ibid. chs. 6 passim, 10. 5–14, *V. Pl.* 16. 8–9). Finally, there was their view of themselves as saved by nature, which led them to neglect moral discipline and even (in the antinomian Gnostic schools) to give themselves over to vice (II. 9. 15 passim, 17. 27–9). The existence of significant resemblances between the two systems Plotinus admits, explaining them (on the whole correctly) as the result of borrowing from Plato (II. 9. 6. 6 ff.). And we must remember that both Platonism and Gnosticism were heterogeneous movements; Numenius of Apamea's dualism, for instance, came very close to Gnosticism on many points (cf. pp. 33–35), while conversely not all Gnostics took as unfavourable a view of the creator as Plotinus' opponents.[1] None the less in the light of such divergences as his polemic reveals, and especially the two movements' contrasting evaluations of philosophy and revelation, the classification of Neoplatonism as a form of Gnosis, even when no more than a general 'Gnostic tendency' is claimed, would seem to cause more confusion than it is worth.

In conclusion we must consider the vexed question of 'Orientalism'. The view, common in the nineteenth century and still often defended, that Neoplatonism marks the capitulation of Greek philosophy to Oriental influences, gains in plausibility when we consider the nationalities of the school's leading members. For instance the seven 'Greek philosophers' who went to Persia on the closure of the Academy include a Syrian, two Phoenicians, a Gazaean and three natives of Asia Minor (a Cilician, a Phrygian and a Lydian) (cf. Agathias *Hist.* II. 30). Plotinus' alleged Egyptian birth may be doubtful (cf. p. 37), but Iamblichus' and Damascius' very names betray their Syrian origin,[2] while Porphyry was a Phoenician from Tyre, his Greek name being a translation of his Semitic name Malchus (*V. Pl.* 17.6 ff., Eunapius *VS* 456). Even Proclus, though born in Constantinople, was by descent a Lycian from the city of Xanthus (*V. Pr.* 6), while his biographer and successor Marinus was a Samaritan from Neapolis (modern Nablus) in Palestine (*V. Is.* 141). But before this is taken as proof of 'Oriental degeneracy' we should recall, first, that Alexander's conquests had long ago established Hellenism as the culture of the educated classes throughout the Near East, secondly, that the proportion of Greek and Oriental blood in the citizens of those lands during our period is impossible to determine, and thirdly that it was the areas in question (Asia Minor, Syria and Egypt) that formed the most civilised parts of the Roman Empire and, with contemporary India and China, constituted one of the three major civilised areas of the globe.

The question of Orientalism decomposes on examination into three questions. First, does Neoplatonism involve abandonment of the Greek

---

[1] Cf. J. Zandee, *The Terminology of Plotinus and of Some Gnostic Writings, Mainly the Fourth Treatise of the Jung Codex*, Istanbul 1961, esp. pp. 24–6.

[2] Syrianus, however, despite his name, was by birth an Alexandrian.

tradition of rational, critical thought? Secondly, were any of its main
doctrines or practices of Oriental origin? Thirdly, can the distinctive
tone of Neoplatonism as opposed to earlier thought, on which we have
commented, be ascribed to Oriental influence? To the first question
alone the answer seems clear, and that answer, if our analysis is correct,
is 'no'. We have just noted Plotinus' criticism of the Gnostics' refusal
to state their position rationally and we shall find other Neoplatonists
taking a similar stand against the Christian appeal to faith (cf. p. 101).
The position is less clear-cut as regards Iamblichus and his followers;
yet, even when philosophy had at their hands acquired a more avowedly
theological purpose, the philosopher was still obliged, as Proclus'
Elements shows, to demonstrate its truth on rational grounds. Iamblichus' demand that philosophical and theurgic matters must be kept
separate (*Myst.* I. 2, II. 11 p. 96. 6–10) prevented the swamping of
philosophy by religion, while his *De Mysteriis* was to offer a rational
justification even of theurgic ritual. Nor did the Neoplatonists' recognition of a realm transcending conceptual thought—a view they shared
with Plato, Kant and Wittgenstein—involve any slackening of critical
rigour within the bounds of reasoning or in determining those bounds.
As evidence of their opposition to treating mysticism as an excuse for
irrationalism, Plotinus' declaration that 'to set oneself above Intelligence is to fall away from it' (II. 9. 9. 51–2) is echoed by that of Isidorus
that 'those who would be gods must first become men' (*V. Is.* 227). To
demonstrate this is one of the objects of our account.

Our second and third questions are much less easy to answer. From
their earliest days Greek philosophy and science had drawn freely on
the ideas of the Near East, which they had habitually given new
meaning by organising them in a conceptual system hitherto lacking,
and it is therefore to be expected that the Neoplatonists should have
done the same. Whether we can determine exactly where this has been
done is another question; allegedly Oriental doctrines have been
generally shown to be explicable in terms of earlier Greek thought, and
it is only those which explicitly conflict with traditional Hellenic ideas,
as does, for instance, Numenius of Apamea's view that evil is present in
the celestial spheres,[1] for which an Oriental origin can be plausibly
inferred. Claims by the Neoplatonists themselves of an Oriental origin
for their ideas are more often to be explained as a reading of Pythagoras
or Plato into the Oriental sages. The case is a little happier as regards
some of the later Neoplatonists' theurgic practices; for instance the

[1] Cf. p. 35 and A. H. Armstrong, *Entretiens Hardt V*, p. 53.

Egyptian origin of 'telestic', the magical animation of a divine statue, seems fairly securely established.[1] But the philosophical concepts by which theurgy was justified appear to be mainly Greek; Ptolemy and others had similarly justified Chaldaean astrology in terms of Greek scientific theory.

The picture is, if anything, even murkier as regards our third question. It seems certain, however, that only Indian thought bears sufficient resemblance to Plotinus' introspective mysticism to be taken seriously as a possible source. It has been shown on the one hand that cultural contacts were quite possible both before and during our period, on the other that Plotinus' views could have arisen simply by reflection on earlier ideas, notably the Aristotelian account of Intelligence, in the light of his own experience. And the tendency of the mystical experience to express itself in similar ways at all times and in all civilisations must also be taken into account. But it is doubtful whether all the resemblances between the similes used by Greek and Indian writers can be explained in this way; for instance the Neoplatonic comparison of divine activity to the effortless and unpremeditated radiation of light by the sun is also widespread in Indian texts.[2] But a final verdict on such points must await future research and it cannot, of course, be assumed that any borrowings must have been on the Greek side. In the meantime, though parallels between Greek and Indian thought deserve serious study, Neoplatonism must be treated as a development of the preceding Greek tradition. It is that tradition, and the Neoplatonists' use thereof, that will form the object of our second chapter.

[1] Cf. E. R. Dodds, *The Greeks and the Irrational*, pp. 293–4. For an attempt to distinguish Platonic and Oriental elements in the *Chaldaean Oracles* cf. H. Lewy, *Chaldaean Oracles and Theurgy*, chs. 6–7, pp. 311–441.

[2] Cf. for instance the use of this and other similes to illustrate the unpremeditated nature of the Buddha's activity by the Tibetan writer Gampopa (*Jewel Ornament of Liberation*, ch. 21, trans. Guenther, pp. 271–4), following the Indian Buddhist philosopher Asanga (*Uttaratantra IV*, 58–60). The sun simile recurs in the modern Hindu mystic Ramana Maharshi (*Collected Works*, p. 46). For another parallel cf. E. Bréhier, 'Les Analogies de la Création chez Çankara et chez Proclus', *Etudes de Philosophie Antique*, pp. 284–8. For a survey of scholars' views on possible connections between Plotinus and Indian thought, with full bibliographical references, cf. J. F. Staal, *Advaita and Neoplatonism* (Madras 1961), pp. 235–49.

CHAPTER TWO

The Sources of Neoplatonism

BEFORE we consider Neoplatonism's philosophical sources it may be desirable both to remind readers of the doctrines whose source we are seeking and to clarify the sense in which the term 'sources' is being used. Attentive readers will in fact observe that our approach differs somewhat from one part of this chapter to another. In the first part our concern will be with the Neoplatonists' use of Plato, Aristotle and, to a lesser extent, the Stoics, with a view to pinpointing both those doctrines which they actually derived from those sources and those which they believed themselves justified in inferring from them. But the scanty remains of the Neoplatonists' immediate predecessors prevent our doing the same in their case. The latter part of the chapter will therefore be primarily concerned with significant anticipations by them of Neoplatonic ideas, without in most cases attempting to decide exactly which Neoplatonic doctrines derive from each individual thinker.

The main doctrines whose source we are seeking have already been summarised in Plotinus' theory of the three levels of Reality, or 'Hypostases' (cf. p. 2). The first or highest of these is the formless, ineffable principle known as the One or the Good; next comes Intelligence, a timeless, self-contemplating divine mind containing the Platonic Forms (or 'Ideas'); finally, mediating between eternity and time, there is Soul, producer and orderer of the sensible cosmos, which in its turn constitutes an image of the Forms cast by Soul on the formless substratum of Prime Matter. A full explanation of the above terms must be reserved for our chapter on Plotinus; for the present we are concerned with their origin in earlier thinkers.

That Plotinus' contemporaries, notably the scholar Longinus, were impressed by his originality, Porphyry's *Life* makes clear (*V. Pl.* chs. 17, 19–20). Proclus similarly recognises him as having inaugurated a new development in the Platonic tradition (*PT* I. 1 p. 6. 16 ff.). But this originality Plotinus himself regarded not as a totally fresh departure, but as a restoration of Plato's own doctrine, which previous interpreters had distorted. Reference may be made on the one hand to his use of the single Greek word *phēsi* ('he—i.e. the master—says') in reporting Plato's words, on the other to his rebuke to the Gnostics for abandoning Platonic teaching (*Enn.* II. 9. 6. 24–8, *V. Pl.* 16. 8–9).[1] In later times Augustine's praise of Plotinus as 'a man in whom Plato lived again' (*C. Acad.* 3. 18) is well known. And while the later Neoplatonists rejected some of his interpretations, they did not doubt the sincerity of his intentions. Their own reverence for Plato was such as to lead Proclus to describe his philosophy as a divine revelation to men (*PT* I. 1. p. 5. 6 ff.); as such it must, of course, be reconciled with other revelations, notably the *Chaldaean Oracles*. The latter will be discussed in a later chapter; here it is the Neoplatonists' philosophical sources that concern us. Inevitably the Neoplatonists' attitude to those sources will appear more monolithic than it really was, but we shall try to give due attention to at least the major differences between Plotinus' approach and that of his successors.

That many Neoplatonic doctrines had not been explicitly propounded in the Platonic dialogues, but were drawn from Aristotle and the Stoics, the Neoplatonists themselves were well aware. Porphyry for instance refers to the presence in the *Enneads* of 'hidden Stoic and Peripatetic (i.e. Aristotelian) doctrines' and claims in particular that they incorporate a condensation of Aristotle's *Metaphysics* (*V. Pl.* 14. 4–7). But, convinced as they were that all important truth had been discovered by Plato, they strove, wherever possible, to extract such doctrines from hints dropped in obscure passages of the dialogues or in Aristotle's account of Plato's oral teaching. Such an attitude had a powerful traditional sanction, as we shall see in considering cases like those of Antiochus of Ascalon (p. 28) and Albinus (p. 30) among the Neoplatonists' forerunners. Apparent contradictions between the dialogues, for instance regarding the problem how the soul enters the body (*Enn.* IV. 8. 1. 27 ff.), must similarly be explained away. At such points Plotinus apparently regards Plato in the same light as he regards Heraclitus of Ephesus, the celebrated 'riddler' of antiquity, as an intentional propounder of enigmas leading us to seek the truth for ourselves. This at least is what both his incidental comments on the two thinkers and his general treatment of Plato suggest.[2]

That the Neoplatonic Plato is far from being the whole Plato is clear

---

[1] Cf. also III. 7. 1. 13–16, v. 1. 8. 10–14, VI. 2. 1. 4–5, VI. 4. 16. 4–7.
[2] Cf. for instance IV. 8. 1. 11–17 (on Heraclitus) with v. 8. 4. 51–4 (on Plato).

even from a casual comparison. Plotinus' Plato omits Plato's mathematical and political interests (though Plotinus recommends the
practice of mathematics and had himself a full knowledge of the subject,
Enn. I. 3. 3. 5–10, *V. Pl.* 14. 7–10) and ignores the early Socratic
dialogues' inconclusive search for ethical definitions. The mathematical
interest recurs in later Neoplatonism, sometimes in the form of number
mysticism, but also including serious research on the foundations and
scientific application of mathematics; a good example is Proclus'
defence of Plato's geometrical conception of physical matter.[1] But the
other two limitations remained. And the Neoplatonists were similarly
selective with regard to some of the doctrines they did retain. Thus the
theory of Forms, as we have remarked (p. 4), had been designed to
answer both the logical problem of universals—justifying, for instance,
the use of the common term 'beautiful' by the assumption that all
particulars legitimately so designated 'imitate' or 'participate in' the
eternal Form of Beauty—and the need for ideal standards in ethics and
aesthetics; finally in the *Timaeus* they had provided the model on which
the mysterious Divine Craftsman (or 'demiurge') shapes the sensible
world.[2] That the requirements of the theory's various aspects conflict
had been seen by Plato himself; thus the logical theory requires Forms
wherever a common term is used (*Rep.* 596A) and hence of such things
as hair, mud and dirt, which are absurd on the aesthetic theory (*Parm.*
130C–D). The Neoplatonists' answer was to concentrate on the Forms'
aesthetic and cosmological functions at the expense of their role as
universals and to jettison Forms that conflicted with these aspects of the
theory.[3] They thus achieved a separation between logic and ontology
that was ultimately of immense benefit to both; though Plotinus rated
Aristotelian logic poorly in comparison with Plato's dialectic (*Enn.* I.
3. 5. 10 ff.), later Neoplatonists were thereby enabled to produce a logic
rather surprisingly less restricted by ontological commitments than
Aristotle's had been.

---

[1] Discussed by S. Sambursky, *The Physical World of Late Antiquity*, pp. 44–61;
cf. also T. Whittaker, *The Neoplatonists*, appendix 3, pp. 225–8, and S. Breton,
Philosophie et mathématiques chez Proclus (Paris 1969, dealing primarily with
Proclus' extant commentary on the first book of Euclid's *Elements* and including a
French translation of an essay on the same subject by N. Hartmann).

[2] On the theory's various aspects cf. R. C. Cross and A. D. Woozley, *Plato's
Republic: a Philosophical Commentary*, pp. 180–95.

[3] Cf. Albinus *Epit.* IX. 2, Plotinus *Enn.* V. 9. 10–14, esp. 14. 7 ff., Syrianus *In
Met.* 105–8, Proclus *In Parm.* 730–2, 815–38. On Neoplatonic logic cf. A. C.
Lloyd, 'Neoplatonic and Aristotelian Logic', *Phronesis I* (1955–6) 58–72, 146–59,
and *Cambridge History of Later Greek and Early Medieval Philosophy*, pp. 319–22.

To see what is left of Plato, we may usefully refer to two lists of dialogues, the former that provided by Henry of the works most quoted by Plotinus,[1] the latter the official curriculum of works prescribed by Iamblichus for reading in the later school. The former list runs: *Timaeus, Republic, Phaedo, Phaedrus, Symposium, Theaetetus, Philebus, Sophist, Parmenides.* The latter, in the order prescribed for reading, is as follows: *Alcibiades I, Gorgias, Phaedo, Cratylus, Theaetetus, Sophist, Politicus, Phaedrus, Symposium, Philebus, Timaeus, Parmenides* (*Anon. Prol.* 26). The disciple was thus supposed to proceed from simpler to more difficult dialogues until he reached the two dialogues which Iamblichus regarded as containing the whole of Plato's philosophy, the *Timaeus* dealing with physics, the *Parmenides*, as we shall see, with theology (*Anon. Prol.* 26. 13–16, Proclus *In Tim.* I. 13, *PT* I. 8. p. 32. 14–18). The *Republic* and *Laws* were excluded from the curriculum by Proclus on account of their length, the *Letters* because of their style (*Anon. Prol.* 26. 6–8), though he recognised the importance of some sections of them, for instance, the theological discussions in *Laws* X and *Republic* II (*PT* I. 5. p. 24. 20–3, cf. ibid. I. chs. 13–21). The *Alcibiades* and *Gorgias* were introduced to provide the necessary ethical basis for the course; Plotinus had several times referred to the most important passage of the *Alcibiades* (129–30), identifying man with his soul. A notable difference between the two lists is the importance assigned by later Neoplatonists to the *Cratylus*, whose discussion of language accorded with their logical interests, and whose account of divine names—concerning which the school displayed its usual blindness to Plato's irony—was vital to theurgy. For the rest (except for the *Politicus*) the two lists are identical.

Prominent in both lists, as we should expect, are the metaphysical dialogues of Plato's middle and later periods, the *Phaedo, Phaedrus, Symposium* and, especially, the *Timaeus*. It is these that form Neoplatonism's genuinely Platonic substratum in their discussions of the theory of Forms, the immortality and destiny of the soul, the ascent to the Intelligible world through Love and the *Timaeus'* account of the divine formation of the sensible cosmos and the soul animating it. The *Republic* contributes the further important idea that the Forms' existence depends on a more ultimate principle, the Form of the Good. But construction of a systematic philosophy on the basis of these dialogues encounters the difficulties, recognised by the Neoplatonists,

[1] Introduction to MacKenna's translation p. xxxix n. 2; cf. Schwyzer *RE* article 'Plotinos', col. 551.

that on many points Plato is silent, while on others his remarks seem contradictory. Two problems are of outstanding importance. First, how is Soul related to the Forms and, more particularly, how is the *Timaeus*' Divine Craftsman (or 'demiurge') related to his Ideal model and to the *Republic*'s Form of the Good? Since the majority of Neoplatonists agreed in identifying the Craftsman with Aristotle's divine Intelligence (cf. Proclus *In Tim.* I. 299–319), the problem for them concerned that principle's relation to the Forms on the one hand and the One on the other. Secondly, how does the *Timaeus*' doctrine of the sensible world's goodness square with the *Phaedo*'s insistence on the body's harmful effects, and is the soul's presence here the result of a divine mission (*Timaeus*) or of a moral lapse (*Phaedrus*)? The Neoplatonists had of course no conception of a development in Plato's thought, nor would this have removed, though it would have mitigated, the latter difficulty; as we have observed (pp. 5–6), the ambivalent status of the sense-world is a problem inherent in Platonism. Two other problems posed by the *Timaeus* that had vexed Plotinus' Middle Platonic predecessors, whether Matter is a principle independent of God and whether the cosmos had a temporal beginning, were unanimously answered by the school in the negative.

Insofar as they try to fill such gaps modern scholars turn to the accounts of Plato's oral teaching in Aristotle's *Metaphysics*. These accounts were certainly not without influence on Neoplatonism, for instance in shaping Plotinus' doctrine of Intelligible Matter (cf. p. 66) and the later schools' treatment of Limit and Infinity (pp. 148–9). But they are subordinated to what the modern mind regards as much more dubious sources, most important among them being the *Parmenides*. The first part of this dialogue, exhaustively discussed in recent years, propounds a series of objections to the theory of Forms. First, there is the problem, already referred to, of the extent of the world of Forms. Then there is the question how we should understand Plato's description of particulars as 'participating' in the Forms; for it seems equally absurd to regard the Form as simultaneously present in its entirety in each of the particulars it characterises or alternatively to suppose it cut into parts distributed among those particulars (*Parm.* 131A–E). Thirdly, should we regard the Forms as ideal particulars; e.g. is the Form of Man a perfect man? An affirmative answer once again generates absurdities; how, for instance, can the Form of Magnitude be itself a magnitude, if Forms have no spatial dimensions (cf. 131C–E)? Yet what other explanation can be given of the alleged resemblance of particulars to the Forms (132D–133A)? The Neoplatonists were to devote much space to these questions; for example, the basis of their answer to the second of them was Plato's tentative suggestion that the Forms might resemble the day in being simultaneously in many places (131B), an idea developed at length in one of Plotinus' most impressive treatises (*Enn.* VI. 4–5).[1] But it was the much more problematical second part of the dialogue that they regarded as containing Plato's profoundest teaching (*Enn.* V. 1. 8. 23–7, *PT* I. 7–12).

In this part of the work Parmenides, starting from the hypothesis 'that there is a One', first 'proves' that if its absolute unity is to be upheld, nothing, not even existence, can be predicated of it, and then, by a reverse procedure, that if the One exists (i.e. partakes of existence), all predicates can be ascribed to it. The third and fourth (or, as the Neoplatonists regarded them, fourth and fifth) hypotheses similarly deduce contradictory consequences from the existence of a One for what are enigmatically called 'the other things', while hypotheses five to eight go on to derive similar contradictions from the non-existence of the One, first for the One itself, then for 'the others'. In the pre-Plotinian period there had been much debate whether the series of hypotheses contained metaphysical teaching or was merely a logical exercise (Proclus *In Parm.* 630 ff., *PT* I. 8); among those taking the latter view was the influential Middle Platonist Albinus (*Isag.* ch. 3). It was only Plotinus' authority that secured victory for the former position, though the interpretation he offered was, as we shall see, traditional. In Parmenides' first hypothesis (137C–142A) he discovered his supreme One, describable only in negative terms; the denial of existence he linked with the *Republic*'s reference to the Good as 'beyond Being' (509B). His Second Hypostasis, Intelligence, he saw described in the *Parmenides*' second, affirmative, hypothesis (142B–155E), while the last part of this hypothesis, dealing with becoming in time (155E–157B), was chopped off and elevated into a separate hypothesis of its own, dealing with the Third Hypostasis, or Soul. The same triad of realities Plotinus saw alluded to in an obscure passage of the *Second Platonic Letter* (312D–313A), while his Second Hypostasis, combining Plato's Intelligible world with Aristotle's self-thinking Intelligence, he saw prefigured in the *Timaeus*' reference (30C ff.) to the world's Ideal Model as an 'intelligible living creature' and in the *Sophist*'s ascription to True Being of motion, life, and intelligence (248E–249D).

---

[1] On the resemblance of particulars to the Forms cf. *Enn.* I. 2. chs. 1–3; on Ideal Magnitude cf. below p. 49.

The *Sophist* (254D ff.) was also the source of Plotinus' defence of the five Platonic 'categories' (Being, Rest, Motion, Identity, Difference) as alone applying to the Intelligible world in place of Aristotle's ten, a point on which we shall find later Neoplatonists taking issue with him.

Plotinus' followers were also faced with the task, which he had not attempted, of extending the Neoplatonic interpretation of the *Parmenides* through the whole series of hypotheses. Proclus records explanations by Amelius, Porphyry, Iamblichus and an otherwise unknown 'philosopher from Rhodes' (*In Parm.* 1052–8),[1] but it was not until Plutarch and Syrianus, the founders of the Athenian School, that a generally acceptable interpretation was found (ibid. 1058–64), and the place of the *Parmenides* vindicated as Plato's systematic treatise on theology. Of this we shall have more to say in due course.

Our account of the *Parmenides* has already brought out the major difference between Plotinus' treatment of the dialogues and that of his successors, that Plotinus makes no attempt to interpret the whole of Plato's text, but confines his attention to a limited number of the best-known passages from his works. Thus his discussions of the *Republic* deal almost entirely with the central, metaphysical books and the Myth of Er and, even within these limits, his quotations are very restricted. An even more extreme case is the *Theaetetus*, represented almost entirely by Plato's well-known affirmation of the necessity of evil and the need to escape by seeking assimilation to God (176A–B). Anthologies of such passages were in common use at the time and have clearly left their mark on Plotinus, though it is hard to believe that he had not read the whole of Plato, especially in the light of the careful study of Aristotle that the *Enneads* exhibit. Equally high-handed is Plotinus' treatment of difficulties in the Platonic text. Thus confronted with apparently contradictory declarations as to whether the earth has a soul, he devotes all his attention to determining the 'reasonable view' of the matter (IV. 4. 22. 5–13), the assumption being that Plato's view will not contradict the reasonable one. Typically, once the reasonable view is discovered, it is reconciled with Plato's text by a far-fetched interpretation of the latter; take, for instance, Plotinus' explanation of the *Philebus'* inclusion of pleasure in the good life (*Phil.* 21D–E, cf. *Enn.* VI. 7. chs. 25. 1–16, 30 passim). With Plotinus' attitude his successors, committed as they were by their more scholastic temperament to the task of commenting at least the 'select' dialogues in full, could not rest

[1] On the authors of the interpretations discussed by Proclus cf. Saffrey and Westerink, *Théologie platonicienne I*, pp. lxxx ff.

content. Nor, however, could they ignore the fact that even those dialogues contain much that conflicts *prima facie* with the Neoplatonic interpretation and many passages dealing with topics like politics in which they were not particularly interested. Porphyry's explanation of such points was felt to be insufficiently systematic and it was left for Iamblichus to formulate elaborate principles of interpretation by which the above difficulties could be circumvented. Since these principles depend on Iamblichus' metaphysical views, they will be discussed in connection with those views.

This said, however, it may be well to issue a warning against treating the Neoplatonists' interpretation of Plato as totally worthless. It was Proclus, after all, who suggested to modern scholars the correct interpretation of *Timaeus* 35A on the construction of the World-soul, and there are numerous points on which so un-Neoplatonic a modern commentator as Cornford has to invoke his authority. From the *Enneads* reference may be made to Plotinus' refutation of the Stoicising interpretation of *Philebus* 30A–B as making individual souls parts of the World-soul (*Enn.* IV. 3. 7). And, if the Neoplatonic interpretation of the *Parmenides* is unacceptable, Proclus' refutation of the view of its second part as a mere logical exercise is devastating (*PT* I. 9). For the rest, if the Neoplatonists' interpretation of their sources seems wearisome and frequently childish, we should recall that its effects were immensely beneficial in preventing the Neoplatonists, as it prevented the Medieval Scholastics after them, from remaining a mere carbon copy either of the Classical philosophers or of one another. In short, in an age dominated by authorities, it was only on this basis that genuinely original thought was possible.

It was a much-debated question both before Plotinus and for long afterwards how far Plato and Aristotle could be represented as in agreement. That there was no essential difference was a plausible view as long as Aristotle was known mainly through his early, more Platonic writings and one which received considerable support even after interest shifted to his 'mature' school works, as was predominantly (though not entirely) the case for the Neoplatonists. In the face, as we shall see, of conflicting Middle Platonic opinions, Plotinus attempted to steer a middle course. On the one hand he accepted several of Aristotle's basic principles, notably his conception of Intelligence, much of his psychological vocabulary and his analysis of reality in terms of the matter-form, potentiality-actuality antitheses, though even these points were generally not left unmodified; thus for Plotinus 'potentiality'

(*dynamis*) has more commonly the active sense of 'power' than
the passive one of 'susceptibility to change', which had been more
usual in Aristotle (cf. II. 5. 3. 19–22, V. 3. 15. 33–5 and below p. 60).
On the other hand he regarded Aristotle as having perpetrated serious
errors. In logic his categories were inapplicable to the Intelligible world
(VI. 1. 1–24) and even in the sensible world his list of ten could be
pruned to five (VI. 3. 3); his psychology made the soul inseparable from
the body (IV. 7. 8⁵), his ethics made happiness dependent on external
prosperity (I. 4. 5 ff.), and his theology failed to recognise the need for a
principle beyond Intelligence (V. 6. 2–6, VI. 7. 37–42, etc.). But the
difference between Plotinus' attitude to Aristotle and his attitude to
Plato can perhaps best be seen from his treatment of two problems in
natural philosophy. The treatise II. 1 is a defence of the view of the
heavens as composed of pure fire, a view equally in conflict with Aristotle's theory that they are composed of a fifth element and with the
implication of the *Timaeus* that their fire is mixed with earth (*Tim.* 31B,
40A). But whereas Plotinus devotes two chapters (II. 1. 6–7) to
reconciling the *Timaeus* with his own position, Aristotle's view is
dismissed in a mere three lines (ibid. 2. 12–14). A similar contrast
characterises his discussion of the two philosophers' definitions of time
(III. 7. chs. 9, 12–13, esp. 13.9 ff.). It is a remarkable consequence that
Plotinus' discussions of Aristotle show a much closer acquaintance with
his text and a much better understanding of his thought than do those
of Plato. Indeed some of his criticisms of Aristotle, notably of his
alleged plurality of Intelligences (V. 1. 9. 7–27) and of his distinction
between motion (*kinēsis*) and activity (*energeia*) (VI. 1. 16), anticipate
the conclusions of modern scholarship.

To the later Neoplatonists, however, Plotinus' attitude to Aristotle
seemed too severe. Porphyry wrote a work (now lost) to demonstrate
Aristotle's agreement with Plato (Elias *In Isag.* 39. 6 ff.) and his defence
of Aristotle's categories against his master's attack was to remain
definitive for the later schools (Simplicius *In Cat.* 2. 5 ff.). Iamblichus'
attitude seems to have been even more accommodating (cf. Elias *In Cat.*
123. 1–3). On the whole Aristotle was regarded as the supreme master
in logic and (with the *Timaeus*) in natural philosophy, and in the school
curriculum study of his treatises formed a preliminary to the reading of
the Platonic dialogues, the supreme authority in metaphysics (cf. Elias
In Cat. 123. 7–11). Awkward points like Aristotle's polemics against
the Forms could be evaded by supposing these to refer only to the
sensible world or to misunderstandings of the theory (cf. e.g. Asclepius

In Met. 69. 17 ff., 166. 24 ff.); the reader will have noted their absence from our list of Plotinus' criticisms. But whether the two philosophers were in full agreement remained a matter for debate. As a later chapter will show, the Athenian School tended to take a more reserved attitude towards Aristotle than their Alexandrian contemporaries.[1] In fact Aristotle's criticism of the Forms was bitterly attacked by both Syrianus (*In Met.* 80. 4 ff.) and Proclus (cf. Philoponus *Aet. M.* II. 2. 31. 7 ff.), who composed a work answering Aristotle's objections to the *Timaeus* (*In Tim.* I. 278–9, Simplicius *De C.* 640. 20 ff.). On the whole we may say that, despite their Platonising bias, the school's surviving Aristotle commentaries are superior, *as an interpretation of their source's actual meaning*, to its commentaries on Plato. But the school's greatest service to modern scholars in the historical field is, of course, Simplicius' preservation, in his commentaries, of numerous fragments of the Presocratics that would otherwise certainly have been lost.

The Stoics must be dealt with more briefly. Their influence on Plotinus is most conspicuous in his conception of the sensible world as a living organism, developing from the seed-principles (*Spermatikoi Logoi*) within the World-soul and with an organic harmony (or 'cosmic sympathy') linking all its parts. His theodicy (*Enn.* III. 2–3) similarly takes over many of their arguments. The Stoics, however, go wrong on two fundamental points, first in making the World-soul the highest deity and secondly in conceiving even Soul in material and spatial terms (cf. p. 50). In fact by treating God and the Soul as modes of matter, the Stoics commit the cardinal error of making the more perfect ontologically posterior to what is less so (*Enn.* II. 4. 1. 11–13, IV. 7. 4, 8³, VI. 1. 26–27; cf. V. 9. 4. 3–12). Similarly in ethics, while the Stoic conception of the sage contains much of value, notably in making happiness independent of external goods, the school erroneously sees man's highest end in moral action in submission to the Fate governing the sensible world instead of in contemplation of the Intelligible order, to which his true self belongs (cf. pp. 82 ff.). Plotinus' vitalistic conception of the Intelligible world also seems to owe much to the Stoics; scholars disagree exactly how much (cf. p. 55). But Stoic influence certainly underlies his advocacy, in contrast to Plato and Aristotle, of the existence of Forms of individuals (cf. p. 54).

The Epicurean influence on Neoplatonism is by contrast minimal. It

---

[1] Cf. Damascius *V. Is.* 35–6, Proclus *In Parm.* VII. 73. 10 ff., and below pp. 143–4. From an earlier period cf. Julian *Or.* v. 162c.

is most pronounced in the theological field, where the Neoplatonists have to answer Epicurus' objection that exercising providence would be a burden for the gods (*Enn.* IV. 4. 12. 39 ff., Sallustius *DM* IX. 3, Proclus *PT* I. 15 p. 74. 17 ff.) and where Plotinus turns the Epicurean question whence God can have derived the idea of making a world (Lucretius V. 181–6) against the doctrine of a deliberate creation (*Enn.* V. 8. 7. 1–12). But the criticisms of the Sceptics, formulated largely by the Academic Carneades (213–129 B.C.), were more important. Their influence on Neoplatonism is fundamental on at least three points, the relation of knowledge to its object, the doctrine of impassibility and the distinction of divine wisdom from its human counterpart. With regard to the first point, the Sceptics appealed to the basic difficulty confronting any empiricist epistemology. In the typical Greek account of sensation the soul receives 'impressions' from external objects and it is these impressions that form the object of her knowledge. Hence her knowledge is confined to the images of external objects, and how far these resemble their originals must remain unknown (Sextus *PH* II. 72–5, *Math.* VII. 191–8, 357–8, etc.). And all knowledge must be of the external, for self-knowledge in the strict sense is impossible; all that is possible is knowledge of one part of the self by another part (*Math.* VII. 310–12). Hence Plotinus' concern to answer the first objection by placing the Forms within Intelligence (V. 5. 1–2) and his defence, in answer to the second, of self-knowledge in the sense maintained by Aristotle (V. 3. 1. 1–14, 5 passim).

The problem of impassibility brings us to Carneades' theological criticisms. All living beings, he argued, God included, must be subject to substantial change (for instance the modification of the sense-organs involved in sense-perception) and to emotional disturbance; but susceptibility to change entails susceptibility to destruction (Sextus *Math.* IX. 138–47, Cicero *ND* III. 29–34). Whether or not the argument applies to God, its applicability to the human soul is obvious and persuaded the Stoic Panaetius of the latter's mortality (Cicero *Tusc.* I. 79). Hence the object of Plotinus' doctrine of the impassibility of incorporeal beings was to defend their immortality by exempting them from change in either of the two offending senses (cf. *Enn.* I. 1. 2. 9–13, III. 6. 1. 28–30). Carneades further took over Aristotle's argument excluding moral virtue from the gods on the grounds that such virtue presupposes either a human type of society or the mastery of unwholesome tendencies inconsistent with divine perfection (*EN* X. 8. 1178b; cf. Sextus *Math.* IX. 152–77, Cicero *ND* III. 38–9). Carneades' contribution was to extend the argument to practical wisdom. The latter involves skill in deliberation; but deliberation is a search for information of which one is initially ignorant and cannot therefore be ascribed to God (*Math.* IX. 167–73, *ND* III. 38). To the reply that God does not have to deliberate since he is omniscient by nature, Carneades counters that in that case his operations will be indistinguishable from those of Nature (*physis*), the unconsciously purposive force to which Aristotle had made over the sublunary world and which he had seen best exemplified in the teleological operations of the lower animals and plants (*Phys.* II. 8. 199a 20–30). The order which for a Stoic proves the world's divinity could just as well be due to Nature, Carneades argued, as to an intelligent God, for to regard the world's excellence as proof of its rationality is as anthropomorphic as assigning it the art of grammar (Cicero *ND* III. 21–8, *Ac. Pr.* 121, Sextus *Math.* IX. 108). Hence Plotinus' concern to formulate a conception of divine wisdom which avoids both horns of the dilemma (IV. 4. 12–13; cf. below p. 63).

Of the results of the Sceptical challenge two concern us here. Since Chrysippus' Stoicism had shown itself too vulnerable to the Sceptical attack, the first was a revival of interest in Plato and Aristotle, a process further boosted by Andronicus' publication during the first century B.C. of Aristotle's school treatises. The second was a closing of the ranks by the rival schools (the Epicureans alone excepted) in the face of the common enemy, in the conviction that what united them was more important than their divisions. This attitude gained strength from the increasing pressure on philosophy to teach a dogmatic way of salvation, and could manifest in one of two forms. Popular philosophers tended to propound an eclectic philosophy combining what was felt to be the best of Platonism and Stoicism (along with less important Aristotelian elements), a combination found, along with Jewish, Egyptian and Gnostic ideas, in the Hermetic corpus, a series of treatises composed during the early centuries A.D. by Greeks resident in Egypt in the form of a revelation by the Egyptian god Thoth, under his Greek name of Hermes Trismegistus (Thrice-Greatest Hermes). A similar eclectic mixture is applied by the Jewish writer Philo of Alexandria (*c.* 25 B.C.–*c.* A.D. 50) to the interpretation of the Old Testament and by Justin Martyr (*c.* 100–65) and Clement of Alexandria (*c.* 150–215) to the formulation of Christian theology. All these authors are important as evidence for ideas that were in the air at the time, but, since their influence was exercised in Christian circles or, in the case of the *Hermetica*, at the Renaissance, they fall outside the scope of this book.

The second reaction, manifested by professional philosophers committed to one or the other school, was to borrow ideas from their rivals to buttress the weak points of their own system. Such borrowings were often unacknowledged owing to the conviction that, if all philosophers agreed, the ideas in question must already be implicit in one's own school. The most extreme example was that of Antiochus of Ascalon (*c.* 130–68 B.C.), who restored dogmatic teaching in Plato's Academy after a period in which Scepticism had been dominant. Maintaining that Plato, Aristotle and Stoicism, if correctly understood, were in essential agreement, he taught as Plato's a doctrine far more Stoic than Platonic.[1] More generally, Platonists would incorporate Aristotle's logic and his account of Intelligence, Stoics tended towards a more Platonic psychology and Peripatetics (the Aristotelian school) tried to find in Aristotle some recognition of divine providence. Our survey will show examples of all three procedures.

Among Stoics such tendencies are especially pronounced in Posidonius of Apamea (*c.* 130–46 B.C.). We know that his admiration for Plato led him to explain some passages of the *Timaeus* (Sextus *Math.* VII. 93, Plutarch *Procr. An.* 22, 1023B), while Plotinus opposes his interpretation of *Phaedrus* 245–6 that only the World-soul is immortal (Hermeias *In Phdr.* 102, *Enn.* IV. 3. 1. 33–7, 7. 12–20). He must therefore be responsible for much of the Platonising Stoicism in Cicero and late Stoic writers, notably Seneca, and underlying many passages of Plotinus. But reconstructions of his thought can only be speculative and the view that he turned Stoicism in a more otherworldly direction finds little support in texts referring to him by name (though cf. Seneca *Ep.* 92. 10). The only part of his philosophy on which we are well informed is his psychology, thanks to the quotations from his work incorporated in Galen's *Precepts of Hippocrates and Plato*. In place of the traditional Stoic conception of a unitary rational soul, in which emotional disturbance is identified with a false judgment, Posidonius returned to Plato's view of the soul as divided into rational, spirited and appetitive parts (Galen op. cit. 405. 9 ff.). Here he followed Plato more closely than the Neoplatonists, who treated Plato's tripartite division as merely a classification of motives for the purposes of moral philosophy and hence as of limited application.[2] More important for Plotinus was Posidonius' stress, following Aristotle (*De An.* I. 1.

---

[1] Cf. Sextus *PH* I. 235, Cicero *Ac. Pr.* 69–70, *Ac. Post.* I. 43, *ND* I. 16, etc.

[2] Porphyry, quoted by Stobaeus *Ecl.* I. 350. 19–25, Iamblichus, quoted ibid. 369. 9–12, Proclus *In Remp.* I. 233. 25–8; for Plotinus cf. below p. 74.

403a–b) on the influence of man's bodily constitution and of the climatic and other forces shaping the former on his irrational soul (Galen op. cit. 442. 7 ff., Plutarch *De Lib.* ch. 6). Of these researches Plotinus' psychological works make abundant use (cf. pp. 74–5).

We must now turn to the second-century A.D. Platonic and Aristotelian commentators whom we know to have been read in Plotinus' school, and of whom Porphyry provides a list, which is certainly not meant to be exhaustive (*V. Pl.* 14. 10–14). It is also a representative selection of the commentators mentioned by later Neoplatonists and includes the names, among Platonists, of Severus, Cronius, Numenius, Gaius and Atticus and, among Peripatetics, of Aspasius, Alexander of Aphrodisias and Adrastus. Of the latter group Alexander is by far the most influential and the only one whose doctrine we know relatively well. First there is his systematisation, in his treatise *De Anima* ('On the Soul') and in the essays collected under the title *De Anima Mantissa*, of Aristotle's psychology. Here Alexander sets his face firmly against the Stoics' corporealist view of the soul in line with his bitter criticisms of the Stoa in other treatises; and some of his arguments, for instance his denial that the soul is spatially present in the body, are echoed by Plotinus (cf. *De An.* 13. 9 ff., *Enn.* IV. 3. 20). But Alexander insists equally, against the Platonists, that soul, as the 'form' or 'actuality' of its body, is inseparable from that body (*De An.* 17–21). Of particular importance was his interpretation of Aristotle's Active Intelligence doctrine. The Active Intelligence, which he identifies with God, he regards as operating on the human mind in its role as the supremely Intelligible object. He agrees with Aristotle that this must be a form which is independent of matter; and since in Aristotelian doctrine thought and its object are identical, it follows that by thinking of God we attain identity with him and so come to share in his immortality (*De An.* 87–91, *Mant.* 106–10). Here Alexander's very clear formulation of the doctrine of the identity of Intelligence with its object was a major influence on Plotinus' account of the Intelligible world. Also of importance was Alexander's treatment of providence, now being recovered from works preserved only in Arabic. Like Aristotle he regards God's only operation on the world as that of inspiring love of himself in the celestial spheres. But unlike Aristotle he regards God as knowing and approving the general features of the world-order due to him. Hence providence is neither deliberately contrived by God nor merely an incidental consequence of his self-contemplation (*Quaest.* II. 21). But that God should know all the world's infinite details is in

Alexander's view impossible, since neither the infinite nor the contingent, the existence of which he defends against Stoic determinism, is a possible object of knowledge (*De Fato* 200. 12 ff., *Met.* fr. 36 Freudenthal). Here Alexander posed a formidable problem for later theologians (cf. pp. 56, 149–50, 165).

Evaluation of Plotinus' Middle Platonic sources is made difficult by the fact that not a single complete work survives by any of the Platonists in Porphyry's list. The position would not be greatly altered were that list complete, since almost our only surviving Middle Platonic writings are those of popular philosophers like Plutarch of Chaeronea and Maximus of Tyre among the Greeks and Apuleius, better known for his novel *The Golden Ass*, among the Latins; of these only Plutarch is mentioned by the pagan Neoplatonists and almost entirely for his notorious view that the world had a temporal beginning. All these writers are, however, of value in enabling us to reconstruct the general Middle Platonic world-picture, and to them must be added the anti-Christian polemicist Celsus, whose treatise has been substantially preserved in Origen's refutation. It seems best, however, to concentrate here on a few systems of Middle Platonists whom Plotinus and his successors are known to have taken seriously.

Of the authors in Porphyry's list we know next to nothing of the doctrine of Gaius. Two short works survive, however, by his pupil Albinus, who taught at Smyrna in the second century A.D. and had among his pupils the well-known physician Galen of Pergamum; these are the *Isagoge*, an introduction to Plato's dialogues, and the *Epitome* or *Didascalicos*, a summary of Albinus' interpretation of Platonic doctrine. The major influence on Albinus is Aristotelian; this leads him to ascribe to Plato (without acknowledgment) the whole of that philosopher's logic (*Epit.* ch. VI). It also underlies Albinus' identification of his Supreme Deity with Aristotle's self-contemplating Intelligence (who is further identified with Plato's divine Craftsman and with his Form of the Good). But he also hints that God may really transcend Intelligence and his stress on the Supreme Deity's ineffability (on which, however, he is once again equivocal) rather prefigures Plotinus' One (*Epit.* ch. x). That God transcends Intelligence was more emphatically proclaimed by Celsus (Origen *C. Cels.* VII. 45). Of the theory of Forms Albinus accepts a common Middle Platonic interpretation first found, among extant authors, in Philo of Alexandria (*Op. M.* 5), which makes the Forms the thoughts of God, and thus partially anticipates Plotinus' combination, in his Second Hypostasis, of Plato's Forms with Aristotle's

Intelligence (*Epit.* ch. ix). The Supreme Deity Albinus describes as ordering the World-soul by arousing it to contemplate his own perfection (*Epit.* x. 3); like most other Middle Platonists he denies that Matter and the World-soul are produced by God, but he anticipates Neoplatonism in denying that the world had a temporal beginning (*Epit.* xiv. 3). Stoic influence on his thought, though subordinate, is pronounced, for instance in the Stoicising language of his account of Plato's view of knowledge as Recollection (*Epit.* iv. 6). Lastly we may note that the mystical side of Platonism is almost wholly lacking in Albinus, a good example being his interpretation of *Theaetetus* 176B's exhortation to seek assimilation to God through virtue. This cannot mean the Supreme Deity, Albinus argues, for he transcends virtue; the goal of our assimilation should rather be the World-soul (*Epit.* xxviii. 3), a view attacked by Plotinus, who denies that even the World-soul exercises the moral virtues and argues that virtue can assimilate us to a God beyond virtue (*Enn.* i. 2. 1. 5 ff.).

In contrast to Albinus, Atticus is the leading anti-Aristotelian among the Middle Platonists. Prominent among the objects of his attack is Aristotle's alleged confinement of providence to the celestial spheres, a doctrine Atticus regards as worse than that of Epicurus; against Aristotle's view of the sublunary world as governed by irrational Nature (cf. p. 27), Atticus endorses Plato's insistence that the world is planned by divine reasoning and his identification of 'Nature' with 'rational soul' (Eusebius *PE* xv. 5. 798C ff., xv. 12. 814A ff.; cf. *Laws* x. 892A–C). Others of his criticisms concern Aristotle's denial of virtue's self-sufficiency for happiness (Eusebius xv. 4. 794C ff.), his view of the heavens as composed of a fifth element (ibid. xv. 7. 804B ff.), his psychology, which denies the soul's immortality and, Atticus charges, comes close to denying its existence (ibid. xv. 9. 808D ff.), and his rejection of the Forms (ibid. xv. 13. 815A ff.), which Atticus, unlike Albinus, places on a level inferior to the Divine Craftsman (Proclus *In Tim.* i. 431. 14–20), though he agrees with Albinus in identifying the latter with Plato's Form of the Good (ibid. i. 305. 6–16). Finally there was Aristotle's denial of a temporal beginning of the world (Eusebius xv. 6. 801C ff.). Atticus' literal interpretation of the *Timaeus* as teaching such a beginning and his location of the source of evil in a pre-existing disorderly World-soul are points on which he agrees with Plutarch, with whom his name is frequently linked by their Neoplatonic critics (cf. Iamblichus quoted by Stobaeus i. 374. 21 ff., Proclus *In Tim.* i. 276. 30 ff., 381. 26 ff., etc.). Some of Atticus' criticisms of

Aristotle are identical with those we have noted in Plotinus, but his unrestrained anti-Aristotelianism and his anthropomorphically literal interpretation of Plato's theology are points on which he and the Neoplatonists are irreconcilably opposed. Despite his 'fundamentalist' approach to Plato, Atticus exhibits fairly strong Stoic influence, notably in his stress on the ethical bearing of Plato's philosophy. Stoic influence of another type seems to have been prominent in Severus, to judge from our scanty information about his teaching; for instance he interpreted Plato's *Politicus* literally as teaching the Stoic doctrine of a series of world-periods (or 'cosmic cycles'), each of which repeats the same events in identical form (Proclus *In Tim.* 1. 289. 6 ff.). That the Stoicisers formed an influential group among the Middle Platonists the *Enneads* make clear, since the Stoic influences on Plotinus are obviously mediated through their writings, while he frequently criticises Platonists whom he judges too influenced by Stoic materialism. The loss of their writings is therefore particularly to be deplored.

Another influential school during the early centuries A.D. was that of the Neopythagoreans (who would, of course, have rejected the 'neo-' prefix as vehemently as the Neoplatonists.) Some of the representatives of the Pythagorean revival were primarily ascetics and miracle-workers and made no contribution to theoretical philosophy; best known of this group was Apollonius of Tyana, whom a later generation of pagans tried to set up as a rival to Christ. Others, such as Nicomachus of Gerasa (*fl. c.* 150 A.D.), were primarily concerned with mathematics and number-mysticism; in Nicomachus' *Theological Arithmetic* (partially preserved in Photius *Bibl.* 187 and imitated by Iamblichus) numbers are identified with the traditional Hellenic gods. Nicomachus' works received much attention in the later Neoplatonic schools and Proclus even believed himself to be his reincarnation (*V. Pr.* ch. 28). Neopythagoreanism's metaphysical doctrines are not easily distinguished from those of Middle Platonism and some of its representatives, like Numenius of Apamea, are indifferently assigned by our sources to both schools (*T.* 4–5). It is, however, interesting, though probably coincidental, that the closest anticipations of Plotinus' doctrine known to us among his predecessors were propounded by Neopythagoreans or Platonists under strong Pythagorean influence. One of the closest of all is the system ascribed by Porphyry (quoted by Simplicius *Phys.* 230. 34 ff.) to the first century A.D. Neopythagorean Moderatus of Gades. This anticipates Plotinus first in regarding Matter as produced by God, secondly in teaching the doctrine of three divine Hypostases (identified respectively, as in Plotinus, with the One beyond Being, the Intelligible world and Soul) and thirdly in apparently deriving these from Plato's *Parmenides*. Indeed Moderatus' interpretation of that dialogue seems more elaborate than that of Plotinus in that it covers the first five (affirmative) hypotheses, the object of the fourth being identified with the forms in Matter and the fifth with Matter itself (cf. p. 145). That Matter is produced by the One had been earlier maintained within Pythagoreanism before the first century B.C. (cf. Diogenes Laertius VIII. 25) and was accepted by the Pythagoreanising Platonist Eudorus of Alexandria (*fl. c.* 25 B.C.) (Simplicius *Phys.* 181. 10 ff.). But most important of all was Numenius of Apamea, whose doctrines Plotinus was accused of plagiarising, with the result that his pupils had to write a defence (*V. Pl.* 17 ff.). For this reason, and because Numenius is now commonly recognised as the most important and influential thinker of the second century A.D., he deserves special attention.[1]

Numenius' most striking anticipation of Plotinus lay first in maintaining the existence of three divine principles (*T.* 24 = Proclus *In Tim.* I. 303. 27 ff.), and secondly in correlating the second and third of these with two distinct levels of mental activity, those respectively of intuitive and discursive thought (*T.* 25 = Proclus *In Tim.* III. 103. 28–32). As we shall see, he differs from Plotinus in not placing his first God beyond Intelligence, but the tone of his account of the vision of that God (fr. 11 = Eusebius *PE* XI. 22. 543B ff.) prefigures Plotinus' accounts of mystical union.[2] Even more important is a passage of Iamblichus, which, as we shall see, is fundamental for the understanding of Neoplatonism (*T.* 33 = Iamblichus *De Anima*, quoted Stobaeus *Ecl.* I. 365. 5 ff.). Here Numenius is described as having maintained the doctrine, fundamental to Neoplatonism, that among incorporeal realities 'all is in all, but in each appropriately to its nature', which he interpreted as entailing the presence of the whole Intelligible world within each individual soul. This latter interpretation of the doctrine, as we shall see, was accepted by Plotinus and his pupils, but rejected by Iamblichus, who regarded it as denying any fundamental difference of rank between different classes of souls (cf. pp. 119–20). Iamblichus similarly objected to Numenius' further conclusion that in her pure state the soul is indistinguishable from the Intelligible principles whence

---

[1] Our meagre information about Cronius, the fifth Platonist in Porphyry's list, suggests that his doctrine was very similar to that of Numenius.

[2] But Numenius' use of the phrase 'alone with the alone' (cf. *Enn.* VI. 9. 11. 50–1, etc.) is probably not significant, since it was a commonplace among ancient religious writers.

she derives (*T.* 34 = Stobaeus I. 458. 3–4). Here again Plotinus and
Porphyry, despite their protestations, were judged by their successors
to have followed Numenius too closely.

Plotinus departed, however, from Numenius' view of the first God
as an Intelligence, more precisely as 'Intelligence at rest' (whereas the
second God is 'Intelligence in motion'). With apparent inconsistency he
is identified with the *Timaeus*' 'ideal animal' (the sensible world's
Intelligible model) and called 'Being itself', yet is also described as
prior to Being and Form (cf. *T.* 25, frs. 24–6). The solution may be
that Numenius, like some later Neoplatonists, regarded the Forms as
pre-existing in unmanifested form in the First Hypostasis, whence they
are brought forth by Intelligence (Proclus *In Parm.* 1106–8). Certainly
we shall have occasion to note the influence of this side of Numenius'
theology in the Porphyrian school (cf. p. 117). Unlike Albinus and
Atticus Numenius distinguishes Plato's Good (whom he identifies with
his first God) from his Craftsman (identified with his second God) (frs.
25, 28–9). The former is said to contemplate by making use of the latter
(*T.* 25); hence, though essentially inactive (fr. 21 = Eusebius *PE* XI. 17.
537C), he is able indirectly to take part in shaping the cosmos. Hence
though Numenius anticipates Plotinus' doctrine of 'undiminished
giving', that creation causes no diminution of substance in the divine
Hypostases (fr. 23 = Eusebius XI. 18. 538C ff.), he does not use it, like
Plotinus to exempt the gods from attention to their products (cf. pp. 62–
63). This emerges even more clearly in his views on the second and third
Gods.

Indeed for Numenius it is less a question here of two Gods than of
two phases of the same God (fr. 20 = Eusebius XI. 17. 536D ff.), the
higher of which remains in perpetual contemplation, while the latter
proceeds to order the sensible cosmos. Hence while the first God is
concerned solely with the Intelligible world, the second has a double
activity, being concerned with both sensibles and Intelligibles. But this
in its turn seems to be true only at one phase of the world's evolution; at
another he is said to revert wholly to contemplation (frs. 21, 24–5).
Just as the first God uses the second to contemplate, so the latter uses
the third God (his own lower phase) to shape the sensible world. And,
though he unifies Matter, the latter in its turn 'splits him' (presumably
into the two phases referred to) and, while the transcendent contemplation of his higher phase is described in terms Plotinus could not have
bettered (fr. 27 = Eusebius XI. 18. 539C–D), his lower phase is said not
merely to give deliberate attention to the sensible cosmos (fr. 21 =

Eusebius XI. 17. 537C–D), but as a result to 'become forgetful of himself' and to cease to dwell in the Intelligible world (fr. 20 = Eusebius XI. 17. 537A–B). The implication that Matter can affect a divine being for the worse and rob it of Intellectual contemplation was too offensively Gnostic for Plotinus, who uses significantly similar language in describing the fall of the human soul, whose relation to its body he carefully contrasts with that of the World-soul (IV. 3. 17. 21–31, cf. p. 79).

Numenius' view of Matter and the sensible world was also unacceptable to the Neoplatonists. Opposing the monists of the Neopythagorean school, he regards Matter as existing independently of God and (unlike Plutarch and Atticus) identifies it with Absolute Evil (*T*. 30 = Chalcidius *In Tim*. CCXCV ff.). From these two opposing forces, whose conflict is permanent and does not, as in Plutarch and Atticus, terminate in an eventual harmony, originate the two conflicting souls, rational and irrational, within man (*T*. 35–6 = Iamblichus *De An*. 350. 25 ff., 374. 24–5). Numenius is thus the most extreme dualist among the Middle Platonists, and it is a natural corollary that he should regard embodiment as always an evil for the soul (*T*. 40 = Iamblichus *De An*. 380. 14–19). He adopts the view, common among late Stoics and Platonists, that the soul descends into this world through the planetary spheres, in which she acquires successively greater degrees of impurity and a successively denser 'astral body'. A passage in the Latin Neoplatonist Macrobius, which is probably based on Numenius, speaks of pure souls as inhabiting the heaven of the fixed stars and ascribes their descent here to a subconscious attraction towards this world, an anticipation of Plotinus' speculations on the unconscious (*In Somn. Sc*. I. 11. 10 ff. = T. 47; cf. *Enn*. IV. 4. 3–4). Numenius' account of the soul's descent was used by Porphyry in his essay *On the Cave of the Nymphs* and other works now lost, and later influenced Proclus' *Republic* commentary and that of Macrobius on Cicero's *Somnium Scipionis* (cf. *T*. 42–7). But none of them could accept Numenius' view that the matter of the planetary spheres, and hence the soul derived from them, was evil (*T*. 30 = Chalcidius CCXCIX; contrast *Enn*. I. 8. 5. 30–4, II. 9. 8. 34–6), and Oriental influence here seems hard to question. Certainly Numenius, like many contemporary philosophers, believed in the Oriental origin of Greek philosophy; in particular he had some knowledge of the Old Testament, and to him is due the description of Plato as 'Moses talking Attic'.[1]

---

[1] *T*. 1, fr. 10 (= Clem. Alex. *Strom*. I. 22, Eusebius *PE* IX. 6. 411A); cf. *T*. 46, frs. 9, 18–19, 32.

It will thus be apparent that Numenius' thought was a major stimulus to Plotinus, both where the latter accepted his doctrine and where he reacted against it. On Porphyry and his school his influence was even more profound, while much of Iamblichus' doctrine marks a reaction against his teaching. Thanks to Macrobius and to the summary of Numenius' doctrine on Matter in Chalcidius' Latin commentary on the *Timaeus*, his influence was to last into Medieval times.

The death in 180 of the philosopher-emperor Marcus Aurelius marks a turning-point in ancient philosophy, as well as in ancient history. Chairs in philosophy for all four of the traditional schools (Platonists, Peripatetics, Stoics and Epicureans) had been established by Marcus at Athens, but by the end of the second century all but Platonism were a spent force. The few Stoics of whom we hear in the next century are mere names, and Epicureanism similarly vanishes into obscurity. In the fourth century we find the Peripatetic school represented by the Aristotelian paraphrases of the rhetorician Themistius, in which Neoplatonic influence is relatively small. But only Platonism possessed sufficient depth to meet the age's spiritual needs and, after Plotinus had assured it a firm intellectual basis, the doom of the other schools was sealed. Not that the Plotinian version of Platonism was by any means universally accepted; in particular it was not until the fifth century that the Athenian Academy, home of the official 'successors' to Plato, capitulated to its influence. But of rival versions of Platonism we know little. The story of Greek philosophy from the third to the sixth century is the story of Neoplatonism, and it is to this that we must now turn.

CHAPTER THREE

Plotinus

I. LIFE AND WRITINGS

WITH the possible exception of one point, all our factual information about Plotinus' life comes from Porphyry's biography, which is included in all modern editions and translations of the *Enneads*. Unfortunately, while Porphyry is a first-hand source, his reticence on many points, and especially concerning the period before he joined Plotinus' school, is extremely irritating to the modern reader. According to Porphyry this stems from Plotinus' indifference to his earthly circumstances, which led him to keep silent about them (*V. Pl.* 1. 1–4, 2. 37–40). But the obscurities in Porphyry's account even of such events as he does relate are hardly less exasperating; however, since modern discussions are available of such points, notably in the two most recent English accounts of Plotinus, we can deal briefly with most of them. The only statement about Plotinus in our ancient sources which may be true and which is not found in Porphyry concerns his birthplace, which Porphyry says he never mentioned, but which later writers name as Lycopolis (modern Asyût) in Upper Egypt (Eunapius *VS* 455, David *In Isag.* 91. 23. ff.; cf. Proclus *PT* 1. 1 p. 6. 19–20). The source of this information none of these authors reveals, and its reliability is therefore questionable. Nor is the point of much importance, for, whatever Plotinus' birthplace or racial origin—and these are, of course, two distinct questions—his culture is thoroughly Greek and his philosophy seems free of any significant Egyptian influence. Of Egyptian religion indeed he shows less knowledge than Plutarch, and a famous passage misinterprets hieroglyphic symbolism (v. 8. 6. 1 ff.). From Porphyry's information we may fix Plotinus' birth in A.D. 204 or 205 and his death in 270 (*V. Pl.* 2. 29–31). For the rest Porphyry records only a single incident in his master's life, until, at the relatively late age of 28, he took to philosophy, trying one after another of the professors at Alexandria and returning disillusioned from them all, until someone directed him to a Platonist called Ammonius, to whom later authors give the nickname 'Saccas', of uncertain interpretation.

On hearing him Plotinus exclaimed, 'That is the man I was looking for!' and stayed with him for the next eleven years (*V. Pl.* 3. 6–21).

Of the teaching of Ammonius, who wrote nothing (cf. *V. Pl.* 20), very little is known, though many imaginative conjectures have been made, and we cannot therefore say exactly why he impressed Plotinus, though we may guess that he surpassed his rivals both in intellectual power and in putting his philosophy into practice.[1] A quotation from Porphyry in the Church historian Eusebius (*EH* vi. 19) states that he had been brought up a Christian, but later abandoned Christianity, and that the Christian theologian Origen (A.D. 185–254) was one of his pupils. Doubts are, however, raised about this information by inaccuracies both in the passage and in Eusebius' comments thereon, and by the presence among Ammonius' pupils of a pagan Origen, who seems, along with Plotinus and an otherwise unknown Erennius, to have belonged to the school's inner circle (*V. Pl.* 3. 24–35). The only point that seems certain is that the two Origens were different people, but divergent opinions persist concerning the remainder of our information. Nor is it possible to reconstruct Ammonius' doctrine by comparing Plotinus' teaching with that of the Christian Origen, even if the latter was really Ammonius' pupil, for the two have little in common that is not also found in the Middle Platonists. But on the (doubtful) assumption that the late Neoplatonist Hierocles' statement is correct that Ammonius maintained the agreement of Plato and Aristotle (Photius *Bibl.* 461A; cf. p. 143), he will have differed on at least this point from Plotinus, whose criticisms of Aristotle we have observed. We know in any case of disagreements between Ammonius' pagan pupils, for the pagan Origen regarded Intelligence as the highest principle and rejected Plotinus' One (Proclus *PT* II. 4. 90), while the title of one of his writings, 'That the King is the Only Creator' (*V. Pl.* 3. 32), is plausibly interpreted as a polemic against Plotinus' hierarchy of Hypostases. Doctrinal disagreements are also attested between Plotinus and the only other pagan pupil of Ammonius of whose teaching we know anything. This was Longinus, the learned literary critic who in later life became the minister of Queen Zenobia of Palmyra, and to whom an erroneous tradition has ascribed the treatise *On the Sublime*. Plotinus described Longinus as a 'scholar, but not a philosopher' (*V. Pl.* 14. 18–20), while Longinus, though he eventually acquired a considerable respect for Plotinus (*V. Pl.* chs. 19–20), still rejected his

---

[1] Cf. further Dodds' discussion in *Entretiens Hardt V*, pp. 24–32, where earlier theories are critically examined.

location of the Forms within Intelligence, maintaining instead the (equally un-Platonic) view that they were on a level *inferior* to Intelligence (Proclus *In Tim.* 1. 322. 24). Porphyry, who had studied under Longinus at Athens (Eunapius *VS* 455–6), relates how he had himself upheld this doctrine on entering Plotinus' school and how Plotinus had smiled and detailed his chief disciple, Amelius Gentilianus of Tuscany, to explain his own position. Amelius did so; Porphyry wrote a reply and, after three repetitions of this procedure, was converted to Plotinus' opinion, wrote a recantation and was admitted to the school's inner circle (*V. Pl.* 18. 8–23; cf. 20. 86 ff.).

On leaving Ammonius in 243, Plotinus joined the emperor Gordian's expedition against the Persians, perhaps as a member of the scientific staff that often accompanied armies in ancient times, hoping to make contact with the sages of Persia and India. (The presence of the religious teacher Mani in the opposing Persian army has aroused comment.) Plotinus' attempt was, however, a failure; Gordian was assassinated in Mesopotamia, Plotinus escaped with some difficulty to Antioch and he never made another attempt to reach the East (*V. Pl.* 3. 15–22). Nor did he return to Ammonius, of whom our sources make no further mention. Instead he proceeded to Rome, where he remained for a further ten years, giving only oral instruction until 253, when his pupils finally persuaded him to start committing his thoughts to writing (*V. Pl.* 3. 22–35, 4. 9–11).

Porphyry's arrival in the school did not take place for another ten years (*V. Pl.* 4. 1–3). It was shortly after his arrival that Plotinus' dispute with the Gnostics broke out (cf. pp. 12–13). Against their doctrine he composed a treatise in four parts (*Enn.* III. 8, v. 8, v. 5 and II. 9), assigning to Porphyry and Amelius the detailed scholarly criticism of the books on which the Gnostics based their alleged revelation (*V. Pl.* 16). Porphyry describes the Gnostics as Christians, and modern research suggests that they should be identified with the Sethians, a sect whose teaching stood very close to that of the Christian heretic Valentinus. The post-war discovery of a Sethian library at Nag Hammadi (ancient Chenoboskion) in Upper Egypt has brought to light treatises with titles identical to those mentioned by Porphyry, and future research seems likely to confirm that we now possess several of the treatises of Plotinus' opponents in a dispute that proved a major stimulus to his thought.

Prominent among Plotinus' patrons during these years were Gallienus, sole emperor from 260 to 268, and his wife Salonina. Though their favour towards Plotinus has probably been overstressed, it was such that he hoped to persuade them to re-found an ancient city of philosophers in Campania, to be named Platonopolis and governed according to Plato's *Laws* (*V. Pl.* 12). Here Plotinus and his school were to have moved and, though a city rather than a monastic community seems to have been intended, it was clearly they who were to have been the city's most important members, with the rest of the citizens supplying them with economic security. It is certainly in this light that Plotinus—regrettably to modern taste—regards the mass of humanity (cf. II. 9. 9. 6–11), and the episode does not therefore conflict with the Neoplatonists' normal aversion to politics, typified by the senator Rogatianus, who renounced office, house and property and by an ascetic discipline cured himself of gout (*V. Pl.* 7. 31–46).[1] In any case opposition at court prevented anything from coming of the project.

Porphyry's stay with Plotinus lasted only the six years from 263 to 268 and it is these years of which his biography of Plotinus presents such a vivid picture. At the end of this time he became depressed and contemplated suicide. Plotinus, displaying an insight into character he had shown on other occasions, guessed what was wrong and (again very typically) gave Porphyry the practical advice to go away for a holiday. Porphyry proceeded to Sicily and was still there at Plotinus' death two years later (*V. Pl.* 11. 11–19).

Another blow befell Plotinus in 268 with the assassination of Gallienus, whose successors were military men with no time for Greek culture. At the same time an illness from which Plotinus had previously suffered (probably a form of leprosy) became worse, and fear of contagion led most of his disciples to withdraw from his presence (*V. Pl.* 2. 1–17). Plotinus therefore left the city for a dead friend's property in Campania, where he died in 270. Of all his pupils only the doctor Eustochius (cf. *V. Pl.* 7. 8–12) was present at his death. To him Plotinus addressed his last words, 'Try to bring back the god in you to the Divine in the universe'[2] (*V. Pl.* 2. 17–31). His pupils were consoled by an oracle of Apollo describing Plotinus as enjoying celestial bliss in company with the gods and the philosophers of old (*V. Pl.* 22).

Of the fascinating details related in Porphyry's biography we can discuss only those relevant to our understanding of the *Enneads*. Since these are like nothing else in philosophical literature, the Neoplatonic

---

[1] Cf. also *Enn.* I. 5. 10. 15–18, VI. 9. 7. 26–8, etc.
[2] On Plotinus' last words cf. P. Henry, 'La Dernière Parole de Plotin', *Studi Classici e Orientali II* (Pisa 1953) 113–30.

writings included, and since their peculiarities echo features of Plotinus' oral teaching described by Porphyry, some account of that teaching is desirable. There is, however, the difference that Plotinus' lectures were open to a wider audience than his writings, which were strictly confined to the inner circle of his disciples (*V. Pl.* 4. 14–16, 7. 1. ff.). The most important members of this inner circle were Amelius, Eustochius and Porphyry, of all of whom we shall have more to say. The wider circle was largely made up of senators and, like many ancient philosophical schools, included women (*V. Pl.* 7. 29 ff., 9. 1–5). It was in the house of one of these, the widow Gemina, that Plotinus lived, taught and looked after the orphans of senators entrusted to his care (*V. Pl.* 9. 5–16). It is in this context that Porphyry notes Plotinus' remarkable ability to combine inner meditation with external activity, a quality we shall find equally involved in his way of writing (*V. Pl.* 8. 19–23, 9. 16–22).

The major points common to Plotinus' lectures and his writings are three. First, he prefers to deal with individual philosophical problems rather than expound his thought in a formal system (cf. *V. Pl.* 4. 10–11) and it is impossible to imagine him writing a work like Proclus' *Elements of Theology*. Similarly in his classes, Porphyry tells us, Plotinus allowed his audience to raise any problems they wished (*V. Pl.* 3. 35–8), while Porphyry once questioned him for three days on end over the soul's union with the body, so provoking a protest from a visitor who would have preferred a formal lecture. Plotinus replied that if Porphyry's difficulties remained unsolved, there would be nothing to put in that lecture (*V. Pl.* 13. 10–17). Plotinus' aversion to formal systems is equally due to the conviction he shares with Plato that Reality eludes expression in rigid formulae. This conviction is best shown by his continual qualification of his accounts of spiritual being by such Greek words as *hoion* or *hōsper* ('so to speak'). But in contrast to Plato Plotinus' treatises exhaust the resources of language in endeavouring to attain successively closer approximations to what remains finally inexpressible. Hence too his tendency to conclude passages of arid dialectical discussion with one of his vivid descriptions of contemplation or of mystical experience, and his stress that only in the light of such experiences can all difficulties be resolved. Also relevant in this context is Plotinus' use of imagery, especially of the so-called 'dynamic images', in which processes drawn from the material world are used to illustrate the activity of the spiritual order. We may note in particular his insistence on the need to purify such images of their material limitations before applying them to the Intelligible world; much-quoted examples are those provided in VI. 4. 7.—a hand's control of a plank and a small body of light illumining a large sphere— in illustration of how the whole Intelligible order is simultaneously present throughout every part of the material world. Further instances need not be listed here, since the most important example, that of emanation, will later be analysed at length (cf. pp. 61 ff.) and will show just how central some of these images are to Plotinus' thought. Equally remarkable is the resemblance between Plotinus' recommen- dations regarding the 'purification' of his images and the spiritual exercises of contemplatives in other traditions; take, for instance, the instructions in V. 8. 9 to visualise an image of the sensible universe and then think away (and not just attenuate) its spatial and material limita- tions. At the same time, since for Plotinus spiritual discipline coincides with philosophy, such images are equally an integral part of the latter.

A second point on which Plotinus' treatises resemble his lectures is in taking their start from a passage of Plato or Aristotle as interpreted by one of the commentators discussed in our last chapter, though, Porphyry adds and Plotinus himself confirms, he did not keep sla- vishly to the traditional interpretation (*V. Pl.* 14. 10–16; cf. *Enn.* IV. 8. 8. 1 ff.). A good example is Henry's demonstration of how *Enn.* IV. 7. 6. 8–19 goes back from Alexander (*De An.* 61–3) to the original Aristotelian text (*De An.* III. 2. 426b–7a).[1] Detection of such cases is, however, exceedingly difficult owing to our loss of most of the works of the commentators in question and of Plotinus' refusal to refer by name to any philosopher later than Epicurus.

A third point where the *Enneads* echo Plotinus' oral discussions is in the form they frequently take of a dialogue with an imaginary inter- locutor. Most remarkable is the sense of rapid interchange between questioner and respondent, which MacKenna's version brings out very successfully in such passages as the discussions of the One in III. 8. 9 and the later chapters of VI. 7. At other times Plotinus' opponent will be given a set speech of anything up to a whole chapter, which the master then answers in his own person. Confusion can arise from Plotinus' habit of launching into such a passage without any indication that it does not contain his own views; nor is it always easy to see exactly where his reply starts or how much of the interlocutor's position he means to reject. And this brings us to the general stylistic difficulties of the *Enneads*.

[1] 'Les Sources de Plotin', *Entretiens Hardt V*, pp. 429–49.

These are best summarised in Porphyry's comment that Plotinus 'is concise and abounds more in thoughts than words' (*V. Pl.* 14. 1–2). Unfortunately his indifference to stylistic grace went beyond avoidance of the high-flown rhetoric that passed in contemporary circles for elegance; it extended to a neglect of the principles of calligraphy and orthography, a defect further aggravated by his poor eyesight, which did not permit him to revise what he had written (*V. Pl.* 8. 1–8). But these blemishes Porphyry's editorial labours have removed from our texts. Far more serious are Plotinus' more general stylistic peculiarities. Here his ability to combine inner meditation with external activity becomes relevant. According to Porphyry, Plotinus would work out the plan of his treatise in advance and then write it straight out, as though copying from a book. Even more impressive was his ability to break off and engage in conversation, returning afterwards to take up his writing where he had left off, and all the while keeping his train of thought (*V. Pl.* 8. 8–19).

The positive results of this procedure should not be overlooked. First, it means that we should look for a general plan in Plotinus' treatises even where it is least apparent; in fact even apparently 'episodic' treatises like the *Problems of the Soul* (*Enn.* IV. 3–4) show on analysis a very definite train of thought running through them. Secondly, it gives his work the vigour of a mind with all its forces bent on the pursuit and communication of truth. But on a first reading the negative consequences are most apparent.

First, Plotinus' sentences are poured straight out in rapid succession without any indication of the logical structure and divisions of his argument and the contribution each section of it makes to the whole. All this apart from the difficulty already noted of distinguishing Plotinus' views from those of his opponents. Secondly, the *Enneads* are written in what is in effect a philosophical shorthand, compared with which even Aristotle is often a model of prolixity. Sometimes it is a question of supplying words (such as verbs) to complete Plotinus' sentences, at others of filling out brief philosophical allusions whose point is no longer readily apparent. That Plotinus is free with the rules of Greek grammar is well known; whether he is positively ungrammatical is a much-debated point, which largely depends on which modern edition one uses. Fortunately there are few passages in which Plotinus' grammar obscures understanding of his thought.

Even Plotinus' contemporaries found his style disconcerting, and Porphyry relates how Longinus regarded the treatises brought him by

Amelius as full of scribal errors, when they were really the most accurate copies that could be procured (*V. Pl.* 19. 19 ff., 20. 5–9). And Plotinus' unsystematic manner of exposition further obscured the logical interconnections of his thought (*V. Pl.* 18. 6–8). A large part of his successors' task lay in fact in the clarification of Neoplatonism's logical structure. For the modern reader, who finds himself in the same position as a Western European trying to read Aristotle not just before Ross, but even before Aquinas, matters are naturally much worse. But those who are tempted by these difficulties to doubt Plotinus' greatness should follow Dodds' advice to compare him with his contemporaries[1] or Armstrong's more concise suggestion to compare the *Enneads* with the *Hermetica*.[2] The superiority of his synthesis of earlier Greek thought to that of his predecessors should then be apparent. Perhaps even more impressive is his ruthless exposure of the inadequacy of anthropomorphic conceptions of God or of man's inherent tendency to conceive spiritual reality in spatial terms (cf. *Enn.* VI. 4–5, e.g. VI. 4. 2. 27 ff.). Or take the remarkable chapter VI. 8. 11, in the course of a discussion whether the One's nature derives from will, necessity or chance. Such questions, Plotinus declares, result from an erroneous imposition of limiting conditions on the Absolute; it is like positing an empty space, introducing God therein and asking how he came there. It is such passages that for the modern reader best illuminate Porphyry's references to Plotinus' ability to 'detect and consider what was relevant' (*V. Pl.* 13. 1–2) and to 'explain the meaning of some deep subject in a few words' (ibid. 14. 17).

It is some compensation in the face of the difficulties we have related that the student of Plotinus possesses one advantage not enjoyed by students of any other major Greek philosopher, that Porphyry's biography supplies two full lists of his writings, one in the chronological order in which they were written (*V. Pl.* 4. 16–6. 25), the other in the order in which his edition arranged them (*V. Pl.* 24. 16–26. 27). We can thus be sure at the outset that we possess everything Plotinus wrote and conversely that all the writings in our possession are genuine.[3] It is true that, since all Plotinus' writings were composed during his last seventeen years, they show no such pronounced development as do

---

[1] *CQ* xx (1928) 142.

[2] Introduction to Loeb *Plotinus*, vol. i., pp. xiv–xv.

[3] The *Letter to Flaccus*, ascribed to Plotinus in modern studies of mysticism, is in fact not a work of Plotinus himself, but one composed out of phrases taken from the *Enneads* by the nineteenth-century author R. A. Vaughan, and published in his *Hours with the Mystics*.

those of Plato and Aristotle. It is none the less useful to be able to
correlate the subject-matter of individual treatises, or groups thereof,
with the external events of Plotinus' life. And that Porphyry's chronological order is correct is on the whole confirmed by cross-references
between the treatises, though a few doubts remain, notably regarding
the treatise III. 9 (no. 13 in Porphyry's list), in fact a collection of short
notes on miscellaneous topics. Nor is there reason to regard any
substantial part of any treatise as spurious (the longest suspect
passage being II. 3. 12. 12–32).[1]

Porphyry's chronological list divides the treatises into three groups,
those written before his own arrival in Rome (253–63, twenty-one in
number), those dating from his stay there (263–8, totalling twenty-
four), and the nine composed during Plotinus' last two years (268–70).
Generally speaking, it is the works of the first group that provide the
best introduction to Plotinus' thought, since the picture of reality they
present is simpler and more orderly, though on some points less
adventurous, than those of the second group. Treatises of this type
include I. 6 on Beauty, IV. 8 on the Descent of the Soul, VI. 9 on the
One and V. I on the Three Hypostases. Several of the group, notably
IV. 7 on the Immortality of the Soul, III. I on Fate and V. 9 on the
Ideas, show a strong influence of traditional scholastic Platonism,
though even in these Plotinus' own spirit continually breaks through;
thus IV. 7's traditional arguments for immortality are crowned by an
appeal to the experience of contemplation as furnishing the best proof
(IV. 7. 10. 3–11. 2). The early works of the second group are preoccupied with the Gnostic menace and in particular with the problem of
eliminating materialism and anthropomorphism from one's conception
of God and the spiritual world. Among them are VI. 4–5 on the
Integral Omnipresence of True Being, III. 6 on Impassibility, IV. 3–5
on the Soul and the anti-Gnostic quartet III. 8, V. 8, V. 5 and II. 9. The
treatises VI. 7 and VI. 8 on the One mark a transition between the anti-
Gnostic group and the last works of the second period, which are
concerned with anti-Aristotelian polemic; most important among these
are VI. 1–3 on the Categories and III. 7 on Time and Eternity. Throughout his second period the need to define his position vis-à-vis rival
systems provokes some of Plotinus' most brilliant critical insights, and

---

[1] F. Heinemann's attempt (in his *Plotin*, Leipzig 1919) to prove several treatises
spurious and to rearrange the order of the remainder so as to produce a substantial
development in Plotinus' thought has been generally rejected; cf. Bréhier's
introduction to the Budé *Plotinus*, pp. xviii–xxvi.

to this extent Porphyry's judgment that they contain his best work has some validity (*V. Pl.* 6. 32–4). Some of them also display superior consistency in rehandling themes previously dealt with in Plotinus' early works; a good example is the superiority of iv. 3. 9–17's account of the soul's descent to that given earlier in iv. 8. Finally, the treatises of Plotinus' last two years are largely concerned with ethical themes, with evil and theodicy, with the influence of the stars and with the philosopher's serenity and its psychological basis; they thus attest Plotinus' own search for serenity in the face of death. Only v. 3 of the last group is primarily concerned with the three Hypostases, while iii. 5, an unusual departure for Plotinus, attempts an allegorical interpretation of the *Symposium*'s myth of the birth of Aphrodite.

Porphyry's own edition of Plotinus' works did not appear until the first decade of the fourth century—more than thirty years after Plotinus' death. In the interval Eustochius had produced an edition of his own, arranged on different principles from those Porphyry was to follow and which is now lost, though it may have been the source of the extracts from Plotinus found in Eusebius' *Praeparatio Evangelica*. A common feature of both editions was their division into two or more parts of some of the longer treatises, though not always the same ones; those divided by Porphyry were iii. 2–3, iv. 3–5, vi. 1–3 and vi. 4–5, while the four parts of the anti-Gnostic work (iii. 8, v. 8, v. 5 and ii. 9) were placed by him in different Enneads. By this division he obtained fifty-four treatises, which he divided into six groups of nine ('Enneads') a combination of mystical numbers that delighted him. This division he regarded as producing a systematic ordering of the treatises according to subject-matter, progressing from the easier questions to the more difficult (*V. Pl.* 24. 11–16); we may compare Iamblichus' attempt at a systematic ordering of the Platonic dialogues (cf. p. 19). To the first Ennead Porphyry assigned the treatises he regarded as concerned with Ethics, to the second and (more doubtfully) the third those concerned with Physics, to the fourth, fifth and sixth those concerned respectively with Soul, with the three Hypostases and Intelligence, and with the Categories and the One. But Plotinus' unsystematic manner of philosophising makes any rigid division between his treatises impossible; in fact most treatises deal with more than one of the above topics and Porphyry has to admit that his third Ennead lacks unity (*V. Pl.* 25. 2–9). Readers are therefore better advised to follow the chronological order of Plotinus' works, as is done in Harder's modern German edition and translation. For similar reasons the titles of the various treatises (added by Plotinus' pupils, *V. Pl.* 4. 16–19) are only a rough guide to their contents.

To his edition Porphyry further added explanatory material of his own (*V. Pl.* 26. 29–37) of which nothing now survives, except part of his table of contents to *Enn.* IV. 4, preserved at the start of the Arabic *Theology of Aristotle*.[1] He also corrected Plotinus' spelling and other surface blemishes (*V. Pl.* 26. 37–40; cf. ibid. 7. 49–51), but there is no reason to believe that his alteration of his master's words went further. And the result of the labours of recent editors, notably Henry and Schwyzer, has been to provide us with as accurate a representation of the words of Porphyry's edition as we are likely to acquire and to ensure that few of our remaining textual problems affect our understanding of Plotinus' thought. It is this which must now claim our attention.

II. THE THREE HYPOSTASES

The first difficulty confronting an expositor of Plotinus' system concerns the order of exposition. An obvious suggestion is to begin from the summit of the metaphysical hierarchy with the One and proceed downwards through the successive stages of his universe to the material world, and thence to follow the soul's return to the One. But this procedure is more appropriate to Proclus, whose system is presented as a logical deduction from the abstract principle of unity, than to Plotinus, who normally begins from the world of everyday experience, whether of the external world or of man's inner life, and proceeds upwards to the One. But this approach encounters difficulties of its own, notably that the procession of lower realities from the One is hardly intelligible without some previous understanding of the One itself; in fact treatises concerned with this subject commonly follow the 'descending' order of exposition. The present account is a compromise between these two approaches; it will begin with an outline of Plotinus' system, following the ascending order and, in particular, dealing somewhat summarily with the level of Soul. Then, after as full an account of the One as space permits, we shall descend again, following the outflow of Reality from the One to the sensible world. Finally, after a detailed discussion of Plotinus' views on the individual soul, we shall deal with his conception of the philosopher's return, ending with his account of

[1] Many scholars believe that Porphyry's commentary is also the source of the non-Plotinian material preserved in the *Theology* itself (cf. p. 163).

mystical experience. The unsatisfactoriness of such an approach is obvious; in particular it means dividing our account of the Intelligible world into three parts (pp. 52–7, 65–7, 85–7). On the other hand it has at least two merits. First, the reader may find it helpful to obtain a general conspectus of each level before filling in its details; secondly, we shall reproduce the unsystematic form of Plotinus' own treatises.

The fundamental principle of Neoplatonism, that reality consists in a hierarchy of degrees of unity, is a systematisation of the Pythagorean-Platonic tradition's identification of goodness and order with form, measure and limit, which in their turn imply number and mathematical ratio and hence ultimately the presence of an organising unity (cf. *Enn.* I. 6. 2); in Plato's oral teaching, as reported by Aristotle, the Forms were conceived as resulting from the imposition of Unity on the Indefinite Dyad (*Met. A.* 6. 987b 18 ff., etc.). And following a Stoic argument Plotinus maintains that unity is necessary for a thing to exist at all (VI. 9. 1. 1 ff.); for any plurality, however indefinite, is always a plurality of things, each of which is one, since plurality without any unity could be only the utter indeterminacy of Matter. And, if we examine the material world, it is obvious that its unity is a very imperfect one.

First of all, being extended in three-dimensional space, bodies are subject to the divisions, restrictions and mutual exclusiveness imposed by such extension. Secondly, and here the Platonists accept Aristotle's 'hylomorphic' analysis of material objects, bodies are composed of two elements, matter (*hylē*) and form (*eidos* or *morphē*) (cf. IV. 7. 1. 8–19, V. 9. 3. 9–20). Thus in the case of a gold cup the gold constitutes the matter on which the craftsman imposes the form of a cup, while in change the underlying substratum receives different forms, while itself remaining the same. But since even the simplest bodies, the elements earth, air, fire and water, have each their own form and change into one another, we must carry our analysis further and postulate a common substratum underlying the forms of the elements and remaining unaltered when change between them takes place (II. 4. 6). This is Prime Matter, without any form or quality of its own, and clearly very different from Matter in post-Cartesian thought (II. 4. 8. 1 ff., cf. Aristotle *Met. Z.* 3. 1029a 20–6). Indeed it appears to be nothing at all, but Plotinus, though he entitles Matter 'non-being' in view of its formlessness and utter unsubstantiality (II. 5. 4–5, III. 6. 7. 7 ff.), denies that this means absolute non-existence (I. 8. 3. 6 ff., II. 4. 16. 3).

The consequent paradoxicality of the concept is emphasised in the treatise III. 6 on Impassibility. In particular Plotinus argues that there can be no true union between form and such an insubstantial entity as analysis shows Matter to be; we should rather think of the reflection of images in a mirror (though since the latter has its own form the comparison is still imperfect) (III. 6. 7. 23–43, 9. 16–19, 13. 18–55). 'Matter's every pronouncement is therefore a lie' and the apparent solidity of the material world based on it an illusion (ibid. 7. 21 ff.). In fact what men take to be the most substantial realities are the least so; evidence is the fact that the heaviest and most solid-seeming bodies are the most fragile (ibid. 6. 33–64; cf. v. 8. 9. 28–37). A similar reversal of the views of unreflective common sense will be found at all levels of Plotinus' universe (cf. v. 5. 11. 5–10, VI. 1. 28. 1 ff., VI. 4. 2. 27 ff., etc.).

Plotinus' conviction of Matter's unsubstantiality is not, of course, due primarily to reflection on Aristotle. In fact his account is full of echoes of the mysterious 'Receptacle of Becoming', which the *Timaeus* (48E–52D) had postulated as underlying the unsubstantial flux of the sensible world. Like many earlier Platonists, Plotinus identifies the Receptacle with Aristotle's Matter and rejects in consequence the natural interpretation of the *Timaeus* identifying it with space. That Matter has spatial extension he denies on the grounds that the latter is a definite quality (II. 4. 8–12, III. 6. 16–18); that magnitude is produced by form is shown by the fact that the form of each natural species entails a definite size (II. 4. 8. 25–7, III. 6. 16. 1–11). Magnitude thus originates from the reflection of form upon Matter and belongs to neither form nor Matter taken in isolation. Hence the Platonic Form of Magnitude is not itself a large object (II. 4. 9. 5–7; cf. above p. 20); on the contrary, true Greatness consists in freedom from spatial restrictions, and three-dimensional extension is merely the best imitation sensible matter can receive of the true non-spatial Magnitude of the Intelligible world (III. 6. 17–18). As we shall see, true greatness for the Neoplatonists is a matter of power, not of bulk, and each level of reality fragments and so weakens what its producer had contained in a more concentrated, and hence more powerful, form (VI. 4. 5, VI. 6. 1, VI. 7. 32. 14–21).

The Middle Platonists had disputed whether Matter was an inert, formless and hence ethically neutral entity or an active principle of evil. Plotinus characteristically offers a paradoxical combination of both views. Since goodness consists in form, he argues, it is precisely Matter's lack of any form whatever that proves its identity with Absolute Evil

(I. 8. 10, etc., II. 4. 16. 16–25, III. 6. 11. 15–45). Plotinus, however, is no dualist; his Matter is not an independently existing principle, but the point at which the outflow of reality from the One fades away into utter darkness.[1] Matter's evil is thus not a positive force (though Plotinus sometimes speaks as though it were); it is rather an utter sterility, or 'poverty' (cf. I. 8. 3. 16, II. 4. 16. 19–24, III. 6. 14. 5–15), which communicates its own deficiency to the bodies based on it and thus becomes the source of all the sensible world's imperfections, including, as we shall see, the wickedness of individual souls (I. 8. 4, etc., cf. p. 76).

The question thus arises whence the sensible world derives such order as it is able to attain and what prevents it from dissolving into the utter formlessness of Matter. A more stable, and more unified, principle is needed, and here Plotinus follows the argument from microcosm to macrocosm which had been propounded by the earliest Greek philosophers and had dominated both Platonic and Stoic traditions. According to this the organisation and orderly movement of the cosmos, like those of the body of an individual animal, depend on the presence of a controlling soul (IV. 7. 2. 20–5, V. 1. 2).[2] We must, however, avoid the Stoics' mistake of conceiving Soul in material and spatial terms; for otherwise we are merely adding one more material entity to those requiring explanation instead of advancing to the higher unity we need (IV. 7. 3. 19–35). And not merely is the Stoics' corporealist view of Soul inconsistent with its role as the world's organising principle; there are also many psychological processes that prove its falsity.

Consider, for instance, the case of sensation. There must, Plotinus argues, be a central perceptive faculty to receive information from all five senses and from all parts of the body; otherwise there would be no closer connection between the perceptions of the various senses than between those of two distinct living beings (IV. 7. 6. 1–19, cf. VI. 4. 1. 24–6, 6. 5–13). But how on the Stoic view can that central faculty perceive pain in both finger and toe? The Stoics' answer is that sensations are transmitted from one part of the body to another until they

---

[1] I. 8. 7. 17–23, II. 5. 5. 17–19, III. 4. 1. 8–17, IV. 3. 9. 23–6.
[2] That the Greek word *psychē* is more accurately translated 'life-principle' than 'soul' is well known; in particular the Greek term carries no implication of immortality or of an entity capable of existence apart from the body. The Neoplatonic conception of *psychē* is, however, sufficiently close to the notion of Soul in Christian and post-Christian thought (itself largely a product of the Platonic tradition's influence) for the rendering 'soul' not to be seriously misleading; but the reader will note that the Neoplatonic 'soul' includes physiological as well as psychological processes.

reach the soul's ruling power, which the school locates in the heart. In that case, Plotinus replies, either the pain would be perceived only in the heart, or there would be a succession of pain sensations from the affected member to the heart; in neither case could the original site of the pain be determined (IV. 2. 2, IV. 7. 7). The only alternative is that the soul is present in her entirety at each part of the body, and this is possible only if she is incorporeal and free from spatial restrictions.

Equally to be rejected are views, like Aristotle's, which admit Soul's incorporeality, but deny her separability from the body (IV. 7. 8[5]). By contrast the Platonic view of Soul as an entity intermediate between sensible and Intelligible worlds is summarised in the *Timaeus*' enigmatic description of her as 'blended of the indivisible substance and of that which becomes (and is) divisible about bodies' (35A), a passage whose meaning had been much debated in Middle Platonism. Soul's 'indivisibility' Plotinus interprets as non-spatiality, not as the indivisibility of a geometrical point (VI. 4. 13. 18–26; cf. VI. 9. 5. 41–6). This is Soul's essential nature, but since the bodies she produces and governs are extended in space, her activity on those bodies makes her appear to undergo spatial division (IV. 2. 1).[1] But this should not make us ascribe the body's spatial limitations to the soul herself; the trouble is that men erroneously take the principles of corporeal existence as valid for the whole of Reality (VI. 4. 2. 27–34, VI. 5. 2). In fact it is only Soul's non-spatiality that enables her to be present in her entirety throughout the whole body, as phenomena like sense-perception require (VI. 4. 3. 17–31). That not all her powers appear to be present at every part of the body is due to the physical world's inability to receive the full power of incorporeal Reality (VI. 4. 3. 6–11, 11. 1–10, VI. 5. 11. 28–38); more specifically, as we shall see, not every part of the body is adapted to every faculty of Soul (IV. 3. 23, IV. 9. 3. 19–23; cf. pp. 76–7). We may thus describe incorporeal beings as present 'everywhere and nowhere' (III. 9. 4, VI. 4. 3. 17–19). And since in dealing with non-spatial entities the only sense we can give the preposition 'in' is that of 'dependent on', we should describe the less powerful principles as 'in' the more powerful ones; hence the soul is not in the body, but the reverse, while Soul herself is in Intelligence and Intelligence in the One (IV. 3. 20. 41–51, V. 5. 9. 29–38, VI. 4. 2. 2–12).

Strictly, however, it is only the lowest level of Soul that comes into

---

[1] On *Tim* 35A cf. also I. 1. 8. 10 ff., III. 4. 6. 30 ff., IV 1. passim, IV. 3. 19, IV 9. 3. 10 ff.

direct contact with bodies (IV. 3. 19, IV. 8. 2. 30–3, etc.). In the World-soul this is identical with Aristotle's Nature,[1] while within man, corresponding to the complexity of the body it has to govern, its functions are much more varied; as a later section will show, it embraces the powers of growth and nutrition, the bodily appetites and emotions and (in some passages) sense-perception, in other words all faculties rooted in the living body (cf. pp. 73 ff.). For the present, however, since we are following the philosopher's quest for unity, we may confine ourselves to the soul's higher level, that of discursive reason, which in Plotinus' view has no bodily roots (cf. p. 79). That Soul cannot be the Absolute Unity we are seeking is clear from the fact that the concept 'Soul' is distinct from the concept 'Unity', whereas what we are looking for is not a principle which merely 'participates in' Unity (to use Plato's terminology), but one which is nothing but Unity (VI. 9. 1. 17–43, cf. III. 8. 10. 20–3, V. 5. 4. 1 ff.). Further confirmation results from an empirical analysis of Soul's consciousness. This cannot be extended in space, for it is naïve to regard even the images received by sense-perception as extended throughout the parts of the central perceptive faculty (as the Stoic theory necessitates) (IV. 7. 6. 19 ff., V. 8. 2. 26–8). And the Stoic view is totally inapplicable to the rational soul's contemplation of wholly immaterial objects (such as justice or the other virtues) (IV. 7. 8. 1–26). But that the unity of even this level of contemplation is imperfect is clear if we compare it with the level immediately above it, that of Intelligence, the Second Hypostasis.

The need to postulate an eternally active principle underlying the intermittent contemplation of human thought had been argued in Aristotle's famous chapter on the Active Intelligence (*De An.* III. 5; cf. *Enn.* V. 9. 2. 20–2, 3. 21 ff., etc.) and it is in Plotinus' accounts of his Second Hypostasis that Aristotelian influence is most conspicuous. On the empirical side his distinction between Soul and Intelligence corresponds to that between discursive and intuitive thought. As Aquinas observes (*ST* Ia. 14. 7), thought may be described as 'discursive' in two senses, either as involving reasoning from premises to conclusion or as involving simple transition from one object to another. Human thought is clearly discursive in both of these senses. The divine souls, on the other hand, cannot be conceived as exercising discursive thought of the former type, since such reasoning starts from an initial condition of ignorance (IV. 3. 18, IV. 4. 12) and is hence inconsistent with divine omniscience (cf. above p. 27). On the other hand their thought is

[1] Cf. pp. 27, 67 and *Enn.* III. 8. 2–4, IV. 4. 12–13, 20–1, V. 2. 1. 18–28.

normally conceived by Plotinus as involving change and therefore subject to time (though cf. IV. 4. 15–16, discussed below pp. 81–2). By contrast Intelligence (*nous*) is the level of intuition, where the laborious processes of discursive thought are bypassed and the mind attains a direct and instantaneous vision of truth (cf. Plato *Ep.* VII. 341 C–D). In earlier Greek thought *nous* had been used both of such intuitive insight and in the wider sense of 'reason' in general; nor is it always easy for readers of Plato or Aristotle to be sure which sense they have in mind. Plotinus, on the other hand, is careful to distinguish true Intelligence from the discursive reasoning to which the name is also commonly applied.[1] But since intuitive insight remains for him the culmination of man's rational life, it is preferable to translate *nous* by 'Intelligence' or 'Intellect' rather than 'Spirit', the term used, for instance, by Inge.

The main distinctions between Soul's contemplation and that of Intelligence are two. First, whereas Intelligence embraces the whole Intelligible world in a single timeless vision, Soul's contemplation, as we have seen, is forced to change from one object to another (V. 1. 4. 10–25). Hence once again the lower principle fragments the life of its prior (I. 5. 7. 14–20, III. 7. 11. 20 ff.) and the result in this case is the generation of time, which Plotinus defines as the 'life of Soul in transition from one phase of life to another' (III. 7. 11. 43–5), whereas eternity is the life of the Intelligible world, which in Plato's words (*Tim.* 37D) 'abides in unity', without chronological succession, since Intelligence contains all possible Being and has therefore nothing further to seek.[2] It is by her perpetual restless search for fresh objects of contemplation that Soul attains the closest approximation she can to this life, and it is in this sense that Plotinus interprets Plato's description of time as the 'moving image of eternity' (*Tim.* ibid., *Enn.* III. 7. 11, V. 1. 4. 18–21). The second difference between the two Hypostases is that the perfect self-awareness of Intelligence, based on full identity between subject and object, is impossible on the level of Soul (III. 8. 8. 1–30, V. 3. 2–4). A corollary is that Soul's contemplation is confined to images or verbal formulae reflecting the Forms (IV. 3. 30, etc., cf. p. 80), whereas the objects contemplated by Intelligence are the Platonic Forms themselves, Plato's Realm of True Being.

Of the general Neoplatonic attitude to the theory of Forms we have

---

[1] I. 8. 2. 9 ff., cf. also I. 1. 8. 1 ff., V. 1. 10. 12–13, VI. 2. 21. 27 ff., VI. 9. 5. 7 ff.
[2] III. 7. 3–6, esp. 3. 37–9, 4. 37–43, 5, 25–8; cf. V. 1. 4. 1–25, V. 9. 7. 1–12, VI. 7. 1. 45–58.

already spoken (p. 18). Here we need merely note one class of Form recognised by Plotinus, though not universally admitted by his successors (cf. Syrianus *In Met.* 39. 8–28, Proclus *In Parm.* 824), namely Forms of Individuals. It is unfortunately unclear how consistently Plotinus maintains this doctrine and how far he intends it to apply;[1] the treatise defending such Forms (v. 7) is primarily concerned with Forms of individual men and other living creatures (cf. v. 9. 12), and Plotinus elsewhere proclaims the absurdity of postulating a separate Form of Fire for each individual fire (vi. 5. 8. 39–46). But his fundamental objective is clear, to give the individual personality a permanent place within the Intelligible world. Individuality in his view is emphatically due to Form, not to Matter, and each individual soul is immortal and dependent in its turn on an individual archetype of its own (iv. 3. 5, vi. 4. 4. 34–46).

Plotinus' account of the Intelligible world has its roots in the Middle Platonic view of the Forms as thoughts of God, which, however, he reinterprets in the light of Aristotle's doctrine of the identity of thought and its object, to reach a fundamentally new, and startling, conception. And he also insists that Forms are not thoughts in the sense of being arbitrary concepts without any substantial content of their own. Nominalism must be avoided; the Forms are not dependent for their existence on being thought (v. 9. 7. 11–18, vi. 6. 6.; cf. *Parm.* 132b–c). As Plotinus' successors were to object, however, such declarations are hard to reconcile with some of his other statements (cf. p. 67). We can see the laws governing the Intelligible world by examining the individual intelligence's contemplation thereof. On the one hand, the individual retains his own identity; on the other, his contemplation embraces the whole Intelligible world and everything within it. Hence, since on this level subject and object are identical, each member of the Intelligible order is identical with the whole of that order, and with every other member thereof (iv. 4. 2. 3–14, vi. 5. 7). We here encounter Plotinus' version of the Neoplatonic principle that 'all is in all', which we met in connection with Numenius (iii. 8. 8. 40–5, cf. pp. 33–4). More precisely, each intelligence expresses the whole Intelligible order from its own particular viewpoint (v. 8. 4. 4–11); or, in Plotinus' terminology, each is 'actually' itself, but 'potentially' all the others (vi. 2. 20; cf. iv. 8. 3. 14–16, vi. 7. 9. 31–8). The analogy he suggests is that of a self-contained deductive science, like Euclidean geometry, where

[1] Cf. the discussions of H. Blumenthal, *Phronesis II* (1966) 61–80, J. M. Rist *CQ* n.s. 13 (1963) 223–31.

each theorem has its own specific content, but contains by implication the whole of the science in question.[1] The unity binding Intelligence is, however, closer than the analogy suggests, since the sciences familiar to us belong to the level of discursive thought; it has none the less the merit of emphasising that the Intelligible order is not a mere confused mass. Though within Intelligence 'all is together', its contents are yet clearly distinguished without separation.[2]

Universal Intelligence thus emerges as a unity-in-plurality, a multiple organism containing a plurality of Forms and Intelligences; Plotinus identifies it with the 'all-complete animal' of *Timaeus* 30C ff.[3] Furthermore, he regards the Forms as themselves living, conscious intelligences (v. 1. 4. 26, v. 9. 8. 2–4, vi. 7. 9. 20 ff.). To the modern reader this view of the Intelligible world as 'boiling with life' (vi. 5. 12. 9, vi. 7. 12. 23) and of the Forms as active forces seems a major departure from Plato. Plotinus, however, believed himself justified in inferring it both from the *Timaeus* passage and from *Sophist* 248E ff.'s description of True Being as endowed with life and intelligence (cf. e.g. ii. 5. 3. 22–40, iii. 6. 6. 10–32). A supporting consideration was that as the archetype of the sensible cosmos, which Plotinus like the Stoics regards as a living being, the Intelligible cosmos must likewise be alive (cf. vi. 7. 11–12). Even more important was Aristotle's doctrine of the identity of intuitive thought with its object, reinforced by the Sceptical critique of knowledge of external objects as necessarily imperfect (cf. p. 26). Intelligence, Plotinus argues, must differ from Soul in possessing perfect self-awareness; nor can it share Soul's deficiency of contemplating images of the Forms rather than the Forms themselves. But these conditions are fulfilled only if there is perfect identity between Intelligence and its contents, and hence if the Forms are themselves Intelligences.[4] Any other supposition, for instance that the Forms are verbal formulae, is absurd in itself and fails to meet these criteria (v. 5. 1. 37–50). But Plotinus' conception of Intelligence, like his conception of the One, has empirical as well as metaphysical and traditional roots. That it is based on an actual semi-mystical experience is strongly suggested by the vividness of some of his accounts, notably the treatise v. 8 on

---

[1] v. 9. 6. 3–10; cf. iii. 9. 2, iv. 9. 5, vi. 4. 4. 34–6.

[2] v. 9. 6. ibid., i. 8. 2. 17–19, iii. 8. 9. 35–7, vi. 6. 7. 1–10, vi. 7. 14. 18–23, vi. 9. 5. 16–20.

[3] Cf. *Enn.* v. 9. 9. 3–8, vi. 2. 21. 53–9, vi. 6. 7. 14–19, vi. 7. 8. 27–32.

[4] v. 3. 15. 18–48, v. 5. 1. 19–2. 24; cf. v. 4. 2. 43–8, v. 9. 5. 1–34. On the doctrine's sources cf. P. Hadot, 'Être, vie, pensée chez Plotin et avant Plotin', *Entretiens Hardt V*, pp. 107–57.

Intelligible Beauty, and confirmed by his exhortations to his readers to attain the experience for themselves (v. 8. 10. 39–43, vi. 7. 15. 30–2).[1] To Iamblichus, on the other hand, Plotinus' unrestricted identification of Forms and Intelligences seemed to overemphasise the unity of the Intelligible world at the expense of the distinctions within it (cf. p. 124).

The tension between static and dynamic aspects of Plotinus' thought are particularly clear in his accounts of Intelligence. We shall observe them in his aesthetics (cf. pp. 86–7) and have already remarked their influence on his evaluation of infinity (cf. p. 6).[2] In marked contrast to his Christian contemporary Origen, who under the influence of the traditional Greek equation of finitude with perfection, and especially of the familiar argument that infinity is unknowable even to God (cf. pp. 29–30, 149) had maintained the finitude of God's power (*De Princ.* frs. 24, 38), Plotinus argues that the power of the Hypostases is infinite (iv. 3. 8. 35 ff.; cf. vi. 9. 6. 10–12) and that we should not fear introducing infinity into the Intelligible world (v. 7. 1. 25–6, 3. 20–3). This, however, is hardly an innovation; Aristotle had already maintained the infinity of divine power (*Phys.* viii. 10). And Plotinus denies the existence either of infinite spatial magnitude or of infinite number, regarding the latter as a logical contradiction (vi. 6. chs. 2, 17. 1–3, 18. 1 ff.). The Intelligible world's boundlessness must, of course, in any case consist not in infinite spatial extension, but in complete non-spatiality.[3] But the Forms are specifically declared to be finite in number and, though Intelligence is free from external limitations, it has still, in taking form, imposed a limit on itself (vi. 6. 18, vi. 7. 17. 14–26, 33. 7 ff.). Viewed in this light, as a self-contained, perfectly organised, system containing a finite number of Forms, Intelligence appears as the apotheosis of traditional Greek ideas of perfection (cf. e.g. iii. 6. 6. 10 ff.); in fact Plotinus claims that this was the real meaning of Par-

---

[1] We may further note the resemblances between Plotinus' Intelligible world and modern accounts of experiences produced by psychedelic drugs; common features include abolition of the subject-object distinction and of the restrictions of space and time, and awareness of an animation pervading even objects which common sense regards as lifeless, (though Plotinus, of course, makes clear that his experience is attained through philosophical contemplation *alone*; on the 'spiritual exercises' involved cf. above p. 42). Plotinus' experience is also to be distinguished from what is called 'extrovertive mysticism', involving the sense of a unity pervading the *external* world; Plotinus stresses that his own vision is attained by withdrawing *within* (cf. v. 8. 11. 10–12).

[2] Cf. A. H. Armstrong, 'Plotinus' doctrine of the Infinite and its significance for Christian thought', *Downside Review* 73 (1955) 47–58.

[3] v. 5. 10. 19–23, vi. 5. 11, vi. 6. 17. 11–14, vi. 7. 32. 15–24.

menides' finite, eternal sphere and of his statement that (as Plotinus interprets it) 'thinking and being are the same' (fr. 3, *Enn.* v. 1. 8. 14–23). Where Plotinus decisively breaks with traditional Greek ideas is in regarding the very fact that Intelligence has limits as disqualifying its claim to be the highest reality.

First, it is clear that Intelligence, containing as it does a plurality of Forms, cannot be the Absolute Unity we are seeking. Nor is its self-sufficiency perfect, since it is dependent upon its constituent elements and, deprived of any of them, would be in want (II. 9. 1. 8–11, v. 4. 1. 12–15, VI. 9. 2, 6. 16 ff.); above all, as we shall see, it is deficient in needing to exercise thought. Parmenides had argued that an entity without limitation must be deficient (fr. 8. 30–3); Plotinus regards this as true only for beings that need limits in the first place. And, on the general principle governing the relations between ontological levels, the One must not be a mere reduplication of the Intelligible world, but the transcendent source thereof. Hence, Plotinus argues in terms shocking for traditional Hellenic thinkers, as the source of Form, Measure and Limit, the One must itself be Formless, Unmeasured and Infinite.[1]

Plotinus' conception of the One can best be understood if we recall that in his view multiplicity is never a valuable addition to an initial unity, but connotes rather a fragmentation of that unity (VI. 6. 1, VI. 7. 8. 19–22). Hence at each stage of his universe the descent into greater multiplicity imposes fresh limits and restrictions, disperses and weakens the power of previous stages, and creates fresh needs requiring the development of new faculties previously unnecessary. That, conversely, the Absolute One should coincide with the Absolute Good exemplifies the mystic's paradox that the Undifferentiated Unity he experiences is simultaneously, because of its freedom from all restrictions, the most substantial and satisfying of realities. The negations which Plotinus, following the *Parmenides'* first hypothesis, applies to the One, should therefore be understood not in the same sense as those used of other entities, but as denials of everything inconsistent with the One's excellence, in particular of all plurality and all limitation.

It follows, first of all, that we should not misunderstand these negations, and particularly Plotinus' denial that the One partakes in Being, as meaning that it is non-existent (cf. III. 8. 10. 26–32). We may recall that for a Platonist the world of Being is the world of stable and definite Form; for Plato the main point had been its contrast with the unstable

[1] v. 5. 4. 12–16, 6. 1–11, 11. 1–5, VI. 7. 17. 39–43, 32. 5–10, VI. 9. 3. 37–40.

flux of Becoming that is the sensible world; but it is clear that it equally contrasts with the One (v. 6. 6. 13 ff., vi. 9. 3. 38–40). A simple affirmation of the One's existence is therefore permissible, provided this is not understood as predicating Being of the One.[1] For, first, subject and predicate constitute a duality; secondly, what is predicated is always a definite form, and form connotes limitation (v. 1. 7. 23–6, v. 5. 6. 1 ff.). In other words, significant predication implies denial of everything inconsistent therewith and hence limits the reality to which it is applied. From this follows the fundamental principle of the negative theology, that words can tell us only what the One is not, never what it is (v. 3. 14. 6–7). A corollary is that denial of a particular predicate to the One does not entail affirmation of its opposite; thus to deny that the One is in motion is not to affirm that it is at rest, but to set it on a level where the motion-rest opposition does not apply (iii. 9. 7. 1–2, v. 5. 10. 14–18, vi. 9. 3. 41–9). Finally we must, of course, avoid confusing the negations used of the One with those used of Matter, at the opposite end of the scale of reality, though the two extremes are superficially alike in their absolute simplicity (vi. 7. 13. 3–4). For whereas Matter's negativity consists in total *deprivation* of all form, the One is on a more exalted level than the Intelligible world (v. 3. 14. 16–19) and in its perfect self-sufficiency has no *need* of any form (vi. 7. 32. 9–10). Similarly to deny Aristotle's claim that the Supreme Deity exercises Intelligence means not that the One is ignorant or unconscious, but that it is too perfect to need Intelligence.[2]

We have here the psychological correlate of Plotinus' views on unity and plurality, that psychological faculties arise only where they are needed and are superfluous to beings that can do without them (cf. vi. 7. 9. 38–46). Thus sense-perception is in his view of value only for the practical purpose of assisting an animal's survival or as a source of knowledge for beings that have forgotten their Intellectual contemplation (iv. 4. 24. 1–12). Similarly even Intelligence is only an 'eye for the blind', necessary where multiplicity is present, but superfluous for the One (v. 6. 5. 1–5, vi. 7. 41). To regard Intelligence, with Aristotle, as necessary to divine perfection is for Plotinus to deny that God is perfect by his very nature. For Intelligence entails logical duality of essence and act, of subject and object, which is inconsistent with the

---

[1] v. 3. 10. 34–9, 13. 24–31, v. 5. 13. 11–13, vi. 7. 38. 1–9. Plotinus' argument, of course, needs restating in the light of modern logic's denial that existence is a predicate; he would, however, presumably still wish to maintain that the One's nature excludes the possibility of significant predication.

[2] iii. 9. 9, v. 3. 13, v. 6. 6. 29–35, vi. 7. 37. 24–31, vi. 9. 6. 44–55.

One's absolute simplicity (VI. 7. 37. 1–16). And while in Intellectual vision subject and object are indistinguishable, the contents of that vision are still a plurality (V. 3. 13. 9–36). We may, however, ascribe to the One an absolutely simple self-apprehension (*epibolē*, VI. 7. 38. 25–6), also characterised as an 'awakening' or 'hyper-intellection' (VI. 8. 16. 32–5; cf. also V. 4. 2. 15–19). Alternatively we may describe the One not as having Intelligence, but as being a pure Intellectual Act prior to the emergence of subject and object (VI. 7. 37. 15–16, VI. 9. 6. 50–5). It is in the light of these considerations that we should consider the two main positive terms used by Plotinus of his Supreme Deity, the terms 'One' and 'Good'.

Plotinus stresses that neither of these terms applies to the One as a predicate (II. 9. 1. 1–8, VI. 7. 38. 4–9, VI. 9. 5. 29–34, etc.). In fact the term 'One' connotes strictly only negation of plurality; hence the Pythagoreans were right to name the One Apollo (on the etymology *a* = not, *polla* = many) (V. 5. 6. 26–8). Alternatively, the term may be taken as signifying that the Supreme Principle is attained by unifying our own minds (VI. 9. 5. 38–41). The term 'Good' on the other hand applies to the One's role as the supreme object of aspiration to all lower realities, which in its turn depends on its utter freedom from limitation and hence from want (I. 7. 1, VI. 7. 23. 7–9, VI. 9. 6. 16–39). Our criterion of the Good is thus not merely subjective; the One is desired because it is Good, not Good because it is desired (VI. 7. 19. 1–9, 25. 16–18). But since the One has no needs, it is good only for other beings, not for itself (VI. 7. 24. 13–16, 41. 28–31, VI. 9. 6. 39–42).[1] Finally, 'Good' does not denote a definite form or quality; on the contrary it is just because it is unrestricted by any form that the One is the Good (V. 5. 13. 1–9; cf. V. 3. 11. 23–5). The paradoxical similarity to, and yet utter contrast with, Matter, is here very apparent. Plotinus therefore condemns the folly of seeking to exalt the One by ascribing it a plurality of attributes, since such additions can only mark a diminution of the One's excellence (III. 8. 11. 12–13, V. 5. 13. 9–16). We must rather beware lest there may still be something to remove from our conception of the One (VI. 8. 21. 25–8), a statement, as we shall see later, with both theoretical and practical applications. For all theoretical discussions of the One are finally inadequate, since its true nature is revealed only in the mystical union (VI. 7. 36).

[1] Hence though Plotinus normally describes the One as the only perfectly self-sufficient principle, he sometimes places it beyond self-sufficiency and therefore beyond the Good (V. 3. 17. 12–14, VI. 9. 6. 55–7).

Another very influential side of Plotinus' thought about the One appears in his discussions of its generation of lower realities. To the problem how unity gives rise to plurality his answer is that, since the product is always less than its producer, the One's products can only be a plurality (v. 3. 15. 1–11, vi. 7. 8. 17–32). Why the product must be less than its producer the Neoplatonists never explain; it is an axiom they have to assume to account for the universe's manifest inequalities (cf. Proclus *ET* prop. 7). Pluralisation is thus once again equated with fragmentation; and this in its turn suggests that the contents of the Intelligible world must already be present in the One in 'unfragmented' or perfectly unified form. In fact Plotinus declares that the One is all things in transcendent mode (*ekeinōs* v. 2. 1. 2; cf. vi. 8. 18. 32–41). A corollary is the doctrine introduced into Christianity by pseudo-Dionysius, and fundamental to Thomism, that we can form some conception of deity by analogy from its products, a possibility to which Plotinus also alludes (v. 3. 14. 7–8, vi. 7. 36. 6–8, vi. 8. 8. 1 ff.).[1] For instance he justifies his description of the One as pure Act of Thought on the grounds that the One, though it does not itself think, causes thought in other beings (vi. 9. 6. 52–5). (Similarly, we may recall, the Form of Magnitude is not a magnitude, but Magnitude's transcendent cause; cf. p. 49.) The example shows that Plotinus does not regard such declarations as inconsistent with his statements that the One cannot be identical with any of its products or all of them together (iii. 8. 9. 39–54, v. 5. 13. 17–38, etc.), and hence gives rise to what it does not itself possess (v. 3. 15, vi. 7. 15. 18–20, 17. 1–6). The truth is that the One is 'all things and none of them' (v. 2. 1. 1–3, vi. 7. 32. 12–14), none insofar as within the One they are not yet distinguished, all insofar as it is their cause and must therefore—some passages at least imply—contain them in seminal form; hence Plotinus' description of the One as the '(seminal) power of all things' (*dynamis pantōn*).[2] A final point to note is that to describe the One as 'cause' does not ascribe anything to the One itself, but merely characterises our own relation thereto (vi. 9. 3. 49–51). We here encounter a principle, that causal relations between

---

[1] On the three ways to knowledge of God distinguished in vi. 7. 36 and in Middle Platonism (Albinus *Epit.* x. 5–6, Origen *C. Cels.* vii. 42), those of negation, analogy and eminence, cf. H. A. Wolfson, 'The Divine Attributes in Albinus and Plotinus', *Harvard Theological Review*, 45 (1952) 115–34.

[2] iii. 8. 10. 1, v. 1. 7. 9–10, v. 3. 15. 33, v. 4. 1. 36; the rendering 'potentiality of all things' should be avoided, since it falsely implies (giving 'potentiality' its Aristotelian sense) that the One's products are a more perfect evolution of the One itself; cf. pp. 23–4 and 69.

the One and its products (and between these and their own products) are non-reciprocating, which we shall see to be of fundamental importance for the Neoplatonic universe.

III. EMANATION, LOGOS, SYMPATHY

The generation of Reality by the One is described by the Neoplatonists in terms of their well-known image of Emanation. The image's underlying principle is summarised in the Scholastic maxim that 'good diffuses itself' ('*bonum diffusivum sui*'). In other words, entities that have achieved perfection of their own being do not keep that perfection to themselves, but spread it abroad by generating an external 'image' of their internal activity. Examples Plotinus gives are those of the radiation of heat from fire or cold from snow or—the example that gives the principle its name—the outflow of light from the sun (e.g. v. 1. 6. 28–40, v. 3. 12. 39–44, v. 4. 1. 23–41). But, as always, the image requires correction and 'dematerialisation'. In particular we must avoid conceiving light, with the Stoics, as a material outflow from the sun; on the contrary, the image's popularity with Plotinus stems in large part from the fact that he regards light *not* as a body or (with Aristotle) as a modification of the air, but as a substantial, incorporeal power (iv. 5. 6–7, cf. ii. 1. 7. 26–30).[1] It constitutes in fact the visible manifestation in the physical world of the life of the Intelligible order—or, more precisely, of the radiance cast on that order by the Good (cf. v. 5. 7, based on Plato *Rep.* vi. 507–9, and below pp. 87–8). Even so, the emanation image has certain defects, notably that the sun from which light radiates is a physical body with a definite place and definite dimensions (vi. 4. 7. 45–8. 12, cf. v. 3. 9. 7–20). As always, dematerialisation of our images must be accompanied by de-spatialisation.

Since lower realities tend naturally to reproduce themselves, we cannot, Plotinus argues, suppose that the One, the most perfect of beings, would grudge others a share in its perfection (v. 4. 1. 23 ff.). Its superabundant power therefore overflows (v. 2. 1. 7–9) and the result, since it must be less than the One, is the next most perfect of beings, the unity-in-plurality of the Intelligible world (v. 1. 6. 39 ff., v. 3. 15. 1–11).

---

[1] For other uses of the light analogy cf. i. 1. 4. 12–18 and iv. 3. 22. 1–7 (illustrating the soul's union with the body, discussed below pp. 111–12) and vi. 4. 7. 22 ff., following *Parmenides* 131B (cf. above pp. 21 and 42). Cf. further A. H. Armstrong, *The Architecture of the Intelligible Universe in the Philosophy of Plotinus*, pp. 54–8, and W. Beierwaltes, 'Die Metaphysik des Lichtes in der Philosophie Plotins', *Zeitschrift für philosophische Forschung* 15 (1961) 334–62.

Consistently with his general equation of greater unity with greater reality and power, Plotinus regards the greatest energy as produced by beings that do not squander their power in external activity, but keep it concentrated within themselves (cf. VI. 6. 1. 4–14), a principle most fully exemplified by the tranquil self-contemplation of the divine Hypostases. We have seen how this view of reality had led Plotinus to treat mental states as more real than material objects; conversely, when spatial and material restrictions are abolished, what we have left, he argues, can only be a form of contemplation, or at least something analogous thereto (cf. III. 8. 3. 1 ff., 8. 12–26). It must, however, be stressed that such contemplation need not be 'conscious', at least in the normal sense of the term (cf. pp. 80–1); hence even unconscious Nature has a 'sleeping contemplation', a last vestige of the vision of its priors (III. 8. 4. 15–29), while the One, in virtue of its 'hyper-contemplation', may similarly be described as 'turning its attention towards itself' (V. 1. 6. 18). On every level therefore creation is the result of the energy produced by such contemplation (III. 8. 3–4). For even in artistic creation the motive force is not the craftsman's instruments, but the plan within his mind, and among the Hypostases there is no question of instruments (III. 8. 2. 1 ff., V. 9. 6. 20–4); the outflow of energy from contemplation into creation is completely spontaneous (cf. III. 8. 4. 9–10).

We now come to the point where the need to dematerialise the emanation simile is greatest, the Neoplatonic doctrine of 'undiminished giving'. It is a corollary of the infinite power of the divine Hypostases that creation involves no dissipation of this power among their products nor any diminution of their substance (III. 8. 8. 46–8, 10. 1–19). Here again Plotinus' view of the celestial bodies makes the image more appropriate than may at first appear. For him, as for other Greek thinkers, the sun and stars are everlasting and will continue endlessly radiating heat and light throughout the universe without exhausting their energy (II. 3. 18. 19–22, VI. 4. 10. 22–30, VI. 9. 9. 1–11). It follows that the divine Hypostases, remaining unaffected by what they produce, need give their products no attention or concern. As we shall see, it is only man's deficiency, and that of his body, that necessitate such attention on his part (II. 9. 2. 4–15, IV. 3. 4. 21–37). 'For absolutely blessed beings', by contrast, 'it suffices to remain in themselves and be what they are' (III. 2. 1. 40–2); hence the One, like the other Hypostases, creates 'without inclination, will or movement' (V. 1. 6. 25–7; cf. V. 3. 12. 20–39); it remains self-intent, while its creation proceeds from it, and receives order from it, automatically. Nor have the divine Hypostases any knowledge of their products. The One, of course, transcends 'knowledge' altogether (VI. 7. 39. 19–33), while the lower Hypostases know only the causal principles they contain within themselves, not the products that emanate from these; for instance the World-soul knows its activity on the cosmos only in its unity, not *qua* directed towards the cosmos (IV. 4. 9. 16–18, cf. V. 8. 3. 26–7). But this does not imply any deficiency in their knowledge, since it is superfluous for one who knows the archetypal realities to seek in addition knowledge of their sensible images (III. 8. 4. 43–4, IV. 4. 8. 3–7).

Creation is not therefore the result of a deliberate decision on the part of the divine Hypostases (III. 2. 2. 8–15, V. 8. 7. 1–16, etc.). A further reason for excluding deliberation and choice is the implication they convey of hesitation between opposite courses, and hence of doubt and ignorance. For the Hypostases, by contrast, all happens automatically in the best, and indeed the only, possible way (IV. 4. 12, VI. 7. 1. 21 ff.). Their activity therefore, down to that of the World-soul, is in this respect more like the spontaneous operation of Nature than the laborious deliberations of human craftsmen (IV. 3. 10. 13–19, IV. 4. 11), (though we must not fall into the Sceptics' trap of confusing the sub-rational with the super-rational; cf. IV. 4. 13 and above pp. 26–7). Hence the *Timaeus'* references to divine deliberation can mean only that the world is as good as the best possible reasoning could have planned it.[1] It follows equally that emanation is necessary in the sense that it could neither fail to happen nor happen otherwise than it does. And this brings us to Plotinus' view of free will.

Consistently with this viewpoint, Plotinus, like many subsequent philosophers, denies the existence of free will in any sense incompatible with determinism. It is true that he opposes the Stoics' subjection of man to the Fate governing the sensible cosmos (II. 3. 9. 14 ff., III. 1. 8–10, etc.), but though man's higher soul is independent of Fate, its character, and its whole destiny, are still the expression of an Intelligible archetype and as such ordained by that archetype (IV. 3. 12. 12–30, 15. 10–23; cf. III. 2. 18. 5–29). On the other hand it is no more accurate to describe incorporeal beings as determined by their nature than as producing their nature by their will (VI. 8. 4. 22–32, 7. 46–53, 13. 5–11). All we can say is that within the Intelligible world will and order imply one another; to distinguish one as prior to the other is possible only on a level of greater multiplicity. Freedom for Plotinus consists in tending spontaneously and with full knowledge towards realisation of one's

[1] III. 2. 14. 1–6, VI. 2. 21. 32–8, VI. 7. 1. 28–32, VI. 8. 17. 1–12.

true good, and thus contrasts with actions performed under compulsion or under constraint from man's irrational nature (III. 1. 9, VI. 8. 4. 11 ff.). Choice between opposite courses (or, more strictly, the illusion of such choice) is therefore paradoxically the sign of a lack of freedom; for at such times our irrational nature has clouded our judgment and prevented our seeing and pursuing the right course automatically. True freedom by contrast consists in the absence of any possibility of change for the worse (VI. 8. 10. 25–35, 21. 1–7). It is with these considerations in mind that we should approach Plotinus' references to creation as motivated by divine generosity (IV. 8. 6. 12–13, V. 4. 1. 34–6, etc.) or, to use a less tendentious translation of the term in question (*aphthonia*), by divine 'ungrudgingness'.

The source of such statements is of course the *Timaeus'* account of the divine motive for creation (29E–30A). How close either Plato or Plotinus here comes to the Christian doctrine of divine love has provoked, and still provokes, keen debate. Those who argue that Plotinus envisages something at least analogous to an act of love or free will[1] appeal to the treatise VI. 8, which describes the One as will, and as love, of itself (VI. 8. 13. 5 ff., 15. 1). It must, however, be remembered that Plotinus stresses the inadequacy of such terms (VI. 8. 13. 1–5, 18. 52–3); for instance love (in the sense of Classical *erōs*) implies need, (cf. III. 5. 7. 9–15), whereas the One has no needs. Plotinus' purpose in using them is to refute suggestions that the One, the source of the freedom and order of other beings, owes its own nature to necessity or —the worst blasphemy of all—to chance (VI. 8. 10. 1–18; cf. above p. 44). And not even here is the One said to love anything other than itself. The contrast with Christianity is best revealed by another passage where a reference to divine 'ungrudgingness' is counterbalanced by the declaration that the One has no need of its products and would not care if it had no products at all (V. 5. 12. 40–9). On the other hand the treatise VI. 8 warns us against regarding the One as compelled to create; the truth is that 'will' and 'necessity' are both inadequate terms to use of a process which follows naturally from divine power, but which leaves the One totally unaffected and unconcerned.

A consequence of the One's infinite power is that emanation exemplifies what Arthur Lovejoy, in *The Great Chain of Being*, calls the 'Principle of Plenitude'. First, since the process continues as long as its source exists, it is without temporal beginning or end (II. 9. 3, etc.).

---

[1] Cf. J. Trouillard, *La Procession plotinienne*, passim; J. M. Rist, *Eros and Psyche*, pp. 76 ff. and *Plotinus: the Road to Reality*, pp. 66–83.

That this must be so of the timeless Intelligible world goes without saying (II. 4. 5. 24–8, V. 1. 6. 19–22); similarly Plotinus denies that the *Timaeus'* ascription of a temporal origin to the sensible world should be taken literally (III. 2. 1. 20–6, IV. 3. 9. 12–20, VI. 7. 3. 1–9, etc.). Secondly, the spontaneous outflow of Reality from the One cannot terminate until everything that could possibly come into existence thereby has actually done so. Hence creation cannot stop with Intelligence, but must proceed downwards through all possible levels of reality, and of imperfection, until the darkness of Matter is reached (IV. 8. 6, V. 2. 2. 1 ff.). And each of these levels must be complete in its turn, Intelligence containing the Totality of Being in a timeless eternity (cf. V. 1. 7. 27 ff., and above p. 53), Soul under conditions of temporal succession and the sensible cosmos under those of spatial extension (III. 2. 3. 19–41).[1] The *Timaeus* had already argued that the sensible cosmos would be incomplete if it did not contain all possible living creatures (30C–D, 39E). Hence, since the Principle of Plenitude necessitates production not just of as many beings as possible, but of every kind of being, not all things can be equally good (II. 9. 13. 1–5, 25–33, III. 2. 14. 6 ff., III. 3. 3, etc.). Indeed the universe would be less perfect if they were, just as it may be necessary to a beautiful work of art that not all its parts are beautiful in isolation (III. 2. 11). As Lovejoy has shown, this justification of the world's imperfections was to have an enormous influence.

None the less, since the Principle of Plenitude was linked in Neoplatonism with the view of creation as a natural rather than a voluntary act, which could therefore not be conceived as failing to happen, it was hard for Christian thinkers to accept it without reservations. A similar contrast with Christian ideas is perceptible as regards the beings produced by emanation, a difference summarised in the later Neoplatonists' description of them as 'self-constituted' (*authypostata*, cf. pp. 128–9). In Neoplatonic thought spiritual beings are not thrown into existence by an external creator without any choice on their part. On the contrary, they come forth voluntarily from their source and shape themselves. But it is impossible for them to receive any shape as long as the descent into limitless multiplicity continues unchecked; they must therefore turn back upon themselves and so imitate the perfection of their source to the best of their powers. Thus arise two laws basic both to Neoplatonic metaphysics and to its mysticism. First, every being seeks to

---

[1] Cf. also III. 2. 4. 18–20, IV. 3. 10. 38–42, VI. 2. 22. 42–6, VI. 6. 7. 15–19, VI. 7. 11. 1–4.

return to its cause (III. 8. 7. 17–18); secondly, since this is achieved through introversion, reversion upon one's cause coincides with reversion in contemplation upon oneself (VI. 9. 2. 33–43, cf. ibid. 7. 29 ff.). Two stages may therefore be distinguished in the self-creation of Intelligence (and, on a lower level, of Soul); in the former, that of Procession (*prohodos*), a formless, infinite stream of life flows forth from the One; in the latter, that of Reversion (*epistrophē*), it turns back, contemplates the One, and so receives form and order. The two stages Plotinus further analyses in terms of Aristotle's account of cognition. Thus Procession corresponds to the power of sight at the stage when it is still 'groping for vision', Reversion to the same power when it has become actualised by contemplation of an object (V. 3. 11. 1–16, V. 4. 2. 4–8, VI. 7. 16. 10–22). For Aristotle this had involved reception of the form of the object contemplated; in the present case, however, this is obviously impossible, since the One has no form. The explanation is that Intelligence is unable to receive the vision of the One in its full perfection; it therefore 'fragments' it, and the result is the unity-in-plurality of the World of Forms (VI. 7. 15. 10–24).

The same analogy explains another odd-sounding Plotinian doctrine, his application to the phase of Procession of the term 'Intelligible Matter' (II. 4. 5. 24–37, III. 8. 11. 1–8). His justification lies in Aristotle's description of the soul's cognitive powers as 'matter' for the forms they receive (though the term 'intelligible matter' had been used by Aristotle in quite another sense; cf. *Met. Z.* 10. 1036a 9–10, *Z.* 11. 1037a 4–5, *H.* 6. 1045a 34–6). Why matter must be postulated in the Intelligible world is explained in the early chapters of the treatise II. 4, where Plotinus is careful to stress that it is free from the imperfections of its sensible counterpart; while both constitute the principle of indeterminacy within their respective worlds, Intelligible Matter does not share sensible matter's unsubstantiality and, of course, should not be regarded as evil (II. 4. 5. 12–23, 15. 17–28, II. 5. 3. 8–19). A further obvious corollary is its identification with the 'Indefinite Dyad' postulated in Plato's oral teaching as the basis of the Forms (V. 1. 5. 6 ff., V. 4. 2. 7–8; cf. above p. 48). Also important in this connection is Plotinus' interpretation of the five Platonic 'categories' (*megista genē*) recognised in the *Sophist* (Being, Rest, Motion, Identity and Difference). For Plotinus these express different facets of the eternal life of Intelligence; in particular Motion and Difference are associated with the descent into plurality that occurs at the phase of Procession, the others with the stability acquired through Reversion.[1] We therefore have here several striking instances of a free adaptation of Platonic and Aristotelian concepts to Plotinus' own teaching.

The above account, the reader will have observed, described Intelligence as creating the Forms through its contemplation of the One, a statement which seems inconsistent with Plotinus' denial elsewhere that the existence of the Forms depends on their being thought (p. 54). Plotinus' considered answer seems to be similar to the attitude we have seen him taking to the question of the relative priority of will and necessity within the Intelligible world, that within that world Being and Thought are so closely inter-dependent that, while for the sake of analysis we may describe one as caused by the other, in reality questions of logical priority are meaningless (v. 1. 4. 26–33, v. 9. 8. 8–22). To Iamblichus, however, such an attitude seemed equivocal, and his departure from Plotinian teaching on this point was to constitute one of his most important modifications of Neoplatonic doctrine (cf. p. 124).

Another fundamental late Neoplatonic doctrine was its recognition of a third principle, Life, intermediate between Being and Intelligence. A similar triadic grouping occurs in some passages of the *Enneads*, notably the treatise vi. 6 on Numbers—cf. also v. 6. 6. 20–1—but Plotinus can hardly be said to have a consistent theory on the subject. Indeed he suggests arranging the three in the order Being, Intelligence, Life, assigning the lowest place to Life in view of its association with Soul (vi. 6. 8. 17–22, 17. 35–43). A closer approach to later Neoplatonic teaching is his suggestion that Life should be equated with the Second Hypostasis in its unformed stage (i.e. with Procession) and Intelligence with the stage of Reversion, when it has received form and limit (vi. 7. 17. 14–26, 21. 2–6). But on this point, as on many others, it was left for Plotinus' successors to transform his hints into a rigid theory.

The lower levels of the procession occur in the same way. Sometimes Plotinus treats the generation of Soul as a single process, but he often grants Soul's lowest level the status of a separate entity, which, as we have seen, he identifies with Aristotle's Nature (iii. 8. 2–4, iv. 4. 12–13, v. 2. 1. 18–28; cf. pp. 27 and 52). It is the latter that automatically conveys into Matter the only vestiges of form it can receive. It is also in connection with the generation of Soul that another important principle

---

[1] On the Platonic Categories cf. further ii. 4. 5. 28–35, iii. 7. 3. 8–11, v. 1. 4. 30–43, vi. 2. 7–8. Plotinus' doctrine is well discussed by Hadot, *Porphyre et Victorinus I*, pp. 215–22.

appears, the Logos. The term is the most basic and most complicated in Greek philosophy; originating as the verbal noun of the verb 'speak' (*legein*), it denotes sometimes 'word' or 'speech', sometimes the 'reason', 'thought', or 'principle' expressed therein, elsewhere, by a natural transition, a thing's 'rationale' or 'ordering principle', and much else besides. In Plotinus all these meanings have come together in an extremely rich and multivalent concept which, in consequence, will here be left untranslated. This is the more necessary since Plotinus, like other writers, often intends several of the above meanings simultaneously. Here, however, we can deal only with Logos as a metaphysical term. In this sense, as in most of its other senses, its normal application is to the level of Soul, which is natural in view of its psychological meaning of discursive, as opposed to intuitive, thought. But it is also applied to Intelligence's relation to the One (v. 1. 6. 44–8; cf. however VI. 7. 17. 41–3), and there is the further complication that recognition of two or more levels of Soul sometimes leads Plotinus to distinguish two or more levels of Logoi (e.g. III. 8. 2. 25–3. 10). It is this that distinguishes Plotinus' use of the term from that of Philo and the Christian Fathers; in his view Logos is not a separate Hypostasis (II. 9. 1. 57–63), but expresses the relation of an Hypostasis to its source, its products, or simultaneously to both (cf. e.g. III. 2. 2. 15 ff.). Despite this coalescence, however, the sense, and probably the source, of the two applications is different.

Applied to the relation of an Hypostasis to its products, Logos normally denotes the 'ground-plan' or 'formative principle' from which lower realities evolve and which subsequently governs their development. As such it is especially prominent in Plotinus' accounts of Soul's government of the sensible cosmos (II. 3. 16–17, III. 2–3, IV. 3. 9–16, etc.) and derives from Stoic thought. According to the Stoics, just as the seed of an individual living being contains in its microscopic bulk the causal principles that will later manifest as the fully-formed creature, so the world unfolds from its causal principles within the divine mind, which receive in consequence the name of 'seminal reasons' (*Spermatikoi Logoi*) (III. 2. 2. 18–31, v. 9. 6. 10–24). Since the world, for both Plotinus and the Stoics, is a living organism, the comparison is more than a mere metaphor (cf. IV. 3. 10. 10 ff., IV. 4. 11). And, though the One is never called Logos, the seed comparison can be applied to its role as 'power of all things' (IV. 8. 6. 7–10, cf. above p. 60). But the seed image, like other images, requires correction. First, it hardly needs repeating that the indivisibility of the divine Hypostases is not that of minute bulk; secondly, since creation is an everlasting process, their priority to their products is logical and ontological, not chronological (III. 2. 1. 20–6, V. 5. 12. 37–8). Nor should the seed analogy lead us to infer a false evolutionary view of emanation, making the end-product superior to its cause (cf. III. 7. 11. 23–7, III. 8. 8. 32–40). The affirmation of the Principle of Plenitude that it is good that other things should exist beside the divine Hypostases should not be misunderstood to mean that they add anything to the beatitude of those Hypostases, still less that they are more perfect than the latter. Indeed for this reason, as we shall later see, Plotinus sometimes takes a more pessimistic view of the origin of the lower realities.[1]

The source of the other sense of Logos, that denoting an entity's relation to its producer, is to be found in Platonic and Stoic psychology. The point of this analogy is that, just as external speech (*logos prophorikos*) constitutes the external expression of internal thought (*logos endiathetos*), so an Hypostasis flows forth from its prior and 'expresses' it under conditions of greater multiplicity, so revealing it to the external world (I. 2. 3. 27–30; cf. *Theaet.* 189E, *Soph.* 263E). Universal Soul thus constitutes a Logos of Intelligence (V. 1. 3. 6–10, 6. 44–5) and individual souls Logoi of their own individual intelligences (IV. 3. 5. 8–14). The principles operative within the psychical cosmos are thus Logoi in both senses (and in many others); hence the term is appropriate to Soul's role as an intermediary between Intelligible and sensible worlds, conveying into Matter images of the Forms she receives from Intelligence (cf. III. 2. 2. 15 ff.).

As an image of the Intelligible cosmos, the psychical cosmos is a unity-in-plurality of its own, a multiple Logos containing a plurality of individual Logoi (III. 3. 1, IV. 3. 8. 17–22) and representing the best possible image of the Intelligible world on its own level. But, though all Souls are therefore one (IV. 9 passim; cf. VI. 4. 14. 1–16), we should not follow the Stoics' description of individual souls as 'parts' of the World-soul, since this is once again to misconceive immaterial beings in quantitative terms (IV. 3. 2–3). Moreover the World-soul, possessing as she does the task of administering her own particular body, is herself an individual soul (albeit the most powerful of all); in fact both she and the other individual souls are manifestations of Universal Soul—the Unparticipated Soul of later Neoplatonism (IV. 3. 2. 1–10, 54–9, 4. 14–21; cf. p. 126). Finally, to describe souls as parts of the World-soul

[1] Cf. III. 7. 11. 15 ff., III. 8. 8. 32–40, V. 2. 1. 18–28, VI. 9. 5. 29, discussed below p. 82.

limits them to the sensible cosmos, whereas our higher soul, like the higher level of the World-soul herself, belongs to the Intelligible order (IV. 3. 4. 14–37, 7. 20–30; IV. 7. 12. 2–11). And she exists there as an individual; to suppose otherwise would entail the absurd conclusion that she ceases to exist just when she has attained full beatitude (IV. 3. 5, cf. VI. 4. 4. 34–46).

From the unity of all souls follow two important consequences, both echoed later in the philosophy of Leibniz. First, just as each Intelligence contains the whole Intelligible world, so each soul contains all the principles operative within the psychical order (V. 7. 1. 7 ff.); hence 'we are each of us an intelligible cosmos' (III. 4. 3. 22, IV. 7. 10. 32–7, cf. III. 8. 6. 40) and determine our destiny by choosing which of these principles shall rule our lives (cf. p. 72). Secondly, there is a pre-established harmony linking the destinies of all souls. From this follows Plotinus' view of divine justice. That this operates automatically had already been argued in Plato's *Laws*, where God had been conceived as simply ordaining the law that each individual tends to his appropriate place and leaving the individual's free will to take care of the rest (904A ff.). Plotinus now takes the further step of eliminating the initial divine decision (cf. IV. 8. 4. 38–42) and making the law an automatic consequence of the pre-established harmony. It is this that ensures that, as long as the individual's desires bind him to this world, he will spontaneously gravitate to the environment the World-soul has produced for him (III. 2. 13, IV. 3. 24, IV. 4. 45). The same principle underlies Plotinus' explanation of paranormal phenomena.

In these Plotinus, like virtually all his contemporaries, except the most determined atheists and materialists—by the third century A.D. a very rare species—firmly believed. Where he differed from many of them was in attempting to accommodate such phenomena to a rational, orderly view of the world (IV. 4. 31. 29–32). The basis of his explanation is the Stoic doctrine of 'cosmic sympathy', the view that, since the world is a living organism, whatever happens in one part of it must produce a sympathetic reaction in every other part (II. 3. 7, IV. 4. 32 ff.). It is by studying and applying the relevant forces that magicians produce their effects (IV. 4. 40). The effects of prayer Plotinus explains in the same way. Prayer to the celestial gods cannot touch their higher souls, which are absorbed in contemplation and unaware of anything in the sensible cosmos; it does, however, provoke an automatic response from their lower soul, which grants the petitioner's wish (IV. 4. 40. 27 ff.). Similarly, just as it is possible to discern an individual's character

from his eyes, so human destiny may be read in the stars (II. 3. 7. 4–10)
Nor are the stars mere signs, without any causal agency (IV. 4. 34.
23–6), though their causality is strictly limited, extending only to man's
body and lower soul (II. 3. 9–10, III. 3. 6., IV. 3. 7. 20–30). The actions
of his higher soul they indeed indicate, in virtue of the pre-established
harmony; but, since that soul is an independent principle, those who
live by it escape astral determinism (II. 3. 9. 14–30, IV. 4. 39. 1–5). Finally,
as always, we must conceive the stars' causality neither in materialistic
terms nor as an act of will on their part (II. 3. 1–6, IV. 4. 31. 32–57);
only the Neoplatonic view of an automatically-operating sympathy is
satisfactory (cf. IV. 4. 39. 17–32).

Plotinus is thus emphatic that magic affects the higher souls neither
of gods nor of men (cf. II. 9. 14. 1–11). It cannot therefore aid the soul's
return to the Intelligible order; indeed contemplation puts the philosopher beyond its power (IV. 4. 43–4). Plotinus indeed allows the sage
to resist a magical attack on his psycho-physical organism by counter-
spells of his own (IV. 4. 43. 1–11), and may possibly have followed this
course himself on one occasion (*V. Pl.* 10. 1–13), but such application
of magic is solely for an immediate practical purpose, and is certainly
not a justification of the theurgic rituals of later Neoplatonism. In one
passage he speaks with apparent favour of the theurgic practice of
animating a divine statue (IV. 3. 11), but not even here is it hinted that
this is necessary for the philosopher. Indeed, when Amelius attempted
to persuade him to engage in ritual worship of the gods, Plotinus
refused with the proud, and enigmatic, reply, 'It is for them to come to
me, not for me to go to them' (*V. Pl.* 10. 33–8). He was, however,
once persuaded to attend an evocation of his guardian spirit, which
turned out to be not a mere daemon, but a god; according to Porphyry
it was this occasion that prompted him to compose the treatise III. 4 on
Our Guardian Spirit (*V. Pl.* 10. 14–33). But if the latter information is
correct, it reveals Plotinus' attitude even more clearly. For the 'guardian
spirit' of the treatise in question is not an anthropomorphic daemon,[1]
but an inner psychological principle; more precisely, it is the level above
that on which we consciously live, and so is both within us and yet
transcendent (III. 4. 3–6, esp. 3. 3–8, 5. 19–24). Plotinus will thus have
seized the chance of turning his disciples away from popular religion
towards philosophy.

We may say therefore that magic, while a real force for Plotinus, is

---

[1] In such daemons Plotinus, however, believed; cf. II. 1. 6. 54, III. 5. 6–7, IV. 3.
18. 22–4, IV. 4. 43. 12–16.

yet of limited application and has no place in the philosopher's training. He thus posed a challenge for those, like Iamblichus, who took a more exalted view of theurgy.[1]

IV. THE INDIVIDUAL SOUL

Since experience thus shows the human soul to contain all the divine Hypostases within her, the obvious question arises why she normally remains unaware of this and how she has fallen into her present miserable condition (IV. 8. I. I–II, V. I. I2). To answer this question it is first necessary to discover who 'we' are who ask it.[2] And this question, like others, may be posed either 'statically' or 'dynamically'. Since the soul, as an 'intelligible cosmos', contains not merely all Logoi operative on the level of Soul, but the higher levels of Intelligence and the One (III. 4. 3. 21–7), she can choose to live according to any of these principles, and it is her resulting disposition that will determine her future rebirth. Thus a soul that chooses the rational level will be reborn as a man, whereas one that yields to its lower irrational nature will become an animal or even a plant;[3] alternatively we can transcend the human level and identify ourselves with Intelligence (V. 3. 4, V. 8. 7. 31–5, II. I–24, VI. 5. 7 and 12), so escaping rebirth altogether.[4] Hence from the dynamic standpoint 'we' are identical with the level to which we give most attention. On the other hand, if we pose the question from the static point of view and ask which of these levels is our 'true self', we may mean either (*a*) Which is the distinctively human level? or (*b*) What is the self we discover after purifying ourselves from the accretions gathered in our descent into this world—the 'intruder' that has 'fastened itself round us' (VI. 4. 14. 16–15. 40; cf. I. 6. 5. 22–58, IV. 7. 10. 27–52)? To the former question the answer is clearly 'Rational Soul' (I. I. 7–8, 13, V. 3. 3. 23–45); to the latter, on the other hand, it would seem to be 'Intelligence', which the former answer had treated as something transcendent (cf. I. 4. 9. 28–30, III. 4. 6. 1–5, IV. 7. 10. 30–40). The discrepancy between the two answers is removed if we assume 'Intelligence' in these latter passages to be shorthand for 'Soul conformed to Intelligence',[5] since, as we shall see, the soul in its pure

---

[1] Cf. further A. H. Armstrong, 'Was Plotinus a magician?' *Phronesis* I 1 (1955) 73–9, opposing P. Merlan, 'Plotinus and magic', *Isis* XLIV (1953) 341–8.

[2] Cf. I. 1. 13, IV. 3. 1. 1–12, V. 1. 1. 30–5, VI. 4. 14. 16 ff., etc.

[3] III. 4. 2, IV. 3. 12. 35–9, V. 2. 2. 1–10, VI. 7. 6–7.

[4] Cf. III. 2. 4. 8–11, III. 4. 6. 30 ff., IV. 3. 24. 21–8, VI. 4. 16. 36–47.

[5] Cf. I. 6. 6. 13–21, IV. 4. 1–2, V. 3. 6. 12–15, VI. 4. 14. 17–21.

state is virtually identical with Intelligence (cf. pp. 81–2). But to accept this answer raises a much graver difficulty, namely what grounds remain for distinguishing between pure Soul and Intelligence and therefore between the Second and Third Hypostases? We may, however, at least observe that on neither static nor dynamic viewpoint do we ever cease to be Soul.[1] It is therefore the nature of Soul that must claim our attention.

Of Plotinus' conception of Soul as a metaphysical entity we have already spoken. But it is worth devoting special attention to the details of his psychology, since by common consent this contains some of his most acute and most modern-sounding observations. Plotinus' concern is not, however, to produce a systematic and consistent psychology covering all aspects of the soul's activity. Instead he approaches the various problems individually, generally with the requirements of man's spiritual life in mind; it is this, for instance, that underlies his concern to discover which psychological functions belong to the soul in her pure state and which arise as a consequence of her embodiment. Hence fluctuations and sometimes inconsistencies arise as problems are considered from different points of view. One example we have just seen. Another arises over Plotinus' division of the soul into 'faculties' or 'levels'.

Since Soul in Plotinus' view forms a single living continuum, no sharp separation between such levels can evidently be made, and every division must therefore be somewhat arbitrary. Hence, while Plotinus is often content with a twofold division into higher and lower, or rational and irrational souls (the latter embracing all the functions enumerated on p. 52 above), he elsewhere divides the soul into three, or even more, levels. Confusingly he can at such times use either of two alternative threefold divisions. The first of these recognises sense-perception as a level of its own, intermediate between discursive reason and the 'vegetative soul' (*phytikon*)—so entitled in view of its responsibility for growth and nutrition, but also including the bodily appetites and emotions.[2] The second recognises at the summit of Soul an 'unfallen' level, which remains in eternal contemplation of Intelligence without descending into this world. Plotinus admits his recognition of

---

[1] The most elaborate attempt to reconcile static and dynamic viewpoints is made in VI. 7. 4–7; cf. also I. 1. 12 and VI. 4. 16.

[2] For the twofold division cf. e.g. IV. 3. chs. 4 and 27–32; for the threefold division cf. III. 4. 2, IV. 9. 3. 10–29, V. 2. 2. 4–10, VI. 7. 5–6; even more elaborate developments of the latter are offered at I. 1. 8. 18–23, IV. 4. 27. 11–17, V. 3. 9. 28–35.

such a level to be an innovation (IV. 8. 8. 1–6), and few of his successors were willing to follow it. Confusion is likely to arise from the fact that the 'middle' level of Soul is on the former classification identical with sense-perception, on the latter with discursive reason (II. 9. 2. 4 ff., IV. 3. 12. 1–8), and is made even worse by Plotinus' frequent attempts to maintain the 'unfallen' nature of the rational soul as a whole (cf. p. 76). Attention to the context is therefore necessary to see which classification is presupposed by any particular passage. A threefold classification which Plotinus by contrast hardly ever uses is the Platonic tripartition of the soul into reason, 'spirit' (*thymos*) and appetite (though cf. III. 6. 2. 22 ff.). Identifying the soul's 'spirited part' solely with anger (as against the heterogeneous phenomena included by Plato under that heading), he refuses in consequence to grant it a more exalted status than appetite. Both anger and appetite are in his view manifestations of man's 'vegetative' soul and both are firmly rooted in the physical body (IV. 4. 28).[1]

Plotinus' most detailed discussions of the relation of soul and body occur in connection with the problem of Impassibility. His aim here is to preserve the soul from substantial change and emotional disturbance, in answer both to the Sceptics' charge that a being subject to these cannot be immortal (I. 1. 2. 9–13, III. 6. 1. 28–30; cf. p. 26) and the Gnostics' admission of sin and ignorance into the spiritual world. It is significant that the question first assumes prominence in the early treatises of his second period, when he was preoccupied with the Gnostic menace; it is raised both in the treatise on Impassibility (III. 6. 1–5) and in that on the Soul (IV. 4. 18–29), a third discussion being provided in the very late treatise I. 1. Fundamental to all three works is the doctrine that the soul gives the body a share in her own life (or, in Neoplatonic terminology, an 'image' of that life, I. 1. 7. 1–6, IV. 4. 14, 18 ff., VI. 4. 15. 8–18) and that it is in the animated body that the emotions or 'passions' (*pathē*), a term including such phenomena as pleasure, pain, appetite and anger, have their seat. The viewpoint of the treatises is, however, somewhat different and their details cannot be pursued here. Their major divergence is that the work on the Soul offers a subtler analysis than the other two, distinguishing two stages in the formation of the emotions, their origination in the animated body and their completion by the lower soul (cf. IV. 4. 20–1). The treatise I. 1, on the other hand, simply distinguishes the activities of the pure

[1] For the Neoplatonists' attitude to the Platonic tripartition cf. above p. 28 and n. 2.

soul from those located in the composite entity formed by body and lower soul (the 'Animated Being' of the treatise's title). For analysis shows that the 'passions' can be attributed to neither body nor soul in isolation.

Take, for instance, the appetite for food and drink. It is clear, on the one hand, that it is not the soul, but the body, that needs replenishment; on the other, that inanimate bodies do not feel desire.[1] Plato's wavering on the question is well known, the *Phaedo* attributing such desires to the body, the *Philebus* to the soul. It is even clearer that both physical pleasure and pain (IV. 4. 18. 19–36) and sense-perception (IV. 4. 23) involve the joint operation of body and soul. The upshot of Plotinus' discussion is therefore clear, that change and disturbance have their seat in the animated body and do not touch the soul herself. Its details frequently draw on the observations of earlier thinkers, especially the research of Posidonius and Galen, following Aristotle (*De An.* I. 1. 403 a-b; cf. above pp. 28–9), into the links between man's emotions and his physical constitution (cf. *Enn.* IV. 4. 21. 1–14, 28. 28 ff.). Equally important are Aristotle's denial (developed, as Plotinus fails to mention, in opposition to Plato) that the soul, in order to move the body, must herself be moved (*De An.* I. 3–4. 405b–409a; cf. *Enn.* I. 1. 4. 25–7, III. 6. 4. 34–52) and his approach, in discussing sense-perception, to a distinction between mental and physical acts (*De An.* II. 5. 417b 2 ff.); Plotinus complains, however, not without justice, that Aristotle fails to uphold this distinction consistently and that his account of memory, in particular, tends dangerously towards Stoic materialism (IV. 6. 3). Against the Stoics, the major object of his attack, he argues that knowledge does not involve reception of a passive 'impression' by the soul; in sensation, as in other psychological phenomena, all passive change occurs in the animated body, and the soul's role is the wholly active one of observing the impressions received there. And there can be no question of impressions of any kind in connection with thought and memory, which are completely independent of the body.[2] Hence if we describe the soul as 'changed' when she exercises or ceases to exercise these activities, we should be clear that such 'change' has nothing in common with the passive changes of material objects and is therefore no threat to her immortality (III. 6. 2. 34–54).

---

[1] I. 1. 2. 16–18, 4. 1–10, IV. 4. 20. 1–10, 21. 14–21. This is true, however, only of *physical* desire; the higher soul's desires (such as her aspiration towards the Good) have no bodily roots (cf. I. 1. 5. 26–8, I. 8. 15. 21–3, IV. 7. 8[5]. 23–5).

[2] I. 1. 7. 6–17, III. 6. 1. 8–11, IV. 3. 26. 1–34, IV. 6 passim, IV. 7. 6. 37–48.

So far Plotinus' aims are reasonably clear. The difficulty of his doctrine arises from the ambiguity of the term 'impassibility', which leads him to argue not merely that error and vice cause no substantial change in the soul (III. 6. 2), but that she is not really subject to them at all. The problem will be clarified if we take the soul's various levels individually. Thus Plotinus seems nowhere to contradict his statement that her highest, unfallen level remains unclouded by error and never descends into this world. On the other hand, he generally allows that the irrational soul may sin, at least in the sense of failing to heed the commands of reason, though even here he suggests that vice may be only an unwholesome state of body (III. 6. 2. 65–7). But it is over Soul's middle, rational level that the real difficulty arises. For whereas Plotinus sometimes admits that this may fail to heed the commands of Intelligence or that it may take injury from its attention to matter (I. 8. 4. 17–22), he elsewhere denies that reason is subject to error. In reality, he argues, the cause of error is our irrational nature's failure to listen to reason; similarly a wise elder may fail to sway a disorderly assembly without himself giving way to disorder (I. 1. 9, IV. 4. 17. 19–27, VI. 4. 15. 18 ff.). The difficulties involved in such a view are obvious, and with the best will in the world—which Christian critics have admittedly not always displayed—it is hard to see how they can be met. Plotinus himself is hard put to explain why moral discipline is needed to make the soul impassible if she is already so by nature (III. 6. 5; cf. I. 1. 12, VI. 4. 16). Where he is, however, always emphatic is that the ultimate origin of evil is not the soul, but Matter, which communicates its own weakness to the bodies based on it and so, in view of the interconnection of body and irrational soul, to the latter; finally, the disturbance so created distracts the rational soul from contemplation (I. 8. chs. 4–5, 8, 13–15). It follows that there can be no sin or error in a soul free from the body's influence (I. 8. 15. 12–23; cf. I. 1. 2). But even this claim we shall find hard to reconcile with Plotinus' account of the soul's fall.

Admission of the soul's passibility was one point at which Plotinus regarded contemporary Platonists as too influenced by Stoic materialism. Another concerned a subject of dispute since Aristotle, the interpretation of Plato's reference to the soul as having 'parts', which the *Timaeus* had located in different regions of the body. For Plotinus it was clearly necessary to interpret such statements consistently with his own non-spatial conception of Soul. His answer is, first, that the soul's various faculties are 'present' in their appropriate organs in the sense that their operation takes place there, and that this in turn results from the fact that not every part of the body is adapted to serve as an organ for every power of the soul (cf. above p. 51); for instance only the blood around the heart is a suitable vehicle for anger. In this way he explains Plato's location of anger in the chest and appetite in the belly (IV. 3. 23, IV. 4. 28. 1–18). But reason, in his view, has no bodily organ (IV. 3. 19. 24–7, V. 1. 10. 13 ff.) and is therefore situated in the head only in the sense that its function is to supervise perception and motion, which are 'present' in the brain insofar as their organs, the nerves, have their terminus there (IV. 3. 23. 21–35). Similar reasons explain why the individual soul, while free from spatial limitations, is yet confined to the government of a particular body (IV. 9. 3. 18 ff.); once again, only that body is adapted to that particular soul (and that there must be such a body, as we have seen, is guaranteed by the law of divine justice; cf. IV. 3. 13. 1–5, 24 passim). But while the spatial limitations to which the individual soul appears subject are therefore only apparent, they none the less indicate that her power, unlike that of the World-soul, is unequal to governing the whole cosmos (IV. 3. 6). Moreover the human soul's relation to its body (though not that of the celestial souls to theirs, II. 9. 8. 30–9, IV. 3. 11. 23–7, IV. 8. 2. 38–53) involves an undesirable emotional attachment to that body, which causes her to direct her attention there rather than to the whole universe. And this raises the problem of how she first enters this world.

Like most of his successors, though less definitely, Plotinus accepts the Stoic-inspired doctrine of a succession of cosmic cycles, in each of which the same events are endlessly repeated (IV. 3. 12. 12–19, V. 7. 3. 13–18), the corollary being that the soul must descend into this world at least once during each cycle. Reflection will show that only so can the existence both of an everlasting world and of a finite number of Forms and souls be maintained (cf. V. 7. 1. 11–13; also below p. 94). The problem for a Platonist was to reconcile the *Phaedrus'* view of the soul's descent as the result of a primal sin with the *Timaeus'* declaration that she is here on a divine mission. Plotinus' most detailed attempts at a reconciliation come in the early treatise IV. 8 and in the great psychological work IV. 3–4 of his middle period (IV. 3. 9–17; cf. IV. 4. 3–5). The basis of his solution is to treat the soul's descent as a biological necessity arising out of the Universal Logos.[1] We have seen that as a living organism the psychical cosmos must be governed by a law

---

[1] A point well brought out by E. R. Dodds, *Pagan and Christian in an Age of Anxiety*, pp. 24–6. I cannot, however, agree with him that the 'biological' approach is intended to exclude the notion of a fall.

similar to those causing other organisms to develop the appropriate powers and organs at the appropriate time (IV. 3. 13. 1–17). We can therefore describe the soul as sent here by God in the sense both that her descent is an automatic result of this law and that her government of body into which she descends assists the divine administration of the sensible cosmos (IV. 8. 5. 10–14). The point at which the biological approach links up with the negative view of the soul's descent is that that descent is *instinctive*, and therefore blind; Plotinus compares it to the sexual urge or to the performance upon impulse of an act of bravery (IV. 3. 13. 18–20). Even less favourably it may be viewed as a wilful assertion by the soul of her own identity—('the will to belong to herself', III. 9. 3. 9–16, IV. 4. 3. 1–3, V. I. 1. 5)—or as an act of narcissism, whereby she falls in love with her own image (i.e. with the terrestrial body awaiting her), 'seeing it as if in the mirror of Dionysus' (IV. 3. 12. 1–2, cf. I. 6. 8. 8–16). So considered, her motive may be characterised by the Pythagorean term 'audacity' (*tolma*, V. I. 1. 4). And its consequences are unfortunate, since self-assertion is equivalent to self-isolation; the result is that a soul potentially containing the whole of Reality chooses instead to attach herself to, and so imprison herself in, a small part thereof (IV. 7. 13. 8–13, IV. 8. 4. 10 ff., VI. 4. 16. 22–36). Hence unlike the self-creation of the divine Hypostases the soul's descent cannot be described as voluntary, first because it is not fully conscious, and secondly because it leads the soul to attach herself to an inferior sphere of existence (IV. 8. 5. 8–10). On the other hand, it is not the result of external compulsion, since the law that motivates it is an expression of the soul's inmost nature (IV. 3. 13. 17–32).

By this means Plotinus endeavours to reconcile Plato's conflicting statements. But ingenious as his attempt is, it leaves serious problems unsolved. For if the soul's descent (and ultimately everything she does) is an expression of the Universal Logos, how can the wicked be blamed for their actions? Plotinus' answers cannot be regarded as successful (cf. III. 2. chs. 10, 17–18, III. 3. 3–4). Conversely, how can the primal sin ascribed to the soul in her discarnate state be reconciled with Plotinus' insistence that evil arises in her only through association with a terrestrial body (I. 8. 15. 12–21)? It is probably with such reflections in mind (cf. II. 3. 10. 3–6, III. 4. 5. 4–19) that the late treatise I. 1 suggests that the soul does not really descend into this world, but merely projects an image of herself here (I. 1. 12. 21–8). This obviously will not do, since it fails to explain why we erroneously identify ourselves with this image and need to purify ourselves from its influence. And this would appear to confirm the unsatisfactoriness of Plotinus' doctrine of the soul's Impassibility.

We saw in connection with Numenius (p. 35) the doctrine that the soul descends into this world through the planetary spheres. Plotinus harmonises this doctrine with his own standpoint by the observation that, since the subtler bodies are more suited to receive the soul's activity, the heavens will therefore receive it before the earth (IV. 3. 17. 1–12). But it is only when she reaches the terrestrial body shaped for her by the World-soul that her fall becomes complete. For now a new danger arises. In contrast to the all-inclusive body of the world and the subtle bodies of the stars, the human body is a complex and unstable combination of elements, needing perpetual replenishment and subject to external dangers (IV. 8. 2. 6–14). It is this instability which is the source of the desires and disturbances of man's lower nature, and which necessitates deliberate intervention by his higher soul (cf. IV. 4. 17–21 passim, IV. 8. 8. 17–22); the divine souls' control of their bodies is by contrast an effortless process which does not hinder their transcendent contemplation (II. 9. 7. 1–18, III. 4. 4. 2–7, IV. 8. 2. 14 ff.). Hence their body is not a prison for them, and both the Gnostics' scornful charge that they can never leave it and the Epicureans' claim that exercising providence would be a burden for them rest on false premises (II. 9. 18. 35–48, IV. 4. 12. 39–49). The human soul, on the other hand, faces the danger that she may come to make care for the body and her lower nature her primary aim and so forget the Intelligible world (IV. 3. 17. 18–31). She thus binds herself to the body and dooms herself to future rebirth, until philosophy delivers her (cf. III. 9. 3. 7–16, IV. 8. 4. 10–35, 7. 9 ff.).

A further paradox emerges in Plotinus' treatment of reasoning and memory. He is emphatic that these faculties need no bodily organs (IV. 3. 19. 24–7, 26 passim, V. 1. 10. 13 ff.), countering Aristotle's argument that men's powers of memory vary with their bodily constitution by the Platonic view that the body is not a help, but a hindrance, to man's intellectual powers (IV. 3. 26. 12–16, 50–6; cf. *Phd.* 65A ff.). It thus appears that these will improve on the soul's separation from the body, but in fact this is true only between incarnations (cf. IV. 3. 27. 14–22). For when the soul returns to the Intelligible world, she reverts to intuitive contemplation and has no further need of any lower faculties (IV. 3. 18, IV. 4. 1–2). That discursive reasoning is necessary only to beings whose knowledge is imperfect is argued by Plotinus, following Aristotle, on the grounds that even in this world the more perfect

crafts resort to deliberation less.[1] The case of memory is more complicated and requires a detailed analysis.

Plotinus' starting-point is Aristotle's doctrine that memory involves
contemplation of a mental image. He does not, however, agree with
Aristotle that it is therefore a function of the perceptive soul; in
Plotinus' view rational and perceptive souls have each its own imaginative power (*phantasia*), though their duality normally escapes our
notice (IV. 3. 29–31). The objects of this power may be either mental
images proper or verbal formulae (*logoi*), which represent the pure
Forms on the level of Soul, exhibiting them to her consciousness 'as
though in a mirror'. And this explains why we are normally unaware of
the Intellectual contemplation perpetually enjoyed by our higher self;
the trouble is that the latter fails to reach our 'imagination', where our
attention is concentrated.[2] A further corollary is Plotinus' interpretation of Plato's description of knowledge as Recollection as denoting
not a temporal recovery of what the soul knew in the past, but an
awakening to what her true self knows eternally (IV. 3. 25. 27–34). He
likewise maintains that there are many activities in our lower soul, for
instance desires and memories, of which we remain unconscious.[3]

Of particular importance is Plotinus' observation that the term
'memory' has two applications, one of which denotes conscious
retention of a memory image, the other an instinctive habitual reaction
(IV. 3. 28). By distinguishing the two he avoids both the Stoics'
identification of impulses with judgments (I. 1. 5. 12–21, III. 6. 4. 8 ff.)
and the opposite behaviouristic reduction of memory to mere habit-
reaction. None the less in conscious contemplation the two factors are
interdependent, since contemplation always involves interest in the
object contemplated, or at least in that type of object (cf. IV. 4. 3–4, 25.
1–11). Hence sensations whose objects are a matter of absolute
indifference to us fail to penetrate our consciousness, and intensity of
consciousness is proportional to degree of interest. For instance, if on a
walk we are concerned only with the act of walking and not with the
places traversed, our awareness of those places is proportionately dim.
Hence although the stars are perpetually circling the earth, their whole
attention is directed to the Intelligible world and in consequence
registers nothing within the sensible cosmos (IV. 4. 8). Hence too,

[1] IV. 3. 18. 5–7, IV. 8. 8. 13–16; cf. *Phys.* II. 8. 199b 26 ff., *EN* III. 3. 1112b 1 ff.;
cf. above pp. 26–7, 52, 63.
[2] IV. 3. 30; cf. I. 1. 11. 1–8, I. 4. 10. 1–21, IV. 8. 8. 1–11, V. 1. 12.
[3] III. 6. 3. 19–22, IV. 4. 4. 10–20, IV. 8. 8. 6–11, IV. 9. 2. 12–21.

since memory depends on our disposition, 'we become what we remember' (IV. 4. 3. 6–8), and the objects of our attention are of vital importance in determining our destiny now and hereafter.

It is thus clear that the higher soul's return to the Intelligible world must abolish all interest in the lower soul and sensible universe, and hence all memory of these (IV. 3. 32. 10 ff.). But we can go further, for, as we have seen, perfect identity with one's object of contemplation is impossible on the level of Soul (cf. p. 53). In Plotinus' words, consciousness on this level exercises a 'blunting effect'; he notes, for instance, that reading or acts of bravery go better when we are more absorbed in, and so less conscious of, them (I. 4. 10. 21–33). Its results are not, however, invariably harmful, since, as Plotinus observes, it is those memories of which we are least conscious that take most complete possession of the soul and are therefore most dangerous (IV. 4. 4. 10–14). Indeed the 'audacity' that impels her to leave the Intelligible world may be identified with a subconscious memory of the material world and of her own separate existence therein (IV. 4. 3–4). But viewed in relation to Intelligence, the type of consciousness involved in memory and discursive thought can only be pronounced defective; hence Plotinus propounds the paradox that the philosopher's well-being is most intense when he is least conscious of it (I. 4. 9–10). More precisely, it is only by abandoning the reassuring solidity of our everyday consciousness (called by Plotinus *antilēpsis* or *parakolouthēsis*) that true self-awareness (normally termed *synaisthēsis*) is attained. As Plotinus observes, our knowledge is most perfect when by our normal standards, which are rooted in sense-perception, we seem to know least; similarly sickness, and evil in general, make their presence felt more forcibly than do health and goodness (V. 8. 11. 19–40). The ethical implications of this reversal of common sense values we shall see in our next section.

It follows that, once in the Intelligible world, the soul is wholly engrossed in intuitive contemplation of that world and retains no memory of anything whatever, not even of herself as a separate entity. She knows herself, indeed, insofar as through contemplation she is identified with Intelligence; conversely her self-knowledge is simultaneously knowledge of all that principle's contents. Furthermore, at this stage her contemplation shares in the timelessness of Intelligence (IV. 4. 1–2). Nor is this true merely of the purified individual soul; the World-soul and celestial souls are perpetually in that state (IV. 4. 15–16) and it is only the World-soul's products, not the World-soul herself, that are subject to time (IV. 4. 15. 15–20; contrast III. 7. 11. 59–62).

This further step was clearly necessary if the World-soul was to escape the Gnostics' charge that her contemplation is inferior to the highest attainable by man. But its consequence appears to be the abolition of the distinction between Soul and Intelligence as Hypostases on which Plotinus elsewhere insists, both in his early treatise on the Three Hypostases (v. 1. 4. 1–28) and in the treatise on Time and Eternity, composed at the end of his second period (III. 7. 11). It is noteworthy, however, that in the latter treatise the procession of Soul from Intelligence is characterised almost as a culpable act of self-assertion parallel to the fall of the individual soul (III. 7. 11. 15 ff., cf. v. 2. 1. 18–28). Plotinus is faced, in fact, with an insoluble dilemma. Either the distinction between Soul and Intelligence is valid only for the embodied human soul, and the distinction between Second and Third Hypostases is abolished; or we regard the World-soul as permanently tainted with some of the imperfections of the human condition. And similar problems can be raised concerning Intelligence's relation to the One; while Plotinus refrains from raising them, he can on occasion take a pessimistic view of Intelligence's self-creation and speak of its separation from the One as an act of audacity (III. 8. 8. 32–8, VI. 9. 5. 29). Such problems could, of course, be avoided if the three Hypostases were viewed simply as different ways of looking at the same thing and their distinction as simply an illusion of thought. As we shall see, such a conclusion was soon to be drawn within the Neoplatonic school.

V. RETURN TO THE ONE

The Neoplatonic view of the sensible cosmos thus emerges as intermediate between that of the Stoics and that of the Gnostics. Of Plotinus' opposition to the latter school's view of the world as the misshapen product of an ignorant demiurge we have already spoken (above p. 12). In attacking it he takes over many arguments from Stoic theodicy, for instance that the universe necessarily contains conflict (e.g. II. 3. 16. 41 ff., III. 2. 2, IV. 4. 32) and that what is good for the whole need not be so for the part (II. 9. 7. 33–9, III. 2. 3. 9 ff., etc.). But although the world is the best that could be produced with sensible matter as its basis, it is still for a Platonist decidedly inferior to its Intelligible archetype (II. 9. 8. 16 ff.). The sage will therefore revere its beauty, since no one can truly love the Intelligible world who does not also love its sensible offspring (II. 9. 16. 5–14). But Plotinus' anti-Gnostic polemic takes a decidedly un-Stoic turn when he argues that to censure the imperfections of the sensible cosmos incurs the error of demanding the same perfection in an image as in its original.[1] A similar blending of Platonic and Stoic themes comes in his explanation of apparently undeserved suffering. That it is really undeserved he denies, taking the Platonic view that it is a punishment for sin in a past life (III. 2. 13, IV. 3. 16. 12–25); but he agrees with the Stoics that in any case it cannot disturb the sage's tranquillity (I. 4. 4. 30–6, 7. 7 ff., III. 2. 5. 15 ff.). External events are a mere game or stage-play, unworthy of being taken seriously (II. 9. 9. 1–26, III. 2. 15. 21 ff.). If ordinary men complain when they are wronged, it is their own fault for not training their souls to withstand the blows of fortune. They should not expect the gods to save them when the divine law ordains that happiness is the result of a man's own virtue (I. 4. 8. 24–30, III. 2. 8. 7–9. 19). Whether this is a specific allusion to Christianity is doubtful; its target may just as well be popular religion in general.

Plotinus therefore agrees with the Stoics that happiness is possible on earth and, against Aristotle, that it is independent of external prosperity (I. 4. 4 ff.). But such a view he regards as justifiable only by a Platonic division of man into higher and lower self, which sets happiness solely in the well-being of the former; (it is important to remember that for Plotinus this division is as much between higher and lower soul as between soul and body). Thus the Epicurean claim that the sage can find pleasure in being tortured to death is simply absurd; the point for a Platonist is that the pain felt by his body and lower soul do not affect his true self, which remains absorbed in contemplation (I. 4. 13. 5–12; cf. ibid. 8. 1 ff., III. 2. 15. 47–62). Similarly a modicum of external goods will certainly contribute to the preservation and harmony of man's lower nature (cf. I. 4. 7. 1–8), (though an excess of them will prove a hindrance, ibid. 14. 9–11). Hence the sage will normally give the body what it needs, for instance, to preserve its health, but, once again, without identifying himself with his lower nature (I. 4. 4. 25–30, 16. 13–29). And he will also discipline the body to weaken its influence over the soul to the extent, in appropriate circumstances, of choosing sickness rather than health (I. 4. 14). And even when external misfortunes come unwished, the well-being of his true self remains undiminished (I. 4. 7. 8 ff.). Admittedly Plotinus often suggests that the need to care for a body at all is a regrettable distraction (e.g. I. 4. 6. 21–4). But he insists that such distraction is not sufficient to destroy the philosopher's well-being, and we have observed his success in combining

[1] II. 9. 4. 22–32, 8. 16–18, III. 2. 7. 1 ff., 14. 6. ff., V. 8. 8. 22–3.

contemplation and action in his own life (above pp. 10, 41). Unlike
the Gnostics, therefore, the Platonic sage will not revile the body; he
will rather patiently await his release by death, when he will abandon
it, as a musician finally abandons a lyre that has served him well (I. 4. 16.
13–29, II. 9. 18). But separation from the body, consisting as it does in
emotional detachment therefrom, is not achieved simply through physical death. Hence Plotinus forbids suicide in normal circumstances;
we have seen how he prevented Porphyry from killing himself (above
p. 40), and the few passages that seem to permit it are explicable as
concessions for the sake of argument against particular opponents.[1]

Plotinus further rejects the Stoic view setting man's goal in submission to the Fate governing the sensible cosmos. Since the soul is an
'amphibian', belonging to both sensible and Intelligible worlds (IV. 8. 4.
31–5), this holds good only for our lower soul; our true self belongs to
the Intelligible order.[2] As a corollary Plotinus agrees with Aristotle
against the Stoics regarding the superiority of the contemplative over
the active life (IV. 4. 44). It would of course be impossible to forbid the
sage all external activity; in fact, both in theory and even more in his
own life Plotinus regarded the sage as bound to perform such duties as
come his way and, in doing so, to exercise moral virtue (cf. I. 2. 7. 13–
21). But such activities he must treat as simply a necessary consequence
of the human condition, in full consciousness that the true good lies
elsewhere. Above all, he must not confuse beauty's sensible images—be
they the beauties of material objects or of noble actions—with the
archetypal beauty of the Intelligible world (III. 5. 1. 30 ff., V. 8. 2. 31–5).
To treat moral action as an end in itself, ignoring this distinction, is to
yield to man's irrational nature. It is, quite literally, a case of bewitch-
ment, since the forces used by magicians are simply those which bind
the soul here in the first place (IV. 4. 43. 16 ff; cf. II. 3. 15. 13 ff.). Hence,
on the view of freedom outlined earlier, only the contemplative life is
free (cf. pp. 63–4). Even the sage's actions are not altogether free,
insofar as they depend on external circumstances. On the other hand,
while the man of mere moral virtue will slavishly follow the dictates of
those circumstances, the sage will plan his course in the light of his
inner contemplation, abandoning, if necessary, family, country and life
itself (VI. 8. 6. 1–31). In fact he would prefer to have no occasion to
exercise moral virtue, since this entails the existence of misery needing

[1] Cf. Rist, *Plotinus: the Road to Reality*, pp. 174–7, *Enn.* I. 9 passim, I. 4. 7.
31–2, 8. 8–9; II. 9. 8. 42–3, 9. 16–17.
[2] II. 3. 9–10, III. 1. 8–10, IV. 3. 15. 10–23, IV. 4. 34. 1–7.

relief; the ideal doctor will wish there were no sick people needing his skill—or would, did he not realise that in this imperfect world misery is unavoidable (I. 4. 11. 12–17, VI. 8. 5. 1–20). But not merely is action inferior to contemplation, all action is really aiming at contemplation. For the man of action is satisfied only when he contemplates its results within his own mind, and it is this satisfaction that is his real goal (III. 8. 6). In other words, action *is* a weak form of contemplation, and thus serves as a substitute for the latter for those lacking the refinement to pursue contemplation directly, just as children unequal to academic studies take up handicrafts (III. 8. 4. 31–47, 5. 17–25). Once again man's instinctive search for solidity is misplaced, leading him away from his goal, or, at best, attaining it only by a roundabout route.

Like other Platonists Plotinus identifies the soul's goal with assimilation to God through virtue (I. 2. 1 ff.); without virtue, he maintains against the Gnostics, 'God' is a mere name (II. 9. 15. 39–40). But it is clear from what we have said that such 'virtue' primarily denotes the discipline that purifies the soul for contemplation, though Plotinus admits that it would be unreasonable to deny the social virtues any role in this purification (I. 2. 1. 23–6, cf. p. 98 and n. 2). Since man is divided into higher and lower souls, this discipline is twofold (I. 1. 3. 21–6, I. 2. 5, III. 6. 5. 13 ff.). The higher soul's purification involves turning her attention away from the sense-world towards the Intelligible order, so as to restore her original status as a divine image of that order (I. 2. 3 ff., I. 6. 5. ff., etc.). That of the lower soul aims at calming her passions so that they do not disturb man's higher nature (except perhaps for a fleeting image, to be instantly calmed by reason with a single glance). But once again there must be no violent repression of the irrational soul (I. 2. 5. 21–31, I. 4. 15. 16–25). The aim is first to train it voluntarily to accept the guidance of reason and afterwards to withdraw one's attention from it (IV. 3. 32. 6–18).

Philosophy for Plotinus is therefore far from an abstract academic discipline. For him, as for Plato, the philosopher's training is both moral and intellectual; without dialectic virtue is imperfect, but without virtue true philosophy is impossible (I. 3. 6. 14–24). And though Plotinus insists, and his practice throughout the *Enneads* confirms, that purification involves a rigorous intellectual training, he also makes clear that the philosopher's aim is to transcend abstract formulae (I. 3. 5. 10–23; cf. V. 8. 4. 35–55) and to come to see Intelligence 'as though it were an object of sense' (VI. 9. 5. 12–13). For we are not confined to images of the Intelligible world, 'the laws engraved by Intelligence on our soul'

(v. 3. 4. 1 ff.; cf. 1. 1. 8. 1–8); we can rise instead to contemplation of, and so identity with, the Forms themselves (vi. 5. 7). Simultaneously the soul overcomes attachment to her separate individuality and realises her inner identity with the whole Intelligible world (vi. 5. 12. 16 ff.). There remains the final return to the One.

The part played by love in the soul's return is worth special attention, since it affords an excellent example of a Platonic theme taken over by Plotinus and submitted to some drastic tacit corrections. First of all, he abandons the homosexual associations of Platonic *ēros*. His condemnation of sodomy indeed merely echoes Plato's own attitude (III. 5. 1. 50–5; cf. *Laws* VIII. 836b ff.). But even the Platonic conception of a non-physical relationship between two souls in search of truth receives no attention in the *Enneads*, where the philosopher's ascent is essentially solitary.[1] And even physical heterosexual love is a falling-short of the best (III. 5. 1. 36–8). It is true that Plotinus uses the union of lovers as a symbol of the soul's union with the One (vi. 7. 34. 14–16), but it is still, like all material images, a very imperfect adumbration of the latter (vi. 9. 9. 39–47). As with other external activities, its real aim is contemplation (III. 8. 7. 18–22) and, even more obviously than they, it involves pursuit of a mortal image of beauty in preference to Beauty itself (III. 5. 1. 30–8, v. 8. 8. 12–15). Consistently with this view, Plotinus modifies Plato's characterisation of love as aiming at 'procreation in the beautiful' (*Symp.* 206E). For Plotinus love is more perfect when it does not aim at procreation, since such an aim indicates dissatisfaction with one's present condition (III. 5. 1. 38–50). And these reservations apply even to the 'spiritual procreation' (intellectual or artistic creation) which Plato had encouraged. We should not, however, regard Plotinian love as non-creative; it is not creation, but the *deliberate intention to create* that he disparages, for, as we have seen, to direct one's energies outwards is to dissipate them. Hence, Plotinus maintains, in a passage reminiscent of Far Eastern mysticism, the sensible world's excellence stems from the fact that its creator had no intention of producing it, but 'in not acting achieved mighty results' (III. 2. 1. 34–45).

Further tacit corrections of Plato appear in Plotinus' reflections on beauty and artistic creation. Thus whereas Plato had regarded the artist as confined to the imitation of sensible particulars, Plotinus argues that

---

[1] Cf. in particular 1. 6. 9. 7–15's adaptation of *Phdr.* 252D; in Plotinus the philosopher's concern is with his own moral improvement, not that of his beloved. Cf. also VI. 7. 31. 11–17.

he can base his work on those particulars' Intelligible archetypes. In illustration he quotes the traditional example of Phidias' production of his famous statue of Zeus 'not from any sensible model, but imagining what Zeus himself would look like if he appeared to our eyes' (v. 8. 1. 32–40). But Plotinus' 'dynamic' approach to the Intelligible world leads to even more radical changes. The full implications are not yet apparent in his attack, in the early treatise on Beauty, on the Stoic identification of beauty with symmetry. He agrees, indeed, that beauty consists in symmetry rather than its opposite; but if it were simply *identical* with symmetry, consisting in a harmony of parts, neither incorporeal beings nor incomposite material objects could be beautiful (1. 6. [1]. 1. 20–54). Beauty should rather be identified with Form and ugliness with Matter unmastered by Form (1. 6. 2–3). But a discussion of the same theme from his middle period marks a new departure. For now it is not Form, but Life, in which Plotinus sees the essence of beauty, arguing, for instance, that living ill-proportioned faces have more beauty than lifeless symmetrical ones (vi. 7. [38]. 22. 24–36). More radically still, he argues that even the beauty of the Forms would fail to stir us were they not quickened to life by the radiance cast upon them by the Good (ibid. 1–24). In other words, it is with this radiance, 'the colour blooming' on the Intelligible world (v. 8. 10. 29–30), rather than with Form as such, that true Beauty should be identified. Hence Plotinus goes as far as to declare that Primary Beauty is formless (vi. 7. 33. 37–8), so breaking completely with traditional Platonism.

It would thus appear that the Good, as Beauty's source, must be on a higher level than Beauty itself. In fact Plotinus hesitates a good deal whether the One can be called Beautiful, just as he does over the application of any positive terms; hence his use of equivocal formulae like 'Beauty beyond Beauty' (vi. 7. 32. 29) in this connection.[1] But his most considered discussion (v. 5. 12) argues that the Good is in fact the higher Reality of the two and the object of a more basic desire, which is at work in all beings even during sleep; whereas only those in some degree awakened seek after Beauty or Intelligence (cf. vi. 7. 20. 11–24). Hence love of the Good is free from the violent passions provoked by Beauty, which frequently distract beings from their true goal. That goal is therefore to be set above either Beauty or Intelligence; it lies in assimilation to the Good, since infinite love demands an infinite object (vi. 7. 32. 24–9). It is aspiration after this goal that motivates each level of Reality to revert in contemplation towards its source and thereby to

[1] Cf. also I. 6. 6 ff., esp. 9. 34–43, I. 8. 2. 7–9, V. 9. 2. 8–9, VI. 7. 33. 19–22, 42. 16–18.

attain the maximum unity possible for it. Hence the Stoics are wrong to set a being's good in self-preservation; it consists rather in aspiration after a transcendent goal (VI. 7. 25. 18 ff., 27 3. ff.). Nor is the soul confined to the imperfect unity of her own level; she is able, in the mystical experience, to pass beyond Intelligence, to union with the Absolute One.

The One, Plotinus emphasises, does not need to turn towards us (VI. 9. 8. 33 ff.); it is present whenever we turn within, away from our normal preoccupation with the sensible world, and so come to know ourselves and, ultimately, the One that is our source (VI. 9. 7. 33–4). To see the latter we must 'divest ourselves of everything' (v. 3. 17. 38) or 'put away all otherness', that is, all multiplicity and everything that differentiates us from the One (VI. 9. 8. 33–5). And just as ascent to the Intelligible world involved relinquishment of all sensible form, so now ascent to the formless One requires that the soul 'confound and annul the distinctions of Intelligence' (VI. 7. 35. 33–4; cf. v. 5. 6. 17–20) and make herself formless (VI. 7. 34. 1–8, VI. 9. 7. 5–16). That this goes counter to man's deepest fears Plotinus recognises; fearing that she may be left with nothing at all, the soul seeks to return to the reassuring solidity of the senses (VI. 9. 3. 1–10). Yet we can attain the One only by first passing through the Intelligible world (e.g. VI. 9. 3. 22 ff.). Once there, we must seek to transcend the subject-object duality and merge into the light that illumines both of them, so as to see it without intermediary (v. 5. 7). For spiritual entities are not cut off from one another (cf. v. 1. 6. 48–9); just as the highest level of Soul remains in union with Intelligence, so the highest level of the latter remains in contact with its own source, with which it enjoys perpetual mystical union.[1] In contrast with the 'sober' contemplation of Intelligence proper, this level is termed 'Intelligence in love' or 'Intelligence drunk with nectar' (VI. 7. 35. 19–33); it is also called the 'first (level) of Intelligence' (VI. 9. 3. 27–8) or 'that element in Intelligence which is not Intelligence' (v. 5. 8. 22–3). Having attained this level the soul can only wait calmly and patiently until the One suddenly appears to her (v. 5. 7. 31–8. 7, VI. 7. 34. 12–13) or until 'raised high on the wave of Intelligence, she suddenly sees, though without knowing how' (VI. 7. 36. 17–19).

For, like other mystics, Plotinus stresses that mystical union is incommunicable in words; indeed he declares the silence enjoined on initiates in the Mysteries to be symbolic of this fact (VI. 9. 10. 19–11. 4). Of the metaphysical problem of the One's ineffability we have already

[1] This at least is stated at VI. 7. 35. 27 ff., though v. 5. 8. 16 ff. seems against this.

spoken (pp. 57 ff.), and little need be added here. What has most caught scholars' attention is that, while Plotinus frequently speaks of the mystical experience in traditional Platonic terms as a 'vision', he none the less regards such language as too redolent of duality to be satisfactory (cf. VI. 9. 10. 11 ff., 11. 22–6). Hence his frequent preference for metaphors drawn from the sense of touch as suggesting greater intimacy between the experiencer and his object (e.g. V. 3. 17. 25, VI. 7. 36. 4, VI. 9. 4. 27); elsewhere he refers simply to a 'presence superior to knowledge' (VI. 9. 4. 3.) The problem is in fact identical with the metaphysical question whether the One has 'knowledge' (cf. pp. 58–9); the final truth is, of course, that all these terms are inadequate to express a union which, while it lasts, abolishes all distinction between the soul and the One (VI. 9. 10. 19–21; VI. 7. 34. 13–14).

Union with the One does not, however, result in abolition of the soul's individual existence. In describing the two levels of Intelligence Plotinus declares, (though this is admittedly hard to square with his accounts of mystical union), that the unity-in-diversity of Intelligence persists eternally over and above its contemplation of the One (VI. 7. 35. 27–33). More light is thrown on the question by Plotinus' application of one of his most influential mystical ideas, that contact with the One is made through the centre of our soul (II. 2. 2. 6 ff., V. 1. 11. 9–15, cf. VI. 8. 18. 8 ff., etc.). For he emphasises that this centre is not itself the One; we must go further and seek a centre in which the centres of all these circles coincide (VI. 9. 8. 10–12). The analogy's full implications are revealed when we reflect that the centres of two concentric circles are indistinguishable while they are together, their distinction becoming apparent only when they move apart (VI. 9. 10. 16–18). The One is therefore not our inmost self, but our transcendent source, with which we are united through love (VI. 9. 9. 26 ff.); and, whether or not identity between the two is implied by a few phrases taken on their own, nothing in Plotinus' accounts of mystical union resembles his insistence on the soul's inner identity with the whole Intelligible world (e.g. VI. 5. 12. 16 ff.). Plotinus' interpretation of the mystical experience thus differs from that of 'monistic' mysticism, exemplified, for instance, by the non-dualist Vedanta of Hinduism.[1]

The differences separating Plotinus from Christian mysticism are,

[1] The terms 'monistic' and 'theistic' are due to Zaehner, *Mysticism Sacred and Profane*. I agree with Stace, however, (whose view is endorsed by Dodds, *Pagan and Christian in an Age of Anxiety*, p. 90), that only a difference of interpretation, not of actual experience, is involved. Cf. also Ninian Smart, 'Interpretation and mystical experience', *Religious Studies I* 1. (1965) 75–87.

however, equally fundamental; above all, his mysticism lacks any sense of sin or of the need for redemption. For Plotinus our true self is eternally saved and all that is required is to wake up to this fact, a process requiring self-discipline, but perfectly within the soul's own power (cf. I. 6. 9, esp. 22–5). And it is doubtful whether his mysticism can be classified as 'theistic' without serious qualification. Whether the final union involves anything analogous to grace is a question requiring more space than is available here. The 'suddenness' of the vision is not necessarily proof of grace *in the theistic sense*, since, first, Plotinus is here echoing Plato (*Symp.* 210E, *Ep.* VII. 341C–D), secondly, he stresses that the necessary movement is the work of the soul, not of the One, (v. 5. 8. 13 ff., vi. 9. 8. 33 ff.) and, thirdly, similar declarations occur in non-theistic mysticism, notably in Zen Buddhism. And Plotinus' denial that the One loves its products (cf. above p. 64) would seem to mark a decisive rejection of the fundamental tenet both of Christian mysticism and of theistic mysticism in general, that mystical union involves a reciprocal love-relationship between two persons. In fact, we shall find a conception of divine grace closer to (though far from identical with) the Christian one in Iamblichus and Proclus.

That Plotinus here, as elsewhere, should resist classification in terms of neat oppositions of thought should not surprise those who have followed the above account, still less those who have read the *Enneads* themselves. It is also relevant in this context to recall his oscillation between personal and impersonal terms (notably between masculine and neuter pronouns and adjectives) in speaking of the One. The reason, as always, is not just inability on his part to harmonise a complex tradition, but the fact that, taken by itself, either side of such antinomies fails to do justice to the spiritual world (cf. above pp. 6, 41). Some may find such elusiveness among Plotinus' most attractive features, others will regard it as a simple absurdity. But whether or not the suggestion that it has experiential justification is accepted, there is no doubt that appreciation of the *Enneads* requires a willing suspension of disbelief in what eludes common sense and, in some cases, transcends logic itself.

VI. PLOTINUS AND LATER NEOPLATONISM

It is clear, however, that at every level of Plotinus' universe we encounter a combination of doctrines which, whether or not they are positively contradictory, are at least capable of development in opposing directions. Hence most of the metaphysical divergences among his successors result from their having developed one side or the other of such antinomies to its logical conclusion. We may therefore, before leaving Plotinus, note the most important of such points.

First, there are the problems raised by Matter. We have seen Plotinus' argument that his identification of Matter with Absolute Evil, far from being inconsistent with Matter's lack of all quality, is a necessary consequence of that lack (pp. 49–50). But if Matter is produced by God, can it be entirely evil? Again, while Plotinus had been careful to distinguish the negations used of Matter from those used of the One, he had admitted that the two principles resemble one another in their absolute simplicity (VI. 7. 13. 3–4; cf. p. 58). And this is merely the extreme case of the principle that complexity increases towards the centre of the metaphysical hierarchy, reaching its maximum in the human soul, with Intelligence and Nature occupying an intermediate position (cf. IV. 4. 13). Here was another point that seemed to require explanation.

Of the problems raised by the One we can mention only three. First, how can the One produce what it does not itself contain; in particular how can Unity give rise to plurality? Conversely, if to avoid this problem, we conceive the One's products as pre-existing within it, are we not abandoning its absolute unity? The latter alternative, as we have seen, had raised the possibility of the One's being known by analogy from its products (p. 60). But how does this square with the complete unknowability implied by the negative theology? Indeed can positive terms be used of the One at all? Such a possibility appears to involve bringing the One and its products under a common standard; but this possibility Plotinus denies (V. 5. 13. 20–3). And this brings us to our third problem. In its role as the Absolute, the One, Plotinus rightly insists, must be free from limiting conditions (V. 5. 6. 5–8, VI. 8. 11. 28 ff.; cf. above pp. 44 and 57 ff.). As such it can no longer be merely the supreme term of the metaphysical hierarchy, for to bring it within that hierarchy is to limit it. But if we regard it as utterly transcending any such limits, what relations can there be between it and other things? The full import of this dilemma will become clear in our next chapter (cf. pp. 114 ff.).

Just as critical were the problems posed by the levels of Intelligence and Soul. In some passages we have found Plotinus attempting to establish an order of logical, and hence of ontological, priority within the Intelligible world, whereas elsewhere he insists that the conditions of that world make such attempts meaningless (cf. p. 67). The dilemma we have seen to be most acute regarding the relation of Intelligence to the Forms. And even where Plotinus suggests an order of logical priority, as in his discussions of Being, Life and Intelligence, he offers several alternative, and apparently conflicting, suggestions. Here, as elsewhere, his successors were to insist on a more rigidly-defined system.

From our discussion of Plotinus' psychology we may first recall the difficulties surrounding the soul's impassibility (p. 74 ff.). Particular exception was taken by Iamblichus to Plotinus' postulation of an unfallen element within the soul (above pp. 73-4). But even more serious problems, as we have seen, arise over her descent into this world. Even if we admit the consistency of Plotinus' attempt to show that this is the result both of a universal law and of an irrational impulse, how can such an impulse arise in a soul free from the body's influence (cf. p. 78)? The problem in Plato had been linked with the further question whether the soul in her pure state is wholly rational or contains an irrational element; yet on the origin and final destiny of the irrational soul Plotinus is anything but precise.[1] But perhaps the most serious difficulties anywhere in Plotinus' philosophy arise out of his virtual abolition, in some passages, of any ultimate distinction either between different classes of souls or between Soul as a whole and Intelligence. That there can be no absolute distinction within the world of souls follows from the doctrine that every soul contains all the Logoi operative on the psychical level; it is this, as we have seen (p. 72), that makes it possible for a human soul to transmigrate into animal form.[2] Conversely, since every soul contains the whole Intelligible world, she can rise by her own efforts to complete identity with that world, and so transcend the limits of Soul altogether. And since the divine souls are perpetually in this state, the distinction between Soul and Intelligence as Hypostases appears to be abolished (cf. pp. 81-2). We may note in passing that, if we go further and regard both Second and Third Hypostases as defective ways of viewing the One, the problem raised earlier, of the One's relation to other things, cannot arise. The incentives to such a view were therefore all the stronger.

If it was thus necessary for Plotinus' successors to add precision at

[1] Cf. (in chronological order) IV. 7. [2]. 14, IV. 9. [8]. 3. 23-9, VI. 4. [22]. 14-16, esp. 16. 40-8, IV. 3. [27]. 27-32, (esp. 27. 1-3), IV. 4. [28]. 29, IV. 5. [29]. 7. 49-62, I. 1. [53]. 12.

[2] On the other hand a few passages in the same treatises suggest a more rigid distinction between souls; cf. IV. 3. 6. 10 ff. and VI. 7. 6. 29-31.

points where his thought seemed ambiguous, it was no less essential to clarify the logical structure of his arguments (cf. above p. 44). And, needless to say, his cavalier approach to the Platonic texts aroused equal concern among his successors. Even where this interpretation seemed to them to represent Plato's own meaning, it was invariably based only on part of the original text and often only on a few phrases taken out of context. Similar reflections were aroused by his casual use of Greek mythology to illustrate his metaphysics as required, but without any attempt at a consistent allegorical interpretation (cf. below p. 135). Such an attitude was even more unsatisfactory in the light of the later Neoplatonists' aim of preserving traditional forms of worship, which Plotinus had regarded as unnecessary for the philosopher (cf. p. 71). But did not the common man require an easier way of salvation than Plotinus had allowed him? And, even for the spiritual élite, was philosophy the best way of salvation? Here again, only a minority of later Neoplatonists were to follow the founder of their school.

Later Neoplatonism thus exhibits two main trends: on its practical side a growing stress on theurgy; from the theoretical point of view an ever-increasing scholasticism, manifested both in its rigorous insistence on logical demonstration and conceptual precision and in its strict adherence, at least in intention, to the text, the whole text and nothing but the text of its Classical sources. Hence, though Plotinus was incomparably the greatest philosopher of late Antiquity, he could never become the supreme authority for the later Neoplatonists, even though their metaphysics is in many ways merely a series of footnotes to the *Enneads*. Nor could Porphyry, whose approach, though more scholastic than his master's, was still, as we shall see, insufficiently systematic. It was thus left for Iamblichus to determine the framework of later Neoplatonic thought.

CHAPTER FOUR

Porphyry and Iamblichus

I. NEOPLATONISM FROM PLOTINUS TO THE DEATH OF JULIAN

PLOTINUS' senior disciple, the Tuscan Amelius Gentilianus, appears in Porphyry's biography as a learned and enthusiastic, but pedantic, devotee of the master; his refutation of one of the Gnostic apocrypha, for example, ran to no less than forty books (*V. Pl.* 16. 12–14). That he had more inclination towards ritual than his master we have seen (p. 71). Also of note is his enthusiasm for the prologue of St. John's Gospel (Eusebius *PE* XI. 19. 1; cf. Augustine *CD* X. 29), which does not necessarily mean that he liked Christianity as a whole better than did other Neoplatonists. Insofar as his philosophical teaching can be reconstructed, it seems to have involved the same tendencies as that of Porphyry. On the one hand it tended to abolish the barriers between the Hypostases, notably by accentuating Plotinus' teaching about the unity of all souls and their kinship with Intelligence.[1] On the other it introduced fresh logical distinctions within each Hypostasis, for instance in its Numenian-influenced triple division of Intelligence (Proclus *In Tim.* I. 306). But the most interesting of Amelius' innovations concern the Forms. First, and very unusually for a Neoplatonist, he postulated a Form of Evil, apparently on the grounds that otherwise evil must remain unknown to God (Asclepius *In Nic. Arithm.* 44. 3–5, p. 32 Tarán; cf. Proclus *PT* I. 21. p. 98. 16–20, *In Parm.* 829–31). Secondly he regarded the Forms as infinite in number (Syrianus *In Met.* 147. 2–6) and was thereby enabled to abandon the doctrine of identical cosmic cycles. As we have seen (cf. p. 77), only on this basis could the soul's liberation be regarded as permanent; but whether Amelius maintained the latter doctrine we are not told, though Porphyry is said to have done so (Augustine *CD* X. 30, XXII. 27). But numerical infinity was unacceptable to Iamblichus and his followers and Amelius' innovations were not repeated. His influence is visible in the thought of

---

[1] Cf. Iamblichus *De An.*, quoted by Stobaeus *Ecl.* I. 365. 16–17, 372. 9–12, 23–6, 376. 2–4.

the fourth-century Neoplatonist Theodorus of Asine, but the most influential stream of Neoplatonic thought ran not through them, but through Porphyry and Iamblichus.

Porphyry was born about 232 at Tyre (cf. p. 13) and died early in the first decade of the fourth century, soon after the appearance of his edition of the *Enneads*. To most of the important events of his life we have already alluded, his early studies at Athens under Longinus, his six years with Plotinus, his departure in 268 for Sicily and his marriage late in life to Marcella, the widow of a friend (cf. pp. 9–10). It was to Longinus that he owed his enormous erudition and the critical scholarship that he was later to employ in the task of enlisting the whole of ancient culture under the banner of Neoplatonism (cf. Eunapius *VS* 455–6). Exactly when he returned from Sicily to Rome is uncertain, but it seems to have been in Sicily that his famous anti-Christian polemic was composed (cf. Eusebius *EH* IV. 19. 2). Iamblichus was a native of Chalcis in Syria and it was in Syria where, after a period of study under Porphyry, he founded his own school (Eunapius *VS* 457 ff.). He died about 326, not long after Constantine became master of the Roman world. His chief disciple Aedesius founded a further school at Pergamum (*VS* 461), but neither he nor any other of the followers of Iamblichus who appear in Eunapius seems to have made any substantial contribution to Neoplatonic thought.[1] A more important figure was Iamblichus' pupil and rival Theodorus of Asine (cf. *VS* 458, Julian *Ep.* 12), whose philosophy seems to have combined several streams from earlier Neoplatonism. On the one hand, Theodorus is said to have been influenced by both Numenius (Proclus *In Tim.* II. 274. 10 ff.) and Porphyry (Damascius *V. Is.* 166), and his interpretation of the *Timaeus'* Craftsman is a development of Amelius' view (Proclus *In Tim.* I. 309. 14 ff.), while his psychology harks back to the Plotinian school on several important points, notably in postulating an unfallen level of soul.[2] On the other, he appears to have resembled Iamblichus in his development of such ideas as the Triadic Principle and the Law of Correspondence (cf. Proclus *In Tim.* II. 274. 10 ff. and below pp. 123–4, 130 ff.). A commentary on Aristotle's *Categories* survives by Iambli-

[1] On the other hand, that the school was not wholly given over to theurgy is proved by the unsuccessful attempt of one of its members, Eusebius of Myndus, to persuade the emperor Julian to follow the Plotinian *philosophical* way of purification (*V S* 474–5).

[2] Proclus *In Tim.* III. 333. 28 ff.; cf. ibid. III. 246. 23–8 and Nemesius *Nat. Hom.* 51. 117 (PG. XL. 584). On the other hand, *In Tim.* II. 215. 29 ff. suggests he sided with Iamblichus against Porphyry over the question of Soul's intermediate status (cf. pp. 111–13, 119–20.)

chus' follower Dexippus and another is ascribed to Aedesius' pupil, Maximus of Ephesus (Simplicius *In Cat.* 1. 14–16). But Maximus' major importance lay elsewhere, as spiritual director to Julian the Apostate (sole emperor 361–3) during the latter's attempt to reverse the process begun by Constantine and re-establish the ancient pagan religion in the form of a church with Iamblichean Neoplatonism as its theological creed. The attempt came to nothing, however, with Julian's death in battle, and Maximus, whose ambition had gained him an unfavourable reputation, paid with his life in the subsequent Christian reaction (cf. *VS* 473–80). Several letters and theological essays survive by Julian himself; their philosophy is largely a popularisation of Iamblichus' teaching, as is that of the attractive little 'pagan catechism' by Julian's praetorian prefect Sallustius preserved under the title 'On the Gods and the World'. The work is a summary of Neoplatonic religious teaching for the benefit of educated laymen; its third and fourth chapters on the interpretation of mythology, with their well-known allegorisation of the Attis myth, are of especial interest.

Of Porphyry and Iamblichus, however, no metaphysical work survives in its entirety, and their importance has in consequence been frequently underestimated. Thus Porphyry has been seen as simply a populariser of Plotinus, and it is certainly true that his greatest influence lay in this direction (cf. *VS* 456–7), especially in the Latin West, where his simplification of his master's thought appealed to the practically-minded Romans' distrust of the subtleties of theoretical philosophy. It is therefore his influence that predominates in both pagans like Macrobius and Christians like Augustine, though this should not be taken to mean that the Latin authors did not read Plotinus himself; Augustine certainly read at least some of his works (*De Vita Beata* 1. 4).[1] But it does mean that they read Plotinus through Porphyrian spectacles and that it was therefore Porphyry's version of Neoplatonism that dominated the Western tradition until Eriugena's ninth-century translation of the Dionysian corpus (cf. below pp. 166–7). And certain features of that version stand out clearly both in our Latin sources and in Porphyry's own surviving works.[2] Among these we may mention first of all the *De Abstinentia*, a defence of vegetarianism,

---

[1] On this text and its interpretation cf. P. Henry, *Plotin et l'occident*, pp. 82 ff., correcting the view of Theiler's *Porphyrios und Augustin*. On Augustine's Neoplatonic sources cf. most recently the works of R. J. O'Connell listed in section 6 (iv) of our bibliography.

[2] A few minor works on specialised subjects are omitted from our list. For a complete list cf. P. Hadot, *Porphyre et Victorinus I*, p. 456 n. 1. On lost works cf.

and a Consolation addressed to his wife Marcella on his departure on a journey and offering her moral advice. From these writings we can see Porphyry's enthusiasm for the moral and ascetic side of Neoplatonic discipline and his concern, in which he differed from his master, with popular religious forms. The former tendency is equally visible in his *Life of Pythagoras*, a work which bears witness to the increasing Pythagorean influence on later Neoplatonism, visible in its moral teaching, in its growing concern with mathematics and number-mysticism, and on such doctrinal points as the later schools' teaching on Limit and Infinity (cf. pp. 148–9). The work in question formed part of a great history of philosophy, of which a few other fragments survive. Fruits of Porphyry's religious interests, on the other hand, included his anti-Christian polemic and his attempts at an allegorical interpretation of the traditional myths. The only surviving example of the latter is his essay on the Cave of the Nymphs described in *Odyssey* XIII. The work is also an excellent example of Porphyrian scholastic method which, as we shall see, differs from that of Iamblichus and Proclus. But the most important and influential examples of that method, Porphyry's Platonic and Aristotelian commentaries, are lost, though the fragments of his important *Timaeus* commentary have recently been edited and P. Hadot has made a strong case for ascribing to him some anonymous and extremely interesting fragments on the *Parmenides*.[1] The work which had most influence, however, and which still survives, was the introduction (or 'Isagoge') that he composed to Aristotle's *Categories*; a commentary by him on the Aristotelian treatise in the form of question and answer is also extant. The *Isagoge* was translated into Latin by Boethius, and a passage from it setting out different views on the ontological status of universals (1. 9–14) was to provide a focus for the Medieval dispute between Realism and Nominalism.

From our survey of Porphyry's surviving works three major points have thus emerged: first his role as a populariser of Plotinus, secondly his moral and religious tendencies, thirdly his work as a commentator and scholastic. What has remained largely unrecognised until very recent years is Porphyry's role as a constructive metaphysician. If the current trend is by contrast to over-stress his originality and his

---

also J. Bidez, *Vie de Porphyre*, appendix 4, R. Beutler *RE* article 'Porphyrios', cols. 279–301.

[1] Cf. *Porphyre et Victorinus* passim and his earlier article in *Revue des études grecques* LXXIV (1961) 410–38. Professor A. C. Lloyd informs me that as yet unpublished work of Hadot's pupils has provided additional confirmation of his thesis; in the meantime a certain measure of doubt must persist.

influence on later philosophy, it has none the less correctly shown him as the initiator of a certain development of Plotinus' thought and one which agrees with his other dominant interests. On the other hand, as will be seen, its account of Porphyry's views is probably too mono-lithic; like his master (and indeed like Plato and Aristotle) Porphyry felt himself drawn in contradictory directions and seems to have taken different attitudes in different works. For the present, however, we need merely list the major works, all of them, alas, extant only in fragments, from which Porphyry's metaphysical views must be reconstructed.

Most important among these are the remains of the *Sentences Leading to the Intelligible World* (*Aphormai pros ta noēta*), a collection of 44 aphorisms on metaphysical topics, ranging in length from single sentences to short essays. Most are based on texts from the *Enneads;* some are mere quotations or paraphrases from that work; but, as Lloyd remarks, any idea that they provide an easy introduction to Plotinus is unlikely to survive the experiment.[1] In general the *Sentences* mark a hardening of Plotinus' statements into rigid formulae foreshadowing Proclus' *Elements*. Along with this goes an increased attention to conceptual precision; thus Sentence 22 agrees with Plotinus that each Intelligence contains the whole of Reality, but adds that 'in universal Intelligence even particulars exist in universal form, whereas in particular intelligences both universals and particulars exist in a manner appropriate to a part'. And although the work is incomplete, it is interesting that many Sentences deal with topics that Porphyry admits he himself found perplexing, the relation of Intelligence to its objects (*Sent.* 41, 43–4, cf. *V. Pl.* 18. 8–23) and the soul's union with the body (*V. Pl.* 13. 10–17), with which we shall deal later. As its title implies, however, the bulk of the work is concerned with the distinction between sensible and Intelligible orders and the change in man's intellectual and moral attitude necessitated by this distinction. The latter point is the subject of its best-known section, Sentence 32, which systematises the four classes of virtue distinguished by Plotinus; further classes were to be added by the later Neoplatonists in accordance with their view of theurgy as higher than philosophy.[2] Of Porphyry's other metaphysical

---

[1] *Cambridge History of Later Greek and Early Medieval Philosophy*, p. 286.

[2] The four classes distinguished by Porphyry are the civic (cf. *Enn.* 1. 2. 1. 16–21), purificatory (ibid. 3. 11–19), contemplative (ibid. 6. 22–7) and paradigmatic virtues (ibid. 7. 1–6), a classification followed by Macrobius *In Somn. Sc.* 1. VIII; among later Neoplatonists cf. Marinus *V. Pr.* ch. 3 and Olympiodorus *In Phd.* 45–9, 113–14.

treatises only scanty fragments survive. First there are the extracts from his *Miscellaneous Inquiries* (*Symmikta Zētēmata*) dealing with the union of soul and body incorporated in the treatise *On the Nature of Man* by the fifth-century Christian bishop Nemesius of Emesa (*PG* XL. 592 ff.) and in a work addressed to the Persian King Chosroes by Priscianus, one of the last philosophers of the Athenian School, and now extant only in Latin. Then there are the important fragments on the *Parmenides* ascribed by Hadot to Porphyry; if not certainly by Porphyry himself, they must emanate from his school and will require extended treatment. Finally, we must mention the substantial fragments that have been preserved of works by Porphyry dealing with the philosophy of religion. Three of these are of outstanding importance, the *Philosophy from Oracles*, the letter to the Egyptian priest Anebo and the treatise *On the Return of the Soul* (*De Regressu Animae*) discussed in Augustine's *City of God*. The extant remains of these works differ so widely in tone that scholars have generally assumed that they date from different periods of Porphyry's life and that the first of them, with its uncritical, not to say superstitious, reverence for oracles, must antedate his meeting with Plotinus. While not necessarily wrong, this view has perhaps been more confidently accepted than the positive evidence in its favour warrants.[1] In any case the problem does not concern us here, since we shall be able to deal only with Porphyry's post-Plotinian period, that is, with the second and third of the above works.

With regard to Iamblichus we are even worse served. The most important work of his to survive in its entirety is the defence of theurgy entitled 'On the Egyptian Mysteries' (*De Mysteriis*), whose authenticity, doubted during the nineteenth century, seems guaranteed by the testimony of Proclus.[2] The work does not, however, deal systematically with metaphysics, though some of the author's views emerge incidentally. For the rest we have two mathematical works, another life of Pythagoras, and the *Protrepticus*, an exhortation to

---

[1] The generally accepted chronology (presented especially in Bidez' *Vie de Porphyre*) is challenged in J. O'Meara's *Porphyry's Philosophy from Oracles in Augustine* (Paris 1959), which goes too far, however, in identifying the *Philosophy from Oracles* with the *De Regressu Animae*. Against O'Meara cf. Hadot, *Revue des études augustiniennes* VI (1960) 205–44. Bidez' chronology rests heavily on Eunapius *VS* 457; on the other hand, that the *Philosophy from Oracles* stood closer to the other works than most of its extant fragments suggest is implied by Eusebius *PE* IV. 7. 3. and Augustine *CD* XIX. 23.

[2] Cf. the scholion (by the Byzantine philosopher Psellus) that heads our manuscripts of the work; also *In Tim.* I. 386. 10–11.

philosophy freely incorporating extracts from the works of Classical philosophers, among them Plato's *Gorgias* and *Phaedo* and Aristotle's own lost *Protrepticus*, for which it constitutes our primary source. Finally, there are the fragments of Iamblichus' important treatise *On the Soul* preserved by the anthologist Stobaeus; though its extant portions deal mainly with earlier philosophers' views, much may be learned from Iamblichus' criticisms of their teaching. For the rest we are wholly dependent on the reports of his doctrine in Proclus and other late Neoplatonists. As a result his importance has not always been fully realised; he has been seen as abandoning philosophy for superstition and sober criticism of his views has often been replaced by abuse. Such an attitude contrasts oddly with Julian's assessment of him as Plato's equal (*Or.* IV. 146a) and with the later Neoplatonists' reverence for his 'divine inspiration', which exceeded even their respect for Plotinus. Few will nowadays accept such an estimate; on the other hand there is ample evidence that Iamblichus was a constructive thinker of no mean power, and no doubt at all that it was he who determined the direction of later Neoplatonic thought, at least in the Greek-speaking half of the Empire; in the West, as we have noted, it was Porphyry's influence that predominated. And though the conflict between Iamblichus' religious views and those of Plotinus may be treated as one between superstition and rationalism, it is no less validly, and perhaps more profitably, seen as one between two contrasting and permanently attractive conceptions of man's relation to God. Certainly Iamblichus was concerned, as the *De Mysteriis* makes clear, to justify his religious innovations rationally; nor does our other evidence suggest an uncritical attitude towards superstition on his part. Eunapius admittedly relates several wonder stories about him, but he also reports Iamblichus' amused denial of rumours that as he prayed his body was transfigured and rose in the air (*VS* 458). Exactly how much of the later Neoplatonic system represents Iamblichus' own contribution is impossible to determine with certainty, in view of the loss of his works. On the other hand he deserves our respect, and will receive extended treatment later in the present chapter.

II. ANTI-CHRISTIAN POLEMIC AND THE PROBLEM OF THEURGY

The conflict between pagan philosophy and Christianity had begun in the second century A.D. with the anti-Christian treatise of the Platonist

Celsus, erroneously identified by Origen with an Epicurean of the same name and answered in one of the Christian Father's most famous writings. Julian was himself to compose his own polemic. But of all the Platonists' anti-Christian tracts it was Porphyry's that was judged most dangerous, owing to the scholarship (including an expert knowledge of Hebrew) which he applied to the analysis of the Biblical texts. Though the work was committed by the Church to the flames, our extant evidence proves that its Biblical criticism remained unequalled until modern times. But this regrettably falls outside the limits of our present study. Nor can we deal with the general pagan objections to Christianity, many of which were accepted by the Neoplatonists. We must confine ourselves to the principal philosophical divergences between the two movements, as revealed by the three polemics and the counter-criticisms of the Church Fathers; Plotinus' anti-Gnostic treatise is also relevant, since many of its criticisms apply equally to orthodox Christianity. We may group the relevant topics under three headings. First, there is the problem posed by the Christian elevation of faith above reason. Secondly, there are the three points found unassimilable by the amateur Platonist philosopher Synesius of Cyrene, on his consecration in 410 as bishop of Ptolemais, and discussed in his 105th letter; the same points were commonly found unacceptable by Platonists otherwise sympathetic towards Christianity. Thirdly, there are the problems of the Incarnation (cf. Augustine *Conf.* VII. 9) and of miracles.

That Jews and Christians demanded belief in propositions for which they were unable to furnish proof was a commonplace of Platonic criticism, perhaps most vigorously stated in a famous fragment of Galen.[1] Plotinus, we may recall, had similarly attacked the Gnostics' refusal to propound their views by rational argument (II. 9. 6. 43–52, cf. above p. 12). In later centuries, however, this contrast became blurred, as Christians sought a rational foundation for their views, while Neoplatonism took on more of the features of a religion and in its final form exalted faith as the highest of the virtues (cf. below pp. 154–5). Nor were the later Neoplatonists willing to allow free discussion of subversive ideas; Proclus wished to withdraw from general circulation all books except the *Timaeus* and the *Chaldean Oracles*, to prevent them from harming the uninstructed (*V. Pr.* 38). Although no more than an

---

[1] Quoted by Walzer, *Galen on Jews and Christians*, p. 15. Cf. Origen *C. Cels.* I. 9, III. 75, VI. 11, Porphyry *C. Chr.* fr. 1 (= Eusebius *PE* I. 2. 1 ff.) line 17, fr. 73 (= Eusebius *D E* I. 1. 12), Julian ap. Gregory Nazianzen *Or.* 4. 102 (*PG* XXXV. 637). On the whole problem cf. Walzer op. cit., pp. 48–56.

application of Plato's own teaching, the principle bears a striking similarity to Christian practice.[1] Synesius' three difficulties were harder to overcome, though even on some of these Neoplatonism and Christianity came closer together; they concerned the eternity of the world and pre-existence of the soul, which the Platonists were determined to maintain, and the resurrection of the body, which they denied. In each case the difficulty as stated was merely the last vestige of a fundamental divergence of attitude. And, though other important points were also involved, the basic Neoplatonic criticism once again concerned Christianity's alleged irrationality. That both the world-order and its designer follow perfectly rational principles was fundamental Hellenic doctrine, summarised in Celsus' denial that God can do, or wishes to do, what is either morally shameful or contrary to nature (*C. Cels.* v. 14; cf. Porphyry *C. Chr.* fr. 35 = Macarius Magnes *Apocr.* IV. 2, fr. 94 = ibid. IV. 24), while for the Neoplatonists, as we have seen, the universe was a spontaneous production of the Intelligible order, with no question of an anthropomorphic creator at all. And that Christianity seemed to deny these principles we can see if we consider Synesius' first problem, that of the world's eternity.

This in fact involves two questions, whether the world has always existed and whether it is indestructible, both points, of course, that the Christians denied. The *Timaeus*, by contrast, seemed to declare on the one hand that the world had a temporal beginning (28B–C), on the other that the divine power will henceforth maintain it in existence for ever (41B), and some Middle Platonists were prepared to accept both statements literally (cf. Atticus ap. Eusebius *PE* xv. 6. 802 B ff., Plotinus *Enn.* II. I. I). For the Neoplatonists, however, to regard the world as subject to either temporal generation or destruction was to impute deficiency both to the world itself and to its divine creator. Plotinus' vehement insistence, against Gnostics and Christians alike, on the divinity of the World-soul and the stars has already been noted (above p. 12), and for a Greek the primary attribute of divinity was immortality. But the most serious consequences of supposing a temporal creation concerned the world's creator. That God cannot change had been fundamental for both Plato (*Rep.* II. 380–1) and Aristotle (*De Phil.* fr. 16 Ross = Simplicius *De C.* 288. 28 ff.; *Met.* Λ. 9. 1074b 25–7); yet it was

---

[1] On the other hand, the Neoplatonists do not seem to have encouraged persecution of the Christians, though Porphyry's work was used in support of Diocletian's persecution by the imperial official Hierocles (not to be confused with the Neoplatonist philosopher of that name, on whom cf. pp. 139, 142–3).

not merely change that the Judeo-Christian view seemed to impute to him, but arbitrary change for no apparent reason. The Neoplatonists' basic objection was summarised in a dilemma originally propounded by Aristotle. Either things are better after the world's creation (or destruction), it runs, or they are worse. But it is equally blasphemous to suppose either that God's activity alters for the worse, or that it was initially imperfect and so needed to change for the better. Or if the resulting state is neither better nor worse, any change is totally pointless.[1] Proclus was to compose a famous treatise setting forth eighteen arguments against the Christian position, which the Alexandrian Christian Neoplatonist John Philoponus answered in a work still extant. Augustine's reply, that there was no time before the creation of the world and that the pagans' objections therefore miss the mark (*Conf.* XI. 13, *CD* XI. 4–6, 21), is also celebrated.

The second and third of Synesius' reservations go together. To Neoplatonists it seemed irrational to suppose, with the Christians, that the soul survives death while denying its existence before birth (cf. Augustine *CD* X. 31). And this was because, unlike the Christians, they regarded the soul as endowed with immortality in its own right and not through divine grace. And that here too immortality entailed divinity is shown by a well-known discussion in the Latin Christian writer Arnobius (*Adv. Nat.* II. 11–66), attacking in particular the Platonists' view of the soul as naturally sinless (ibid. II. 14–15, etc.). The latter doctrine indeed was to be toned down in post-Iamblichean Neoplatonism, but as our discussion of the late Neoplatonic term 'self-constituted' will show, the basic contrast with Christianity remained unaltered (cf. pp. 128–9). And in the original Neoplatonic view immortality was reserved for the soul alone, whereas the Christians believed that God would resurrect body and soul together.[2] Here again the two movements came closer together over the years. Though the Catholic Church was not to proclaim the soul's immortality (and not just the final resurrection of the whole man) as a dogma for more than a thousand years, it became the universal teaching of Christian Platonists, some of whom, like Nemesius, even upheld pre-existence (*Nat. Hom.* 45. 104 ff. = *PG* XL.

---

[1] Aristotle *De Phil.* fr. 19c Ross (= Philo *Aet. M.* 8. 39–43), cf. fr. 20 (= Cicero *Ac. Pr.* 119), Porphyry *C. Chr.* fr. 34 (= Macarius *Apocr.* IV. 1), Sallustius *DM* VII. 1–2, Proclus *In Tim.* I. 288. 14 ff. Against a change of mind on God's part cf. Plotinus *Enn.* II. 1. 4. 25–33, II. 9. 4. 4–6, 17–19, V. 8. 12. 15–26, VI. 7. 3. 1–9.

[2] Cf. *C. Cels.* V. 14, Porphyry *C. Chr.* fr. 94 (= Macarius op. cit. IV. 24); also frs. 92–3, Augustine *C D* X. 29, XIII. 19, XXII. 26–7.

572B); Augustine's early works presuppose the latter doctrine, and he was never definitely to deny it.[1] On the Platonic side the later Neoplatonists' doctrine of the immortality of the soul's subtle 'astral' body (cf. pp. 109 and n., 157–8) seemed to offer hope of bridging the gulf. But the contrast between that body and man's gross terrestrial body was still too sharply drawn by the pagans to be acceptable to Christian orthodoxy and, while a standing temptation to Platonising thinkers, the doctrine was condemned as Origenism at the Council of Constantinople in 553.

The doctrine of divine incarnation, in its Christian form, was unacceptable to orthodox Neoplatonism on many grounds, though Porphyry, at least, was willing to regard Jesus as a righteous man admitted to heaven for his virtue (Augustine *CD* XIX. 23). First, the Christian doctrine seemed once again to involve arbitrary action by God at a particular time—the metaphysical problem here reinforcing the moral difficulty of God's seeming unconcern for the pre-Christian generations (cf. *C. Cels.* IV. 7, VI. 78, Porphyry *C. Chr.* frs. 81–2 = Augustine *Ep.* 102. 8, Jerome *Ep.* 133.9). Then the Platonists' repugnance towards the idea of divine union with an unclean fleshly body had to be overcome (*C. Cels.* VI. 73, Porphyry *C. Chr.* fr. 77 = Macarius op. cit. IV. 22, Augustine *CD* X. 28–9). Thirdly, it was well-nigh impossible for Hellenic thinkers to accept a unique once-for-all incarnation of divinity. How hard such an idea was to accommodate to Neoplatonic metaphysics a little reflection will show; more generally, educated pagans were insistent that the supreme deity's glory is best revealed in the multiplicity of subordinate gods he has produced (cf. *Enn.* II. 9. 9. 26–42, Porphyry *C. Chr.* frs. 75–8 = Macarius op. cit. IV. 20–3), and found the new religion's claim to a unique revelation especially distasteful. But perhaps the most serious difficulty concerned the idea of a suffering god, which the Neoplatonic doctrine of Impassibility rendered a contradiction in terms (cf. Methodius = Porphyry *C. Chr.* fr. 84). That no god could submit to the shame of crucifixion was a common pagan charge, echoed by Celsus (*C. Cels.* II. 31 ff., VII. 13–15, etc.), while on a more philosophical level there was the difficulty that to the Hellenic sage all suffering is a matter of indifference; hence Jesus' lamentations before his death attracted particularly unfavourable comment (*C. Cels.* II. 24, Porphyry *C. Chr.* frs. 62–3 = Macarius op. cit. III. 1–2). Finally, there were Jesus' miracles, on which the early Church laid great stress, but which the pagans regarded as due to magic and as such repeatable

[1] Cf. E. Gilson, *The Christian Philosophy of Saint Augustine*, pp. 50–1, 275.

by anyone able to manipulate the appropriate cosmic forces (*C. Cels.* I. 6, etc., Porphyry *C. Chr.* fr. 4=Jerome *Tract. de Psalm.* LXXXI). We thus once again encounter the fundamental antithesis between Neoplatonism and Christianity, that of rational world-order versus supernatural grace. It is this, as we shall see, which distinguishes theurgy from Christian sacramentalism and which was to provide a stumblingblock for Platonically-inclined Christians for many centuries to come (cf. e.g. pp. 161–2).

An invaluable advantage for the Christians in the conflict of religions was their possession of a sacred book. To fill the vacuum on their side, the Neoplatonists turned to the *Chaldaean Oracles*, a collection of turgid and obscure hexameter oracles composed or collected during the reign of Marcus Aurelius by a certain Julian and his son of the same name (entitled respectively the Chaldaean and the Theurgist) and probably originating in the revelations of an ecstatic prophet or prophetess. The first philosopher known to have quoted the *Oracles* was Porphyry; for Plotinus either did not know them or deliberately ignored them.[1] Porphyry further equipped them with a commentary harmonising their teaching with Neoplatonism, and for Iamblichus and the Athenian School they became the supreme authority, exceeding even Plato. While no contradiction between the two sources could of course be admitted, it is significant that it was the writings of the 'theologians' (Orpheus and the Chaldaeans) that formed the culmination of the Athenian School's curriculum, the student approaching them only after thorough study first of Aristotle, and then of Plato (cf. *V. Pr.* 13 and 26). But, needless to say, like all sacred scriptures the *Oracles* needed considerable interpretation, since their theology constituted a pre-Plotinian version of Platonism, having affinities with the doctrine of Numenius, notably in maintaining the existence of two divine Intelligences, the lower of them doubled into an active and a contemplative phase (*Kr.* p. 14; cf. above p. 34). (Scholars disagree whether the *Oracles* are borrowing from Numenius or vice versa, or whether both depend on a common source.) Surprisingly little difficulty was caused by the *Oracles*' Stoicising descriptions of divine Intelligence as a 'fire' (*Kr.* p. 13);[2] for by taking 'fire' as equivalent to 'light' the Neoplatonists were able to 'dematerialise' them (cf. above

---

[1] Though Psellus (*PG* CXXII. 1125 C–D) ascribes the oracle quoted at the start of *Enn.* I. 9 to the Chaldaean collection.

[2] Hence the term 'empyrean' (*Kr.* p. 54); on the doctrine cf. Lewy, *Chaldaean Oracles and Theurgy*, pp. 429–32.

p. 61). The *Oracles'* account of the Supreme Deity raised more serious problems. Like other Middle Platonic texts the *Oracles* wavered between describing the 'Father' (as they called him), as the supreme Intelligence (cf. *Kr.* p. 14) and as the supreme Intelligible object beyond the reach of Intelligence (*Kr.* p. 11, quoted by Damascius, *De Princ.* I. 154. 16–26); the latter view is supported by a more turgid description of the Father as having 'rapt himself away and not enclosed his own fire in his intellective power' (*Kr.* p. 12). Another influential verse described him as 'all things, but in intelligible mode' (*Kr.* p. 19). But most important of all were the *Oracles'* description of him as a trinity-in-unity, and their claim, in such declarations as that 'in every world shines a triad ruled by a monad' (*Kr.* p. 18), that the whole of reality was triadically organised. Basing themselves on a verse of the *Oracles* (*Kr.* p. 12; cf. Proclus *PT* VI. 9. 365), the Neoplatonists saw the supreme triad as constituted by the Father's Existence (*hyparxis*), his Power (*dynamis*) and his Intelligence (*nous*), which they saw as corresponding to Plotinus' Intelligible triad of Being, Life and Intelligence, and to the three phases of Abiding, Procession and Reversion exhibited in the constitution of every reality. For Christian Neoplatonists, such as Synesius or the Latin theologian Marius Victorinus, such a trinity was of course far more attractive than Plotinus' hierarchically subordinated three Hypostases. But for pagans the trouble was that the triad in question was situated on the level of the *Second* Hypostasis; hence the Father described in the *Oracles* could not be identical with the supreme deity. Porphyry's attempt to identify the One with the first term of the Intelligible triad was criticised as destroying the former's transcendence (Damascius *De Princ.* I. 86. 8 ff.); how great the danger was we shall presently see. More influential (though less legitimate) was Porphyry's interpretation of the *Oracles'* references to Hecate. to whom, appropriately in a work concerned with ritual magic, they had assigned a major role, and whom they had identified with the World-soul. Ignoring this and building instead on a verse describing her as 'intermediate between the fathers' (*Kr.* p. 27), Porphyry identified her with Life, the middle term of the Intelligible triad; it is the combination of this doctrine with the one just referred to that explains Augustine's puzzled reference to the intermediary introduced by Porphyry between the first two Hypostases (*CD* x. 23).

On its theoretical side, however, the Chaldaean system contained little that was not equally present in some of its rivals, such as the *Hermetica*. More important was the fact that the *Oracles* taught a clearcut way of salvation through theurgic ritual. The term 'theurgy', with its etymological connotation of 'divine work',[1] seems to have been coined, perhaps by the younger Julian, in deliberate contrast to 'theology', which merely talks about the gods; by the Neoplatonists it is also contrasted with *theoria*, the philosophical contemplation advocated by Plotinus, whose deficiency the theurgists similarly stressed. The methods of theurgy were essentially those of ritual magic, its aim the incarnation of a divine force either in a material object, such as a statue, or in a human being, the result being a state of prophetic trance. Its justification, most clearly expounded in Proclus' little essay *On the Hieratic Art* (*CMAG* VI. 148–51), is the magical 'Principle of Correspondence', the idea, first, that each part of the universe mirrors every other part, and secondly, and more important, that the whole material world is the mirror of invisible divine powers; hence, in virtue of the network of forces linking image to archetype, manipulation of the appropriate material objects brings the theurgists into contact with the deities they represent. The principle rests in fact on the Neoplatonic doctrine, systematised, as we shall see, by Iamblichus, that 'everything is in everything, but in each appropriately to its nature' (cf. pp. 123–4); it justified, for instance, the production (begun long before Neoplatonism) of long lists of stones, plants, animals, etc. expressing the power of Sun, Moon or other celestial gods. And it was common ground for all Neoplatonists that the sympathy linking all parts of the sensible cosmos enabled the magician to draw power from the celestial spheres. What the Plotinian school denied was that the effect of theurgic practices extended to the Intelligible world or to the One (cf. pp. 70–2).

The increasing importance attached to theurgy in later Neoplatonism corresponds to the greater stress laid on ritual in the later, Tantric, forms of Indian religion, and in both cases the contempt with which scholars formerly spoke of the later developments is now giving place to a more respectful interest. This is largely because it is now realised that, whatever may be thought of its practitioners' more extreme claims, ritual, and the symbols it uses, are indeed efficacious on the psychological plane, answering as they do to needs rooted deep within the human mind. The later Neoplatonists' failure in competition with Christianity may in fact have been due less to any capitulation to 'superstition' on their part than to the fact that too many of the rites

[1] Perhaps also 'making gods' (cf. *CH Asclepius* 23–4) or 'making gods of men' (cf. Psellus *PG* CXXII. 721D). On the term cf. Lewy op.cit., pp. 461–6.

they wished to defend were no longer of more than antiquarian interest. Alliance with one of the new saviour-cults, such as that of Isis or
Mithras, might have produced firmer results. We may concede at least
that Porphyry was right in regarding such methods as more immediately helpful than philosophy to the average man. We may be less
inclined to grant Iamblichus' claim that they have higher value even
for the philosopher; yet we should remember that Catholics are advised
to attend Mass in preference to studying theology. In this connection
we may recall Iamblichus' argument that man, as a composite being,
needs a form of worship involving body as well as soul (*Myst.* v.
15–17), an idea echoed in Byzantine sacramentalism (cf. p. 162).
The great difference between Neoplatonic theurgy and Christian
sacramentalism was, as we have seen, that the former regarded itself as
employing forces built into the natural world-order, and not as
dependent on a supernatural divine intervention over and above that
order. It must indeed be admitted that many Neoplatonists, like other
occultists, lost themselves chasing psychic phenomena; yet the final
goal of theurgy was regarded both by the *Oracles* and in the Athenian
School as the mystical union. Proclus is nowhere recorded as having
attained it, but Damascius' *Life of Isidorus* suggests that others, including Isidorus himself, may have been more successful (cf. *V. Is.* 38).
Mystical union is not, however, prominent in Iamblichus' *De Mysteriis*,[1] perhaps because the work depends more on Egyptian than
Chaldaean ideas. And since its theoretical justification, insofar as we
can reconstruct it, depends on ideas peculiar to the Athenian School, it
will be dealt with in our next chapter (cf. pp. 153–5).

Porphyry's attitude to theurgy was, however, decidedly more reserved. In his view, expounded in his treatise *On the Return of the
Soul*, it was merely an easier first step for those unable to pursue
philosophy directly; it was unnecessary to the philosopher and could
not by itself lead the soul back to the Intelligible world (cf. Augustine
CD x. 9 and 27–8). All that it could do was to purify the soul's 'pneumatic envelope', the subtle 'astral' body acquired during her descent
through the heavens. By this means, in virtue of the interconnection of
body and lower soul, the latter could be purified sufficiently to enable
man's higher soul to pursue contemplation without distraction. Theurgy could not, however, confer immortality either on the irrational
soul or on her 'vehicle'; on our return to the Intelligible world both

---

[1] It seems to be alluded to in i. 3, ii. 11, v. 26 and, most clearly, in x. 5–7,
though the work's terminological imprecision makes certainty difficult.

are once again resolved into the spheres whence they originated.[1]
Finally, theurgy can be misused and is always dangerous; not all
daemonic forces are morally wholesome and there is the danger that
the wrong ones will be evoked (cf. Augustine *CD* x. 9). The *Letter to
Anebo* carries Porphyry's criticism of popular religion further.

The Anebo of the title is a (real or fictitious) Egyptian priest, to
whom Porphyry addresses a series of questions concerning the explanation and value of theurgic practices and the nature of the beings
they are intended to evoke. The *Letter*'s critical tone is set in its first
part, which poses the problem of distinguishing the various orders of
superhuman beings and raises objections to any answer that may be
suggested. For does the distinction between gods and daemons (*a*)
correspond to that between the inhabitants of the celestial spheres and
those of the air? But can divine beings be limited to a particular place,
and how does such a view square with the recognition of 'chthonic'
gods, whose habitation is beneath the earth (*Ep.* I. 2a–b = Iamblichus
Myst. I. 8–9)? Or (*b*), is the distinction that the gods are impassible,
the daemons subject to passions? Or (c), should the gods be identified
with Intelligences, the daemons with Souls? But on neither of these
hypotheses can the gods be moved by the prayers and invocations
addressed to them; so what is the use of the latter (*Ep.* I. 2c–3b =
Myst. I. 10–15, Eusebius *PE* v. 10. 10)? Or (*d*), do the daemons have
bodies, while the gods are incorporeal? But then the heavenly bodies
will not be divine (*Ep.* I. 3c = *Myst.* I. 16–17); and so on. The remainder of the *Letter* deals with the theurgic practices themselves, especially
those concerned with divination, and with Egyptian theology and its
symbolism. The sceptical note of some of Porphyry's criticisms, which
go far beyond anything in Plotinus, is remarkable; indeed he even
quotes, without apparent dissent, the Christian view that divination is
the work of deceptive daemons and therefore worthless (*Ep.* II. 7 =
Cyril *Contra Iulianum* IV. 125, *PG* LXXVI. 692, *Myst.* III. 31). The
explanation probably lies in the conventions of ancient polemic, and
we need not suppose that Porphyry wished even here to reject theurgy
altogether, though he would have nothing to do with any practice
involving animal sacrifice, condemned in the second book of the *De
Abstinentia* (cf. *Ep.* II, 8b, *Myst.* v. 1, VI. 1). His queries rather concern the explanation of theurgy and the consequent value to be

---

[1] Iamblichus *De An.* 370. 5 ff., Proclus *In Tim.* III. 234. 18 ff. It is significant
that Iamblichus took the opposite view (cf. *In Tim.* ibid.). On the astral body cf.
Dodds, *Elements of Theology*, appendix 2, pp. 313–21.

assigned to it, and here his attitude is thoroughly Plotinian, that such practices work only through the sympathy governing the sensible cosmos (*Ep.* II. 5d = *Myst.* III. 27) and cannot therefore affect the higher souls of the gods. To suppose otherwise entails the blasphemous conclusion that the gods can be constrained by pressure from men, an idea constantly attacked throughout the *Letter*.[1] Plotinus had taken a similar view of the workings of prayer (cf. pp. 70–2). It follows that theurgy's status is much less exalted than its practitioners claim and that it cannot of itself bring salvation; evidence is the fact that the power of prophecy, which, Porphyry argues, is a purely psychological phenomenon, does not guarantee happiness (*Ep.* II. 5b, 18d = *Myst.* III. 24, x. 4). Such was the dilemma that Iamblichus, writing in the *De Mysteriis* under the name of Anebo's master Abammon, was to have to resolve.

III. THE THREE HYPOSTASES IN PORPHYRY AND THE PARMENIDES COMMENTATOR

Porphyry's critical attitude towards theurgy was possible in view of the confidence which he shared with his master in the soul's power, through her membership of the Intelligible order, to deliver herself by moral virtue and philosophical contemplation. Our main sources for his psychology are, first, some of his Sentences, secondly, the extracts from his *Miscellaneous Inquiries* preserved in Nemesius and Priscianus, thirdly the criticisms of his views in later Neoplatonists, especially in the fragments of Iamblichus' treatise *On the Soul*. We may begin by recalling the important passage from the latter work mentioned in our account of Numenius (Stobaeus I. 365. 5–21; cf. pp. 33–4). We may remember that the view there criticised by Iamblichus involved two objectionable and inter-related views, both of them tending to abolish the barriers between the several levels of the metaphysical hierarchy. The first was that there is no substantial difference between various classes of souls, all of which contain the whole Intelligible order within themselves, the second that there is no ultimate distinction between Universal Soul and Intelligence. The application of Iamblichus' criticisms to Numenius and Plotinus have already been considered (cf. pp. 81–2, 92). And though Iamblichus describes

---

[1] Cf. *Ep.* I. 2c, II. 3a–b, 8a–c, 13b = Eusebius *PE* v. 10. 1–10, *Myst.* I. 12, III. 17–18, IV. 1, VI. 5 ff., VIII. 8. For Plotinus cf. *Enn.* II. 9. 14. 1–11, IV. 4. 30. 26–30, etc. Augustine's charge (*CD* x. 10) that Porphyry himself regarded the gods as subject to human constraint must be a misunderstanding.

Porphyry as having been in two minds, sometimes accepting the doctrines in question, at others vehemently rejecting them, it is certainly the former standpoint that predominates in Porphyry's extant works.

That Porphyry's writings, and those of the Latin authors dependent on him, exhibit a decided simplification of Plotinus' system has often been observed. It is not merely that, compared with the distinction between sensible and Intelligible reality, the differences between the Hypostases take a subordinate place in his works. More positively, he displays a pronounced tendency to abolish any absolute distinction between the Hypostases or, to use Lloyd's expression, to 'telescope' them into one another. For the present it is his 'telescoping' of Soul and Intelligence that concerns us. As we have hinted, the root of the difficulty was the inherent dilemma in the Platonic view of Soul, which was linked in its turn with Plato's equivocal attitude towards the sensible world (cf. pp. 5–6, 20). On the one hand the *Timaeus* had treated the soul as an intermediary between Intelligible and sensible worlds and as responsible for the organisation of the latter; on the other, the more dualistically-inclined *Phaedo* had exhorted her to shun the body and virtually admitted her to full membership of the Intelligible order. That the latter viewpoint should have had more appeal for the ascetically-minded Porphyry is not surprising; in fact it predominates both in the *Sentences*, whose main object we have seen to be the distinction between the two orders of reality, and still more in the *Miscellaneous Inquiries*, where the Soul is termed an 'Intelligible' entity without qualification (cf. Nemesius *Nat. Hom.* 57–9. 129–35 Matthaei).

The object of the main surviving section of the latter work is the union of soul and body. It seemed clear to the Neoplatonists, against the Stoics, that such a union could not resemble that between two bodies. For on the one hand it must be a real union and not a mere juxtaposition; on the other, a substantial fusion between the two would destroy the soul's separate existence and so render inexplicable her activity apart from the body in intellectual activity and dreams. Ammonius Saccas had therefore maintained that the union of Intelligible entities with the body takes place without substantial alteration or intermixture on their part, and so escapes the above dilemma; as a parallel he instanced the union of light with air (*Nat. Hom.* 55–8. 125–34), a comparison repeated by Plotinus (*Enn.* I. 1. 4. 12–18, IV. 3. 22. 1–7). And like his master Porphyry uses the Neoplatonic 'incorporealist' conception of light (on which cf. above p. 61) to defend the

soul's impassibility, at least in the sense that she is exempt from substantial change (cf. pp. 74–6). Like Plotinus he regards the soul's so-
called 'passions' as really activities, and denies in consequence that she
should be regarded as suffering along with the ensouled body (*Nat.
Hom.* 60–1. 137–40, *Sent.* 18, 21).

Equally fundamental to the *Sentences*, as we should expect, is the
denial that incorporeal entities are subject to spatial restrictions; for
Porphyry, as for Plotinus, they are 'everywhere and nowhere' (*Sent.*
27, 31, 38). The soul's 'presence' in the body is therefore not a matter
of spatial location, but consists in a 'relation' (*schesis*) towards that
body. If we ask in what that 'relation' consists, the answer is again
thoroughly Plotinian. First, to say that the soul 'is' somewhere is an
incorrect way of saying that she operates there. Secondly, this depends
on her attitude, since incorporeal realities are where they *wish* to be
(*Nat. Hom.* 58–9. 134–7, *Sent.* 3, 27, etc.; cf. pp. 50–1, 76 ff.). The
soul is therefore present 'in' Intelligence when she exercises intuitive
thought and 'in' her own sphere when she reasons discursively; conversely she 'descends to Hades' if the pneumatic vehicle to which she
has grown attached becomes so coarsened that after the death of the
physical body it sinks to the subterranean regions (*Sent.* 29). For it is
the soul's emotional attachment to the body that binds her there, 'as the
lover is bound by his beloved' (*Nat. Hom.* 59. 135), and physical death,
while separating body from soul, does not necessarily free the latter
from the body's influence (*Sent.* 8–9, 28).

The resulting doctrine would appear to be vulnerable on at least two
grounds. First, there is the problem, noted in connection with Plotinus,
of reconciling the soul's impassibility with her need for purification
(cf. p. 76). Secondly, it would seem to follow from the soul's kinship with the Intelligible world that her union with the body is a mistake. It would therefore appear necessary, in order to avoid a dualism
unacceptable to a Neoplatonist, to treat the lower levels of existence
as a mere illusion. That Plotinus had seemed at times to treat Soul
as a mere appearance of Intelligence we have seen (cf. pp. 81–2, 92).
And an even more decidedly 'illusionist' view has been detected by
Lloyd in certain passages of Porphyry. Most important of these is his
claim that it is only erroneously that place or relation (including by
implication relation to a body) is attributed to Reality (*Sent.* 40); his
consolation to his wife that, though his physical body be absent, his
true Intelligible self is still with her (*Ad Marc.* VIII) also points in this
direction. Apart from these hints, however, there is little in the passages

so far discussed that goes beyond Plotinus; indeed we do not know whether Porphyry went as far as Plotinus had done on one occasion in raising the soul above time. What is true is that such passages represent only one side of Plotinus' thought; for elsewhere he had clearly distinguished Soul from Intelligence. We should remember, however, that Iamblichus regarded Porphyry as having had more reservations about assimilating the two than Plotinus had done. Sentence 5, which propounds the traditional Platonic view of Soul as an intermediary, does not necessarily support this, since Proclus suggests that Porphyry regarded this as applying only to Soul in her relation with the body and not in her pure state (*In Tim.* II. 105. 3 ff.). Where our evidence does suggest hesitation on Porphyry's part is in connection with the relation between different classes of souls, the other half of the thesis attacked by Iamblichus.

This emerges above all from our evidence regarding Porphyry's views on transmigration, a problem where the school's internal disputes came to a head; for Numenius and Plotinus, in accordance with their tendency to abolish the barriers between different classes of souls (divine, human, animal, etc.), accepted the transmigration of human souls into animals, whereas Iamblichus, equally consistently with his own standpoint, rejected it (cf. below p. 120).[1] That Porphyry stood with the Plotinian camp is implied by Nemesius' statement that he regarded both human and animal souls as rational and therefore as members of a common species (*Nat. Hom.* 51. 117 = *PG* XL. 584); on the other hand, Augustine (*CD* x. 30) and Aeneas of Gaza (*PG* LXXXV. 893) state that he rejected animal transmigration, and the latter author ascribes the same reason to him as to Iamblichus, that there is a difference of essence between human and animal souls (cf. Iamblichus *De An.* 375. 24–8). Iamblichus further states that Porphyry drew a clearcut distinction between the operations of Universal and individual souls, which Plotinus and Amelius had tended to confuse (*De An.* 372. 9–14). It is true that even this distinction was insufficient to satisfy Iamblichus; yet that it was not a mere consequence of the soul's embodiment is suggested by another statement that, unlike Plotinus, Porphyry regarded even the disembodied soul as keeping its own appropriate rank (ibid. 457. 11–13). If this is correct, it constitutes a major departure from Plotinus' position towards that of Iamblichus.

[1] Cf. H. Dörrie, 'Kontroversen um die Seelenwanderung im Kaiserzeitlichen Platonismus', *Hermes* 85 (1957) 414–35, though my interpretation of Porphyry differs from his.

Our resulting picture of Porphyry's views is therefore a confusing one, and reveals his position as perhaps less consistently 'monistic' than his surviving works have led scholars to conclude. Such a verdict must, however, be radically revised if Porphyry was indeed the author of Hadot's anonymous fragments on the *Parmenides*, since these go well beyond Plotinus in 'telescoping' Intelligence with the One. In any case, even if not certainly Porphyry's own work, they are heavily under his influence, and have the additional importance that they contain some of the school's profoundest reflections on the One in its role as the Absolute. For this reason they are worth treating in some detail.

In Porphyry's *Sentences* the One plays little part and what is said of it is not on the whole un-Plotinian; this applies, for instance, to the claim that the One contains everything 'non-intellectively and hyper-essentially' (*Sent.* 10; cf. above p. 60). On the other hand Sentence 12 maintains more decidedly than had Plotinus that the One possesses its own mode of life.[1] Finally, Sentences 25 and 26 deal with our know-ledge of the One and in their vocabulary (for instance Sentence 25's reference to a 'non-intelligence superior to Intelligence') come very close to the language of the anonymous fragments. The latter are six in number and deal with various sections of the second part of the *Parmenides*, fragments 1–4 being concerned with the One of its first hypothesis, fragments 5 and 6 with the One Being of its second. Of these fragment 3, a mere exposition of and commentary on *Parmenides* 141A5 ff., may be left aside. A similar doctrine to that of the fragments is also found in the Latin Christian theologian Marius Victorinus. Fragment 1 deals with the problems posed by the name 'One' and by the negative theology. First, there is the need to avoid conceiv-ing the One's absolute simplicity as a deficiency; secondly, there are the opposing pitfalls of on the one hand attributing anything to the One and on the other regarding the negations used of it as signifying a mere void. Nihilism can be avoided, the fragment argues, if we remember that it is the One's superabundant power that has produced the uni-verse; to escape the opposite danger we should reflect that as the cause of all things it can be identical with none of them (cf. *Enn.* III. 8. 10. 23–35), so that even the term 'One' falls short of its nature. To conceive that nature, the fragment maintains, in terms foreshadowing the Medieval notion of 'learned ignorance', we must abide in a 'non-comprehensive comprehension and an intellection that intuits nothing'.

---

[1] For Plotinus' attitude cf. *Enn.* III. 9. 9. 17–18, V. 4. 2. 16–17, VI. 7. 17. 9–14, VI. 8. 16. 34–8.

We may thus arrive at 'an ineffable preconception that represents the One in silence, without awareness of that silence, or consciousness that it is the One's image, or knowledge of anything whatever,' and which constitutes an 'image of the Ineffable that is ineffably identical with the Ineffable'. Fragment 2 turns to the implications of the One's role as the Absolute, in particular that it can have no relation to anything else.

The One, the fragment agrees, is not identical with Intelligence. But we should not on that account describe it as 'other than Intelligence', since otherness, like all relations, implies limitation and can therefore be present only in the One's products, not in the One itself. Like Plotinus the commentator argues that creation adds nothing to the One, which would remain the same whether its products existed or not, since otherwise it would have been initially imperfect.[1] His conclusion that the One has no relation to other things is similarly only a logical extension of Plotinus' views; the commentator compares the references of everyday speech to the sun as rising and setting, which erroneously attribute our relation to the sun to that body itself. It follows that there can be no comparison between the One and other things and that the One must be unknowable to us, since like is known by like. But whereas negative theology speaks of the One as non-existent, in reality, the commentator maintains, in terms that go well beyond anything in the *Enneads*, it is the One that is the only true Existent and other things (including ourselves) that are nothing in relation thereto. He comes closer to Plotinus later in the fragment, where he ascribes to the One a mode of awareness transcending the duality of subject and object and the opposition between knowledge and ignorance (cf. p. 59). And though we here encounter the seeds of a positive conception of the One counterbalancing the negative theology and pointing forward to fragments 5 and 6, for the present the negative theology predominates. It is better, the fragment concludes, to abandon such speculations than risk falling short of the One's absolute simplicity. The greatest stress on the negative theology comes, however, in fragment 4, where it is declared to be superior even to the positive affirmations about God found in the *Chaldaean Oracles*.

Such affirmations, the commentator declares, may be true, but, lacking any adequate idea of the One, we cannot understand how they should be taken; hence they are as valueless to us as descriptions of colours to a man born blind. Moreover their propounders subsequently

---

[1] That the One is without otherness is stated at VI. 9. 8. 33–4; on non-reciprocating causal relations cf. V. 5. 12. 40–9, VI. 9. 3. 49–51, and also above pp. 60 ff.

turn round and proclaim the inadequacy of their own terms; so what is the point of learning such descriptions, only to abandon them so soon afterwards? Since the One transcends both quality and essence, no positive terms can express its nature; hence we cannot know either the One itself or the manner in which lower realities proceed from it. To this radically negative conclusion the more positive theology of fragments 5 and 6 stands in marked contrast.

As stated, the object of the last two fragments is the Second Hypostasis, the One-Being of the *Parmenides'* second hypothesis. This fragment 5 declares in one sense to be identical with the original One, in another not. For as a product and image of the One it retains something of the latter's nature; on the other hand, as One-Being it is no longer the One in its original purity. The most daring development of the fragment, however, comes in its description (with some hesitation) of the original One as the Form of Being, insofar as it constitutes the source of the Being in which Plato describes his second One as partaking. The One is indeed beyond Being and Activity, it is declared; yet, since it is active in its own fashion, it may be characterised as 'Absolute Being beyond Being'. The commentator's point turns on the distinction between the infinitive (*to einai*) and the abstract noun (*ousia*) and is therefore hard to render in English. It may, however, be helpful to recall the Neoplatonists' general treatment of the Forms (for example the Form of Magnitude), which we have seen to underlie Plotinus' references to the One as an 'act of thought that does not itself think' (cf. p. 60), an idea echoed in fragment 2's account of the One's absolute knowledge (cf. also *Enn.* v. 6. 6. 3–8). But Plotinus had never spoken of the One as Absolute Being; and any doubt that this idea is totally un-Plotinian is removed by the commentator's development of it in fragment 6.

Even here, however, the commentator's starting-point is a Plotinian doctrine, that of the two states of Intelligence (cf. p. 88). The first of these, he declares, that transcending the subject-object distinction, is identical with the primal One. The second stage, by contrast, that of Intelligence proper, is no longer simple, but corresponds to the Chaldaean triad of Existence, Life (or Power) and Intelligence. The commentator anticipates Iamblichus in correlating each phase of the triad with a distinct moment in the emergence of reality from the One, associating Life with Procession and Intelligence with Reversion; but he agrees with Porphyry, against Iamblichus, in identifying the first moment of the triad, that of Existence, with the One itself (cf. Damascius *De Princ.* I. 86. 8–10, noted above p. 106). (Hence, though entitled the stage of Rest, this phase strictly transcends the opposition of Rest and Motion.) The One and Intelligence thus turn out to be two ways of viewing the same thing. And the results are oddly ambivalent, according to whether we consider the One in its transcendent or its immanent phase. Both approaches we have seen to involve the un-Plotinian doctrine of the One as Absolute Being. But whereas the former standpoint (that of fragments 1–4) maintains the unreality of everything apart from the One, the tendency of fragments 5 and 6 is rather to treat the One as a mere element in Intelligence and so abolish its transcendence. In either case the consequences for Plotinus' metaphysical hierarchy are equally disastrous.

That the latter viewpoint does not in fact abolish the One's transcendence is argued in the first part of fragment 6, where the One's role in relation to Intelligence is compared to that of Aristotle's central perceptive faculty vis-à-vis the five special senses. The unsatisfactoriness of such a defence of the One's transcendence is clear from the fact that the Plotinian entity of which the commentator's account is most reminiscent is not the One, but Intelligible Matter (cf. above p. 66).[1] It would be untrue, however, to describe his views as utterly alien to Plotinus; for a puzzling passage of the *Enneads* (v. 1. 7. 5–6) appears to describe Intelligence as originating as the self-vision of the One, an idea which seems irreconcilable with Plotinus' insistence elsewhere that the One transcends its products and has no need of Intelligence. The latter doctrines appear to have been directed in particular against Numenius' view that the higher Hypostases make use of the lower ones (cf. p. 34), an idea which seems certainly to underlie fragment 6's description of the One as 'using' the several operations of Intelligence. Other Numenian ideas in the fragments are, first, their conception of the supreme God as Absolute Being (cf. Numenius fr. 26) and as the Idea of the Second Hypostasis (cf. frs. 28–9) and, secondly, their identification of the distinction between the first two Hypostases with that between Intelligence at rest and Intelligence in motion (cf. p. 34). On all these points the fragments mark a return from Plotinus towards Middle Platonism.

Yet, as we have hinted (p. 91), the above difficulties are not merely the result of the commentator's wilfulness, but are inherent in the idea of a metaphysical Absolute. Thus the paradoxes of fragments 1–4 are

[1] Cf. also Rist, *Plotinus: the Road to Reality*, pp. 33–7, though I cannot accept his further conclusions.

a necessary consequence of the axiom that between Absolute and relative there can be no common measure. And if we attempt to re-establish some relation between them by stressing the One's imma-nence, we risk destroying its transcendence. In short the alternatives are either acosmism (denying the reality of anything but the One) or an immanentist pantheism, views equally fatal to the Neoplatonic doctrine of a graded metaphysical hierarchy. The problems posed by the 'negative transcendence' view of the One were to recur in Damas-cius, the last head of the Athenian Academy (cf. p. 158), but were implicit in more subdued form in all later Neoplatonism, whose general response was simply to treat them as a necessary consequence of the One's ineffability, on which the school laid ever greater stress (cf. pp. 150–1). But the Plotinian and Porphyrian schools' 'telescoping' of the Hypostases, of which the commentator's views were merely the extreme example, seemed to Iamblichus to pose a much more serious menace. It was therefore against such tendencies that his metaphysical innovations were directed.

IV. IAMBLICHUS' COUNTER-ATTACK; THE SOUL AND HER SALVATION

Iamblichus' reaction to the Porphyrian school's treatment of the First Hypostasis was not merely to restore the One to its Plotinian status above the Intelligible triad; according to Damascius he went further and postulated a supreme principle transcending even the One, a prin-ciple which he called simply the 'Ineffable' (*De Princ.* 1. 86. 3 ff.). While we cannot be sure of his reasons, he was probably influenced, like Damascius after him (ibid. 1. 5–6), by the consideration that unity has meaning only in contrast to plurality and therefore belongs to the sphere of relative reality. Our information regarding his treatment of the Second and Third Hypostases is much more extensive and suffices to prove his responsibility for most of the basic innovations which we find in writers of the Athenian and Alexandrian Schools. But there is equally no doubt that the doctrines propounded by those authors have undergone substantial post-Iamblichean development. In the absence of any surviving metaphysical treatise by Iamblichus himself it is there-fore impossible to be sure how much later Neoplatonic doctrine was specifically propounded by him and how much represents the con-tributions of his successors. Here we shall not attempt the task. The final three sections of the present chapter will deal with doctrines which there is reason to regard as essentially Iamblichean, even though much of their development may actually have been the work of the Athenian School. Doctrines more likely, as far as we can tell, to have originated in the latter school, will be reserved for our next chapter.[1]

Our starting-point must once again be the passage of Iamblichus' *De Anima* criticising his predecessors (Stobaeus I. 365. 5 ff.). Against them he insists that Soul is a separate self-subsistent Hypostasis, dependent on and inferior to Intelligence (ibid. 365. 22 ff.). In other words she is neither a defective way of viewing the latter nor a full member of the Intelligible order. Hence the *Timaeus'* definition of her as an intermediary concerns her essential nature and not merely her relation to bodies (Proclus *In Tim.* II. 105. 15 ff.). Equally essential to her role as mediator between the two worlds is the later Neoplatonists' view that, while Soul's essence is eternal, her activities take place in time (Proclus *ET* 191); Plotinus had said exactly the same of the human soul (*Enn.* IV. 4. 15. 16–20). But for Iamblichus and Proclus this restriction applies even to the contemplation of the divine souls (*In Tim.* II. 289. 3 ff., etc.). A further corollary of the new view of Soul was Iamblichus' modification of his predecessors' view that 'everything is in everything'. This will be examined in more detail later; for the present we need merely note that Plotinian Neoplatonism seemed to Iamblichus to have given too little emphasis to the fact that an entity contains the whole of reality only in a manner appropriate to its own individual nature (Proclus *ET* 103, 176–7; cf. below pp. 123–4). Thus he was perfectly prepared to admit not merely that Universal Soul reflects the whole Intelligible cosmos, but that each individual soul contains all the Logoi operative within Universal Soul (*ET* 194–5). What he and Proclus were emphatic in rejecting was Plotinus' description of man as an 'intelligible cosmos' (Proclus *In Parm.* 930. 26 ff., 948. 14 ff.; cf. above pp. 70, 72), and this for two reasons. First, since Soul is distinct from Intelligence, the principles she contemplates are *only* Logoi, not the transcendent Forms themselves; the latter, contrary to Plotinus' teaching, no soul can know as long as she remains a soul (*ET* 190. p. 166. 20 Dodds).[2] Secondly—and here we touch on the other basic disagreement with Plotinus—we must not ignore the distinctions

---

[1] The best analysis of how much of Proclus' doctrine is likely to derive from Iamblichus and how much from Proclus' teacher Syrianus is that of Dodds, *Proclus: Elements of Theology*, pp. xxi–xxv.

[2] An important qualification since, as we shall see, what cannot be achieved by the soul's own powers is possible through theurgy.

between different orders of souls; our soul is *not* consubstantial with those of the gods.

For whereas the divine souls are still conceived as each dependent on a transcendent Intelligence enjoying eternal contemplation of the Forms, that this is not true of the human soul is proved for Iamblichus by the fact that man's intellectual powers function only intermittently (*ET* 111, 175, *In Tim.* 1. 245. 17 ff., etc.). For similar reasons, and because of its inconsistency with the Platonic texts, he and all the later Neoplatonists, except Theodorus of Asine (cf. above p. 95), rejected Plotinus' doctrine of an unfallen part of the soul (Proclus *In Tim.* 111. 333. 28 ff., *ET* 211, Simplicius *De An.* 6. 12–17; cf. pp. 73–4). Over the soul's impassibility they differed less from Plotinus than one might expect, agreeing with him that emotional disturbance affects only the compound of body and lower soul and is only erroneously attributed to the soul herself (*Myst.* 1. 10 p. 35. 8 ff., *In Tim.* 111. 330. 9 ff.; cf. above pp. 74–6). They did, however, admit that the whole soul could be affected by error. And it was essential to Iamblichus' rigidly hierarchical universe that no soul ever leaves the order to which it belongs. For this reason he rejected the basic presupposition of Plotinus' account of transmigration, that the human soul could be transformed into that of an animal (Nemesius *Nat. Hom.* 51. 117–18 = *PG* XL. 584, Aeneas Gazaeus *PG* LXXXV. 893; cf. pp. 72, 113); in fact the later Neoplatonists denied that animals have souls at all in the strict sense of the term (cf. Proclus *PT* 111. 128, *Mal. Subs.* 25. 223–4). They therefore interpreted Plato's references to animal transmigration either as meaning merely that the evil man acquires a beast-like character, or at most as allowing that his soul, while remaining human, may become temporarily associated with an animal body (Sallustius *DM* XX. 1, Proclus *In Tim.* 111. 294. 22 ff.).[1] Similar efforts were made by Iamblichus to reconcile his basic standpoint with the possibility, which he admitted, that the soul may rise to angelic rank. In reality, he argued, this comes about not through the soul's own powers or her possession of all Logoi, but through association with her transcendent causes. It is thus the result of 'the gods' good will and the illumination imparted from them' (*Myst.* II. 2). That this is achieved through theurgy is argued at length in the *De Mysteriis*.

The superiority of theurgy to philosophy is upheld in a famous chapter of the latter work denying that thought alone can unite the

[1] We may note that the *Chaldaean Oracles* rejected animal transmigration (Proclus *In Remp.* II. 336. 27 ff.).

philosopher with the gods (*Myst.* II. 11). A theoretical understanding of the powers he invokes is no doubt incidentally necessary to the theurgist, Iamblichus concedes, but the vital union depends not on this, but on performance of the appropriate ritual *actions*. Porphyry's failure to appreciate this was the principal reason for Iamblichus' charge that he failed to keep philosophical questions separate from theurgic ones (cf. ibid. I. 2. p. 7. 2 ff.). His view of theurgy as dependent on the sympathy binding the sensible cosmos was symptomatic of the same failure to distinguish auxiliary causes (*synaitia*) from the true cause of theurgy's efficacy, the power conferred by divine grace on its rituals and on the symbolic objects they employ (cf. III. 26–7, V. 7–10). The power of theurgy is not therefore confined to the sensible cosmos. But this does not mean that the gods can be constrained by men; constraint of superior by inferior is impossible. The truth is that the rituals that invoke the gods work only in virtue of a *voluntary* bestowal of the divine power. And the result is not that the gods are forcibly drawn down into the sensible world, but that they purify their worshippers and draw them up into the Intelligible order (*Myst.* I. 12, I. 14, III. 16–18. p. 138. 6 ff., etc.). The later Neoplatonists' references to divine 'will', it is important to note, do not imply any fundamental change in Plotinus' conception of divine activity. As we have seen, Neoplatonic 'sacramentalism' differs from its Christian counterpart in that it depends solely on the world's basic god-given laws, not on a supernatural intervention over and above those laws—an idea as repugnant to the later Neoplatonists as to all Hellenic thinkers (cf. pp. 102–5). They were equally determined to maintain Plotinus' distinctions between divine will and its human counterpart (cf. pp. 62 ff.), denying that the former involves either deliberation or conscious attention to its products.[1] None the less their references to 'will', where he had spoken merely of divine 'ungrudgingness' (cf. p. 64), mark a significant change in man's attitude towards the divine. And even more important was their conclusion, in accordance with their humbler estimate of the human soul, that salvation is not within man's own powers. To deny this was one of the reasons explicitly put forward by Iamblichus for denying that philosophy could lead to divine union (*Myst.* II. 11. p. 97. 2 ff.). The *De Mysteriis* shows, in fact, both that Iamblichus was fully alive to the charge that he was making salvation a more mechanical process than it had been for the earlier Neoplatonists and that this

---

[1]. Cf. *Myst.* III. 17 p. 140. 6 ff., Proclus *PT* I. 15 p. 74. 17 ff., *In Tim.* I. 399. 17 ff.; also below p. 149.

was far from his intention. On the contrary, the work exhibits a new stress on the need for divine grace, combined with a new humility and receptiveness on man's part towards that grace. Of this we shall see further signs in Proclus.

Particular attention is devoted by the *De Mysteriis* to the problem of divination, of which Iamblichus distinguishes a higher and lower form, of which the former alone concerns the theurgist. His basis is the traditional distinction between 'artificial mantic', based on a reading of signs within the sensible cosmos (such as astrology or the examination of omens), and 'natural mantic' (cf. *Enn.* III. 1. 3. 13–17), in which the soul, released from the body in prophetic ecstasy or dreams, is able to contemplate the causal principles of the universe contained within the divine mind. The distinction between the two had been most fully elaborated by the Stoics, whose views are examined at length in Cicero's *De Divinatione*. Plotinus had devoted many pages to artificial mantic, which he had explained, like the Stoics before him, by the doctrine of cosmic sympathy (cf. pp. 70–1); to natural mantic, on the other hand, he had given little attention, since the object of Plotinian introversion had been union with Intelligence, not prophetic visions. The vital step now taken by Iamblichus was to transpose natural mantic into Neoplatonic terms by treating it as the result of the soul's union with a transcendent Intelligence, and to identify it, so understood, with his higher, 'divine' form of mantic (*Myst.* III. 3). The unreliability of the inferences derived from artificial mantic had long been commonplace, and Iamblichus was thus able to identify it with his lower 'human' mantic and contrast it with the intuitive certainty attainable through ecstatic union with Intelligence. Thus Plotinus and Porphyry were justified in stressing the inferiority of this form of divination; their error lay in identifying it with the divine mantic practised by the theurgists (*Myst.* III. 1, III. 26–7, X. 3–4). Equally misguided was Porphyry's suggestion that natural mantic was a purely psychological phenomenon; once again divine grace is necessary and the prophet's psychological disposition is a mere auxiliary cause (III. 1. p. 100. 10 ff., III. 24, etc.). An associated error was the earlier Neoplatonists' identification of man's guardian spirit with part of his soul or with his individual intelligence (*Myst.* IX. 8, cf. Proclus *In Alc.* 75–8 and above p. 71); since man is no longer regarded as having an Intelligence of his own, such a conclusion is henceforth impossible. Similarly, now that divine mantic is seen as involving union with Intelligence, Porphyry's conclusion that the power of prophecy does

not always bring happiness becomes for a Neoplatonist a contradiction
in terms (*Myst.* x. 4). Such were the consequences for man's salvation
of Iamblichus' new view of the soul. We must now examine the structural principles underlying his general view of the universe.

V. THE STRUCTURE OF LATE NEOPLATONIC METAPHYSICS

The contrast between Iamblichus' conception of the way of salvation
and that of his predecessors was fully recognised by the later Neoplatonists themselves (cf. Olympiodorus *In Phd.* 123. 3–6). An equal
contrast is apparent between the relative simplicity of Plotinus' metaphysical hierarchy and the proliferation of Hypostases, separated by ever
more rigid divisions, in the post-Iamblichean schools. It should, however, be remembered that the 'telescoping' of the Hypostases, which
Iamblichus so vehemently opposed, was only one tendency, albeit the
predominant one, in the works of Plotinus, and probably in those of
Porphyry as well. Hence, despite the general bias of Iamblichus' system,
most of his metaphysical theories can be seen as a mere systematisation
and development to their logical conclusion of ideas already present in
his predecessors. We shall find a particularly striking example of this
in his doctrine of 'Unparticipated' terms (cf. pp. 126–7), but it is no
less true of the general principles on which his system was based. Three
of these are of outstanding importance, first the Realistic Principle, a
corollary of the ontological priority of Intelligible object over thinking
subject, secondly the Triadic Principle, based in its turn on Iamblichus'
Law of Mean Terms, and thirdly the Principle of Correspondence, the
law, with which we should now be familiar, that 'everything is in
everything, but in each thing appropriately to its nature'.[1]

We may take the last-named principle first, since its significance
should be fairly clear from earlier sections. We have seen, in effect, that
it could be applied either 'vertically', to signify the implication of the
Principle of Plenitude that each Hypostasis expresses the Totality of
Being under its own appropriate conditions (cf. p. 65), or 'horizontally', expressing the fact that each member of a particular Hypostasis
mirrors the whole of that Hypostasis (and hence the whole of Reality);
the clearest example of the latter application we saw in Plotinus' conception of the Intelligible order (pp. 54–5; for Iamblichus cf. Proclus
In Tim. I. 423. 9 ff.). Similarly, for all Neoplatonists every soul, in
virtue of its possession of all Logoi, 'is all things, being identical with

[1] Proclus *ET* 103; for Iamblichus cf. esp. *In Tim.* I. 87. 6 ff., 426. 3 ff., etc.

sensible things as their exemplar (*paradeigmatikōs*) and with Intelligible things as their image (*eikonikōs*)' (*ET* 195). But the qualification, 'in each appropriately to its nature' is no less important; a thing is what it is because within it a particular principle (or principles) predominates. Thus, while a man contains all Logoi, it is the Logos of man, and not that of horse, that predominates within him. Plotinus, in Iamblichus' view, had sometimes failed to observe the latter point, for instance in locating the Forms themselves, and not merely their Logoi, within the individual soul (cf. p. 119). For Iamblichus, by contrast, what we have is *merely* correspondences between different orders of reality, no longer the direct presence of one within another. So understood, the principle assumed fundamental importance for later Neoplatonism, not only in metaphysics, but, as we have seen, in theurgy, and, as the final section of this chapter will show, for textual exegesis.

Most important, however, was Iamblichus' principle of Logical Realism. The foundation of this was the doctrine, basic to Greek rationalism, and most emphatically expressed in Plato's *Parmenides* (132B–C; cf. above p. 54), that objects of thought must exist prior to and independently of the thinking of them (cf. Proclus *In Parm.* 753. 8–31, 891–901, 1054. 25–37). That Plotinus' view of the relation of Intelligence to its objects was at least equivocal on the point has already been noted (cf. pp. 55–6, 67). Hence, Iamblichus concluded, Plato's position could be safeguarded only if Being were set on a higher ontological level than the Intelligence which contemplates it and the Second Hypostasis in consequence divided into an Intelligible and an Intellectual Order.[1] More generally, since it is basic to the Realistic Principle that logical distinctions imply ontological ones, and since the Intelligible world is based on an order of logical priority and posteriority, a further reason arises for positing differences of ontological status between its members. As Proclus observes, Plotinus' normal reluctance to admit this was once again the result of a too indiscriminate application of the 'all in all' principle (*PT* I. 10. p. 43. 16–21); yet elsewhere, notably in his most 'realistic' treatise, VI. 6 on Numbers, he had seemed to reach a more 'hierarchical' position, in his distinction of Being, Life and Intelligence and his insistence on the priority of Being both to Thought and to Number (ibid. I. 11. p. 50. 15 ff.; cf. above p. 67). It was such tendencies in Plotinus' thought that the post-Iamblicheans were to develop to their logical conclusion.

[1] Cf. Proclus *In Tim.* I. 308. 17 ff., *ET* 161; for Iamblichus' conception of the Intelligible Order cf. *In Tim.* I. 230. 5 ff., *PT* I. 11. p. 52. 2 ff.

As A. C. Lloyd observes, their metaphysics aimed above all 'to show what things could be said to have *separate existence* and what is their *rational order*'.[1] To the former question their answer was that a real ontological distinction must be postulated corresponding to every genuine distinction of thought, to the latter that ontological corresponds to logical priority. Hence the more universal concepts acquire a higher status in the metaphysical hierarchy, since (transposing logical into ontological terms) they are causes of more effects and hence more powerful (*ET* 25, 57, 60). Hence, for instance, Being must be prior to Life and Life to Intelligence, since not all that exists is alive, nor does all that lives exercise thought (*ET* 101, *PT* III. 126 ff.). And since the more universal concepts are also the simpler ones, the Neoplatonists' correlation of simplicity with greater power and higher ontological status finds its justification (*ET* 61–2). The final development of these principles will be seen in connection with the Athenian School. For the present, it must be stressed that the Iamblichean doctrine was realism in its most extreme form, which treated the Forms not merely, like Aristotelian moderate realism, as principles operative within particulars (*universalia in rebus*), but as self-subsistent substances in their own right, and as such not merely required for the explanation of particulars, but responsible for the latter's very existence. Hence not merely is the whole more than the sum of its parts; but prior to the whole-in-the-parts we must postulate a separately existing whole-before-the-parts (cf. *ET* 67–9, *In Tim*. I. 426. 3 ff.). Another well-known example of the extent to which Iamblichus and his successors were prepared to develop these principles is that of Time and Eternity. Analysis of these concepts, and of the Platonic texts devoted to them, convinced Iamlichus that they must be regarded as logically, and hence ontologically, prior to Soul and Intelligence respectively; hence they can no longer be treated simply as aspects of these Hypostases, but must themselves be granted the status of self-subsistent substances (*ET* 53, *In Tim*. III. 8–34; cf. Simplicius *In Phys*. 792. 20 ff.). And the pedantic and hair-splitting nature of many of the later Neoplatonists' distinctions is equally disconcerting.

As may be suspected, and as we shall see later, their motives in all this were not solely metaphysical. None the less they were in essence simply carrying Platonic Realism to its logical conclusion. And we should recall that their realism was less extreme than Plato's in declining to postulate a separate Form for every common name, and hence

[1] *Cambridge History of Later Greek and Early Medieval Philosophy*, p. 310.

free from some of the worst absurdities in the original theory of Forms (cf. above p. 18). Their identification of true causality with the activity of the Intelligible order (through the intermediary, of course, of Intelligence and Soul), and their consequent reduction of mechanical causes within the material world to mere 'auxiliary causes' (*synaitia*; cf. *ET* 75), are similarly rooted in *Phaedo* 98–101 and *Timaeus* 46C–E; we have already seen the importance of this distinction to Iamblichus' justification of theurgy (above pp. 120–3). But perhaps the most important application of the above principles was Iamblichus' doctrine of Unparticipated Terms, a combination, as we shall see, of a basic Platonic doctrine with ideas drawn from Plotinus.[1]

It was essential to Plato's account of the 'participation' of particulars in the Forms that the Transcendent Form (e.g. of Whiteness) is distinct from the universal, whiteness, immanent in particular white objects; this is implied in the *Phaedo* and follows necessarily from *Timaeus* 52A's denial that the Forms themselves enter the sensible world. Iamblichus was therefore justified in extracting from these passages a triad of Transcendent Form, immanent universal and material particular, terms which he entitled respectively Unparticipated, Participated and Participant (*ET* 24). But a wider application of the doctrine resulted from Iamblichus' extension of 'participation' into a general term for the 'informing' of lower principles by higher ones— e.g. of bodies by souls and of souls by intelligences—and his consequent distinction between Unparticipated (i.e. Universal) Soul, without relation to any particular body, and the individual souls in which bodies participate (*In Tim.* II. 105. 15 ff.), as also between Unparticipated Intelligence and the Participated Intelligences immanent in individual souls.[2] Plotinus, we may recall, had similarly postulated a Universal Soul as the origin of all individual souls, including the World-soul (IV. 3. 2. 5 ff., etc.; cf. IV. 8. 3. 6–21 and above p. 69). What the term 'Unparticipated' seems, however, to deny is Plotinus' stress on the Intelligible order's immanence within the material world (*Enn.* VI. 4. 3, etc.). Needless to say Iamblichus did not wish to reintroduce a *spatial* separation between the two realms; moreover we shall see the Athenian School, if not Iamblichus himself, developing its own, albeit very un-Plotinian, doctrine of divine immanence (cf. pp. 155–7). What

---

[1] *ET* 23, *In Parm.* 1069. 23 ff.; for Iamblichus cf. *In Tim.* II. 105. 15 ff., 240. 4 ff., 313. 15 ff.

[2] *In Tim.* II. 252. 21 ff., 312. 30 ff., *In Alc.* 65. 16 ff.; Plotinus *Enn.* VI. 2. 20.

Iamblichus did wish to emphasise was that the Unparticipated Terms' operation on lower realities is only indirect, through the intermediary of the Participated Terms they produce. We have in fact one more case where Plotinus' doctrine could be developed in the direction of greater stress on either the Intelligible world's immanence or its transcendence, and, as always, Iamblichus' inclination lay in the latter direction (cf. *In Tim.* II. 313. 15 ff.). A final result of the doctrine is its clarification of the structure of the Second and Third Hypostases as a plurality— variously termed an 'order' (*taxis*), 'series' (*seira*)[1] or number (*plēthos*) —of Participated Terms, with appropriate gradations of rank between them, but having in common their derivation from the single Unparticipated Term (or 'monad') at that order's head (*ET* 21–2, 100; cf. *In Tim.* II. 240. 4 ff.). It remained for the Athenian School to extend the principle to the First Hypostasis, by their doctrine of the Divine Henads.

Characteristics of Iamblichus' system revealed by his account of participation are thus, first, his development to their logical conclusion of ideas from his predecessors in such a way as to multiply ontological levels and safeguard divine transcendence, secondly his hypostatisation of the generic concept 'Soul' as the Unparticipated Soul, thirdly his confusion of what we would regard as a logical question, the relation between particulars and the Forms, with the ontological one of that between Soul and body. The latter relation is, however, more complex than the former one in that for Platonists, unlike Aristotelians, the soul is not the body's immanent form (or 'entelechy'), since, if she were, she would be incapable of separate existence.[2] What for a Neoplatonist corresponds to Aristotle's entelechy is rather the body's immanent life, which the school, as we have seen, regarded as an image cast by the soul herself (cf. pp. 74–5). Hence in analysing the body-soul relation we must recognise four terms instead of three, distinguishing the individual soul, which, as a self-subsistent substance is participated by the body without loss of her separate existence (*chōristōs metechomenē*), from her image, or 'irradiation' (*ellampsis*), which is not (cf. Proclus *ET* 64, 81–2, *In Tim.* I. 360. 28 ff.). This is, of course, merely a formalisation of a fundamental Plotinian and Porphyrian principle (cf. pp. 111–12); nor is Iamblichus' similar distinction between

---

[1] Confusingly, however, both the above terms can also be applied to the *vertical* series formed by corresponding individual principles (e.g. intelligence-soul-body) within the several orders.

[2] The complications posed by the soul's subtle, astral body, which, as we have seen, Iamblichus regarded as immortal (cf. p. 109 n. 1), must be passed over.

self-subsistent Intelligence and its 'image' on the level of Soul (i.e. the latter's cognitive powers) much more than this. An un-Plotinian note arose only with Iamblichus' insistence that some bodies, those of animals and plants, have no self-subsistent soul of their own, but only an image thereof (cf. *PT* III. 128, *Mal. Subs.* 25. 223–4), and that the human soul has similarly only an image of Intelligence (Proclus *In Crat.* LXIV. 28. 22–6, cf. *In Alc.* 247. 1–2). And if we analyse the term *authypostatos* ('self-subsistent' or 'self-constituted'), applied by later Neoplatonists to incorporeal substances, we shall see on the one hand that it served to define the Neoplatonic view of such substances against those of other schools, on the other that it points to a fundamental divergence among the Neoplatonists themselves.

The former point can be seen if we consider the term's ambivalence, which precludes translation by a single equivalent; for while its sense of 'self-subsistent' emphasises the independence of souls and intelligences vis-à-vis the body, the point of the related sense of 'self-constituted' is the fundamental principle of the emanation doctrine (cf. pp. 65–6) that an incorporeal substance, though taking its ultimate origin from a higher source, none the less itself 'determines the particular potency that shall be actualised in it',[1] and so takes part in its own creation (whereas a body's whole existence is determined by external causes).[2] In this sense the doctrine's obvious target was Christianity (cf. p. 103); and, since it was fundamental to the Neoplatonic conception of Soul that the latter possesses immortality in its own right, it is only natural that Proclus' discussion (*ET* 40–51) attempts to integrate the most important and influential of Plato's arguments on the subject.

A primary aim of the Middle Platonic tradition had been to restate the far from conclusive arguments of the *Phaedo* and *Phaedrus* in a more systematic and less vulnerable form. The results are most conveniently set out in Plotinus' early, very 'scholastic' treatise IV. 7 on Immortality, whose arguments, repeated with relatively little change by Augustine and others, thus became the common property of the European metaphysical tradition. Perhaps most influential among them were *Phaedrus* 245–6's conception of the soul as self-moved, and hence inherently endowed with life (a development of *Phaedo* 105–6; cf. *Enn.* IV. 7. 9, Proclus *ET* 45–6), and *Phaedo* 78B's argument that the soul is without parts, and hence indissoluble (cf. *Enn.* IV. 7. 12. 12–19, *ET*

---

[1] Dodds, *Elements of Theology*, p. 224.
[2] *ET* 40–1, *In Tim.* III. 39. 2–5, 210. 30–2, Syrianus *In Met.* 116. 6–7, 187. 6–9.

47-9). The dependence of the Neoplatonists' notion of auto-constitution on Plato's doctrine of self-motion is evident enough; their development of the *Phaedo* argument is more complicated. That incorporeal substances must be indivisible followed for a Neoplatonist from their power of self-contemplation; for as Plotinus, accepting the Sceptical challenge, had argued, only beings entirely without parts are capable of such contemplation (cf. p. 26). Hence, Porphyry had maintained, self-knowledge is possible only to those powers, like Intelligence, which have no bodily concomitants and are thus entirely free from spatial division (*Sent.* 41; cf. Proclus *ET* 15-16). A criterion was thus provided for distinguishing those faculties which belong to the self-subsistent soul from those, like sense-perception, which require an external object and/or depend on bodily organs. And it requires only the addition of the law that a being reverts in contemplation upon its cause (cf. above pp. 65-6) to prove that a self-subsistent entity must also be self-caused (cf. *ET* 42-3). But here we touch once more on the Neoplatonists' internal disagreements. For whereas in the Porphyrian school the term 'self-constituted' seems to have carried the implication that the lower Hypostases are a self-manifestation of the higher ones,[1] for Iamblichus its point was the exact opposite, that Soul is a self-subsistent Hypostasis in its own right, dependent indeed on Intelligence but in no way a mere 'appearance' of the latter. Hence his application to the soul of the synonymous term 'self-complete' (*autotelēs*) in his protest against his predecessors' 'telescoping' of the two Hypostases (*De An.* 365. 25-6). The reason for this divergence was, of course, the inherent ambiguity in the notion, common to all Neoplatonists, of the dual origin of Intelligible entities, from a transcendent source and from themselves—yet one more doctrine inviting contrary developments in accordance with a philosopher's individual inclinations.

So far Iamblichus' metaphysical doctrines have been presented as basically a development of the earlier Platonic tradition. But it should be no less apparent that the motives behind many of them are religious as well as metaphysical; we have seen, for instance, the anti-Christian orientation of the notion of auto-constitution and the theurgic application of the Principle of Correspondence. Another striking example is provided by Iamblichus' hypostatisation of Time and Eternity; for the

---

[1] This emerges from Marius Victorinus; cf. Hadot, *Porphyre et Victorinus I*, pp. 297-330. The term 'self-constituted' is not found in our extant Greek texts before Iamblichus (quoted Stobaeus *Ecl.* II. 174. 22), but Porphyry (*Hist. Phil.* fr. 18) uses equivalent terminology of Intelligence.

Chaldaean Oracles had regarded Eternal Time (*aiōn*) as a deity (based on the Persian Zervan) and provided a spell for his invocation (Proclus *In Tim.* III. 20. 22 ff.). Iamblichus' multiplication of Hypostases similarly enabled him and his followers to find room for all the deities, Greek and Oriental, whose worship they wished to further. But this does not mean that their metaphysics was simply a cover for their religion; for, since it was axiomatic for all Neoplatonists that no conflict existed between the two, it is meaningless to ask which of them they regarded as more important (though, as we shall see, sometimes one had to be sacrificed for the sake of the other). The intertwining of the two sources of inspiration, and the complications to which they led, will become yet more apparent if we consider Iamblichus' Triadic Principle and the Law of Mean Terms, on which it was based.

That the structure of reality was basically triadic was explicitly affirmed, as we have noted, in the *Chaldaean Oracles* (cf. p. 106). And particular applications of the principle were available in plenty in the Neoplatonists' philosophical and mythological sources; for the universal appeal of the number three was as keenly felt by the Greeks as by most other peoples. Our discussion will show examples from Plato, Plotinus, the *Oracles* and even Aristotle, as well as from mythology. And needless to say Iamblichus and his successors were no less ingenious in discovering fresh triads and in drawing correspondences between seemingly unconnected triads than they were in other fields. A relatively painless example is Proclus' triadic arrangement, in the first book of his *Platonic Theology*, of the divine attributes set out in various Platonic dialogues; for instance *Phaedo* 80A–B is made to yield two triads (divine-immortal-intelligible and unitary-indissoluble-self-identical), related both to one another and to the basic triad of Being-Life-Intelligence (*PT* I. 26–7). Such correspondences were, of course, vital if the various triads were to be integrated in a single system, though the reader will often discover only the most distant 'family resemblances', if that, between them. A warning must also be issued against attempting to fit the Neoplatonic triads into the Hegelian triadic scheme of thesis-antithesis-synthesis, though Hegel acknowledged his indebtedness to Proclus, and though his system can be made to work with a few of the Neoplatonic groupings, notably the *Philebus'* triad of Limit, Unlimited and the Mixture of the two (cf. pp. 148–9). The fundamental contrast between the two schemes is that in Hegelianism it is the final term of the triad that synthesises the two preceding ones, whereas the Neoplatonists' emphasis falls on the role of the

middle term as a link between the two extremes (cf. *PT* III. 123–4).[1]
This is a result of Iamblichus' Law of Mean Terms, a principle of great
importance even apart from its contribution to our present problem.

The essence of the law in question is that two dissimilar terms must
be linked by an intermediary having something in common with each
of them.[2] Instances from the Platonic dialogues included the role of
daemons as mediators between gods and men[3] and, more important, of
Soul as mediating between eternity and time and between Intelligible
and sensible worlds (Plato *Tim.* 35A, Proclus *ET* 106–7, 190–1). Meta-
physically considered, the law is identical with what has been called the
Principle of Continuity, the doctrine that there is no abrupt transition
from one order of reality to another (cf. *Enn.* V. 2. 2. 26–9, Proclus, *De
Prov.* 20. 163–4). Its importance as a corollary to the Principle of Plenitude emerges clearly from Lovejoy's *Great Chain of Being*; summarised
in the Scholastic maxim that 'nature makes no leaps', it was to dominate
Western thought, especially in biology, for well over a thousand years,
leading, inter alia, to the search for 'missing links' between species.
And it was clearly a powerful factor in the post-Iamblichean
multiplication of Hypostases, leading as it inevitably did to the
recognition of fresh and hitherto unsuspected intermediaries. The
principle's role is in consequence a highly paradoxical one; for while
providing a link between extremes, an Iamblichean Mean Term simultaneously fulfils the opposite role of keeping them firmly apart. Its
function is, in other words, on the one hand to safeguard divine transcendence, while on the other preventing the gulf between God and
man from becoming unbridgeable. Nor should it cause surprise that
this principle, like others, could turn up in very unexpected contexts.
Thus in Sallustius' justification of animal sacrifice the life of the sacri-
ficial victim forms the necessary mean linking our life to that of the
gods (*DM* XVI. 2).

We have already observed that any attempt to force the various Neoplatonic triads into too close a harmony is doomed to failure. A few
guidelines are none the less desirable to assist the reader in approaching

---

[1] Proclus admits, however, that each term of a triad is in its own way a link
between the other two (*ET* 148). Hegel's scheme has probably been influenced
by the prominence of the *Philebus'* triad in *Platonic Theology III*; cf. his *Lectures
on the History of Philosophy* (trans. Haldane and Simson) vol. II, pp. 440–9.
Another modification of the Neoplatonic scheme is provided by the triadic
groupings of Renaissance art (cf. below p. 171).
[2] *ET* 28, 132, etc.; cf. Plato *Tim.* 31 B–C; for Iamblichus cf. *In Tim.* II. 313.
15 ff., *Myst.* I. 5–7.
[3] *Symp.* 202E, *Epin.* 984E; cf. *Myst.* I. 5–7, *ET* 202 and below p. 152.

the most important of them. First, we may say that the basic structure of an Iamblichean-Procline triad, as determined by the Law of Mean Terms, is A–AB–B, or AB–A not B (or B not A)–neither A nor B (cf. Proclus *PT* III. 123–4). Secondly, like the Principle of Correspondence the Triadic Principle may be applied either 'horizontally', to the relation between different aspects of a single Hypostasis, or 'vertically', to the relation between different orders of reality; the relation exemplified in the latter case is that of Participation, in the former that of Procession, while some triads, notably Being-Life-Intelligence,[1] will be seen to have something in common with both groups. Of the purely vertical triads little need be said here, since their most typical example, the triad Unparticipated-Participated-Participant (*ET* 24), has already been considered. With this is linked the doctrine, based on the Principle of Correspondence, that every entity has a threefold existence, causally (*kat' aitian*) in the principle whence it originates, substantially (*kath' hyparxin*) on its own level and 'by participation' (*kata methexin*) in its images on lower levels (*ET* 65). This should by now present no difficulty; it should be easy, for instance, to see its application to the Logoi contemplated by souls (cf. pp. 123–4). The 'horizontal' triads require rather more consideration, since they depend on the later Neoplatonic development of the emanation doctrine.

Plotinus, as we saw (pp. 66–7), had been content to divide the emanation process into the two phases of Procession and Reversion. The anonymous *Parmenides* commentator's description of the generation of Intelligence, on the other hand, had recognised a phase of Rest, anterior to these two, in which Intelligence is identical with the Primal One (cf. pp. 116–17). And though the latter identification was unacceptable to later Neoplatonists, they agreed with the commentator in dividing emanation into three phases, those of Abiding, or immanence in one's cause, Procession from that cause, and Reversion upon it (*ET* 35; for Iamblichus cf. *In Tim.* II. 215. 5 ff.). And this triad is no longer applied solely to the emanation of one Hypostasis from another, but regarded as a law inherent in the structure of everything that exists. It is further equated with (among others) the Plotinian triad of Being, Life and Intelligence (cf. p. 67), the Chaldaean triad of Existence, Power and Intelligence (p. 106), the Aristotelian triad of Substance, Potentiality and Actuality, the *Philebus'* triad of Limit, Unlimited and the Mixture of the two (pp. 148–9) and the mythological triad of Cro-

[1] On this triad cf. *ET* 101–3, *PT* III. 126 ff. For Iamblichus cf. *In Tim.* III. 45. 5 ff.; for Porphyry and Theodorus ibid. 64. 8 ff.

nos, Rhea and Zeus, extracted both from the Orphic poems and (illegitimately) from the *Chaldaean Oracles* (cf. Proclus *In Crat.* CXLIII 81. 2 ff.).[1] That the above groups were regarded as exemplifying the same basic principle does not, of course, mean that the differences between them were ignored; on the contrary, it was just the possibility of finding correspondences between concepts that are not precisely identical that enabled the later Neoplatonists to multiply entities so remorselessly.

For first, as we have seen, Being, Life and Intelligence are no longer aspects of a single reality, but must on the Realistic Principle be treated as hierarchically ordered substances. Corresponding to these three principles the Athenian School was to posit three orders of reality, the Intelligible order corresponding to Being, the Intelligible and Intellectual order to Life and the Intellectual order to Intelligence. But on the Principle of Correspondence each of these orders must be reflected in both the others; hence each of them contain its own triad of Being, Life and Intelligence, though Being predominates in the Intelligible order, and so on (cf. *ET* 103). And since each of the principles so recognised exemplifies the triad of Abiding, Procession and Reversion, we may multiply by three once again. We should thus expect to find three orders of nine principles, to which, following a law to be explained in our next chapter, there should correspond three enneads of gods. And clearly there is no need to stop here; how exhaustive were the later Neoplatonists' subdivisions of their basic triads, and how elaborate their identifications of the members of those subdivisions with entities drawn from Plato's dialogues and deities drawn from Greek mythology, can be seen from the later books of Proclus' *Platonic Theology*; summary tables have fortunately been drawn up by modern scholars.[2] Nor was the attempt to reconcile the school's metaphysical, religious and exegetic aims always without difficulty, and sometimes one had to be sacrificed in favour of another. A good example has indeed already arisen; for, instead of the three enneads of gods which our discussion anticipated, we in fact find two enneads, followed by a hebdomad, or group of seven. And despite Proclus' laboured attempts to justify the asymmetry (*PT* v. 2. 249–52), it is clear that the hebdomad in question is required for religious and exegetic reasons (since a seven-fold god

[1] For correspondences between the various triads cf. e.g. Proclus *In Tim.* I. 17. 23 ff., 371. 13 ff., *PT* III. 135, 144 etc. Damascius *De Princ.* I. 86. 20 ff.
[2] Cf. Lewy, *Chaldaean Oracles and Theurgy*, pp. 483–4 and Saffrey and Westerink, *Théologie platonicienne I*, pp. lxv–lxvii.

formed part of the Chaldaean cult; cf. *In Tim.* I. 34. 21, Damascius *De Princ.* I. 237. 11, Julian *Or.* v. 172D), and that metaphysical consistency has had to give place.

The above, simplified, account of the structure of the late Neoplatonic world-view was based on Proclus—necessarily, since our accounts of Iamblichus' metaphysics consist only of fragments—but it is evidently merely a development of Iamblichus' principles. In fact Proclus ascribes a similar numerical grouping of gods (two orders of nine and one of seven) to Iamblichus himself (*In Tim.* I. 308. 17 ff.). The Athenian School's main contribution to the present problem seems to have been the recognition of the Intelligible and Intellectual order intermediate between the purely Intelligible and purely Intellectual levels. Exactly whose innovation this was remains a mystery; it is found in Proclus' commentaries and *Platonic Theology*, whose fourth book discusses it at length, but does not appear in his *Elements*, which were probably composed earlier in his life. It was none the less required, both by the Law of Mean Terms and in order to obtain a separate order of gods corresponding to the intermediate principle of Life; lacking this refinement, Iamblichus appears to have simply postulated two orders of Intellectual gods.[1] This example suffices to show that the Athenians' role was mainly one of filling such gaps as Iamblichus seemed to have left, though they were probably responsible for more of the detailed elaboration of the above principles than our account has suggested. Iamblichus' basic religious and metaphysical innovations have thus been surveyed; it remains to consider his contribution to the problem of textual exegesis.

VI. TEXTUAL EXEGESIS ACCORDING TO PORPHYRY AND IAMBLICHUS

An oracle of Apollo quoted by the Aristotelian commentator David (*In Isag.* 92. 3; cf. Aeneas Gazaeus *PG* LXXXV. 893) contrasted Porphyry's 'polymathy' with Iamblichus' 'divine inspiration'. Its point was no doubt in part the 'religious' tone of Iamblichus' thought, but it also had in mind what Proclus, in discussing his exegesis of the Platonic dialogues, called its 'epoptic' character (*In Tim.* I. 204. 24–7); in other words, its integration of Neoplatonic metaphysics and scholasticism in a single all-comprehending vision (cf. Simplicius *De An.* 313. 6 ff.). Proclus' aim, like Apollo's, was to point the contrast with Porphyry's 'piecemeal' manner of exegesis (cf. *In. Tim.* I. 174. 24 ff.), and certainly

---

[1] At least if the text of *In Tim.* I. 308. 21 is sound, which seems impossible to determine.

the divergence between Porphyry and Iamblichus is particularly evident in their interpretation of the school's traditional texts.

The problem, as we saw at the end of our last chapter, was twofold: first, to extend the Neoplatonic interpretation to the whole of Plato's dialogues; secondly, to provide a complete and consistent interpretation of the traditional myths. Since Porphyry's Platonic commentaries are lost, our best illustration of his methods is his essay on the Cave of the Nymphs described in *Odyssey* XIII (102–12), which, it has been shown, illuminates Proclus' comments on his Platonic exegesis. Allegorical interpretation of mythology was, of course, nothing new and the Stoics in particular had made abundant use of it. Plotinus, however, had been content to use mythology in illustration of particular doctrinal points as need arose; but without necessarily claiming the sanction of the myths' original authors for his interpretations.[1] How far he had been from treating myths as Holy Scripture is shown by his indifferent identification of Zeus with Soul (e.g. V. 1. 7. 35–7), Intelligence (e.g. V. 8. 4. 40–2) and even in one passage with the One (VI. 9. 7. 20–6). Such fluctuations appear even in his most deliberate essay in allegorical interpretation, *Enn.* III. 5's account of the *Symposium* myth; for instance Intelligence is identified in chapter 2 with Cronos, in chapter 8 with Zeus. The difficulty facing a more rigid interpretation was, of course, that different features of a single myth often seemed to accord with different metaphysical principles. And it was here that the solutions of Porphyry and Iamblichus diverged most radically.

Porphyry's response, as revealed by his Homeric essay, was simply to admit that a single myth or symbol could simultaneously convey several allegorical meanings. Thus several features of Homer's account argue for the identification of his cave with the material world; Matter's recalcitrance is suggested by the cave's rock, Matter's flux by the waters flowing within it, Matter's obscurity by its darkness (ch. 5). But the cave's obscurity can equally symbolise the invisible powers within the material world (ch. 7). And if we take darkness as signifying inaccessibility to the senses, and rock as a symbol of indestructibility, we must understand the cave as a symbol of the Intelligible world (ch. 9). No attempt is made by Porphyry to reconcile his alternative interpretations; what he does sometimes attempt is to arrange them in an order of plausibility. For instance he prefers the 'material world' explanation of

---

[1] Cf. his comments at IV. 3. 14. 17–19 at the conclusion of a chapter interpreting (and on one point radically altering) the Prometheus myth as an allegory of the soul's predicament.

the cave symbol, since it alone of the three suggested possibilities can account for the flowing waters mentioned by Homer (ch. 10). Equally characteristic is Porphyry's ethical interpretation of the olive-tree described by Homer as growing above the cave, and his transition from this to a more general reflection on Odysseus' significance as a symbol of the aspirant to wisdom (chs. 32 ff.; cf. *Enn.* I. 6. 8. 10–20). Exegesis of this kind was, of course, congenial to Porphyry's moralistic temperament, and Proclus suggests that it was equally common in his Platonic commentaries and contributed greatly to their unsystematic character (cf. *In Tim.* I. 19. 24–9, 116. 25 ff., etc.). And it was in these works that the defects of that exegesis, from the Neoplatonic point of view, revealed themselves most sharply.

For, despite the fantastic character of many of his interpretations, Porphyry still took the common-sense view that, while a Platonic dialogue may have a single dominant theme, it still includes discussions of a number of subordinate topics only loosely related thereto (cf. Proclus *In Tim.* I. 204. 24–7). But such 'piecemeal' exegesis was an obstacle if Platonism was to be treated as a systematic philosophy of the same type as Aristotelianism. Hence Iamblichus, in addition to arranging the main dialogues in a formal curriculum (cf. p. 19), had also to formulate new principles for their interpretation. The basis of his solution was the corollary of the Principle of Correspondence that different sciences are really treating the same subject-matter from different points of view (cf. e.g. Proclus *In Tim.* I. 8. 13 ff., 87. 6 ff., III. 173. 2 ff.). The parallel between physics and theology, for instance, is that between image and archetype, whereas physics and politics exhibit the macrocosm-microcosm relationship (ibid. I. 13. 1 ff., 33. 23 ff.). Iamblichus' second main principle was that each dialogue has one and only one theme (*skopos*), to which all its contents must be related (Elias *in Cat.* 131. 10–13).[1] Justification was sought for this in Plato's own recommendations for organising a work of literature (*Phdr.* 264, cf. Hermeias *In Phdr.* 9. 6–10). It was accordingly necessary for successful exegesis of a particular text to determine, first, whether its object was philosophical or theurgic (cf. p. 121) and, secondly, the *branch* of philosophy with which it was concerned. Thus it was unanimously agreed that the *Timaeus'* object was physics; hence even those parts of it apparently concerned with other matters (such as the pro-

[1] Cf. *In Tim.* I. 19. 24–9, 77. 25 ff., *In Remp.* I. 6. 10–12, 24 ff. Further passages are listed by Praechter, *Richtungen und Schulen im Neuplatonismus*, pp. 128–41, and in Westerink's note to *Anon. Prol.* 21.

logue, including the Atlantis myth) must be shown by the Principle of Correspondence to have a physical bearing (cf. *In Tim.* 1. 4. 6 ff., 78. 12 ff., 205. 4 ff., etc.). By such means (often involving far-fetched allegory) a wealth of unsuspected meaning could be discovered in passages of seemingly little Neoplatonic interest. And it was, of course, equally possible to follow the converse procedure and by ascending from image to archetype to extract theological lessons from a physical dialogue (*In Tim.* 1. 8. 2 ff., 24. 17 ff., *PT* 1. 4. p. 19. 6–22). Once again it was only Iamblichus' systematic application of the principle that was new; for, as readers of Plato will be aware, the drawing of such correspondences had been commonplace since early Pythagorean times (cf. *In Tim.* 1. 30. 2 ff.).

It was no less easy to apply the principle to the elucidation of mythology and thereby avoid the problems we have noted. For it might indeed be possible to extract several meanings from a single myth; but as long as these could be related by the Principle of Correspondence, they could all be granted a measure of validity (though the primary one was, of course, that which best agreed with the supposed theme of the work in question). And the difficulties about Zeus could equally be resolved by recognition of several gods exemplifying the same principle at different levels of the divine hierarchy and therefore sharing a common name (cf. Proclus *In Tim.* III. 190. 19 ff.). Thus Zeus, for instance, appears in the Intellectual realm as a member of the triad Cronos-Rhea-Zeus, in the Supercosmic order (the level of Unparticipated Soul) as one of the triad Zeus-Poseidon-Pluto, and among the Intracosmic gods as one of the twelve Olympians.[1] How much of this should be credited to Iamblichus himself is uncertain; its final stage, in the doctrine of the Athenian School, will be seen in our next chapter. It has been observed that among its unintended results was the draining of the traditional gods of such personality as they still retained; hence in seeking to establish traditional worship on a philosophical basis the post-Iamblicheans ironically ensured the triumph of Christianity. But, with few exceptions,[2] Iamblichus' exegetic principles were universally accepted and employed in the later Neoplatonic schools. And since those schools' Platonic and Aristotelian commentaries constituted the overwhelming majority of their output, their importance cannot be overestimated. Hence this innovation alone would have justified Iamblichus' claim to be the dominant figure of later Neoplatonism.

---

[1] Cf. the relevant sections of Rosán's *Philosophy of Proclus.*
[2] Notably, as Pépin observes, Sallustius (*Entretiens Hardt XII* p. 250).

CHAPTER FIVE

The Athenian School

I. NEOPLATONISM AT ATHENS AND ALEXANDRIA

The final phase of pagan Neoplatonism is that of the fifth- and sixth-century schools of Athens, where Neoplatonism at last becomes the official teaching of Plato's Academy, and of Alexandria. We know little of how the movement became established in either city, though this is merely symptomatic of our ignorance both of fourth-century Neoplatonism and of contemporary intellectual life in general. The first Neoplatonic head of the Academy, Plutarch of Athens (cf. above p. 1 n. 1), died in 432 (cf. *V. Pr.* 12), and from that date onwards a continuous succession of Neoplatonic heads of the school can be traced down to its closure in 529.[1] Its greatest renown came under Plutarch's successors, Syrianus (died *c.* 437) and Proclus (412–85), the best known of the later Neoplatonists and the school's greatest systematiser. Proclus' successor and biographer Marinus was by contrast a man of little philosophical talent (cf. Damascius *V. Is.* 144), and with him the school entered on a period of decline lasting until Damascius, the Academy's last head, under whom a recovery took place. It has, indeed, been conjectured that it was Damascius' revival of this last bastion of paganism that determined Justinian to close the school. The story is well known how Damascius and six of his colleagues, including the Aristotelian commentator Simplicius, migrated to Persia, having come to entertain high hopes of the philosophical aspirations of its new king Chosroes, but were quickly disillusioned. They therefore returned home, but not before Chosroes had concluded a treaty with Justinian stipulating that the philosophers were to enjoy freedom from persecution (Agathias *Hist.* II. 30–1). But they were still debarred from teaching philosophy, and it is probably to Simplicius' studies during the enforced leisure of these years that we owe his preservation of so much of the Presocratics for posterity; the general view is that his commentaries were composed

[1] The list (including those whose headship is disputed) runs: Plutarch, Syrianus, (Domninus?), Proclus, Marinus, Isidorus, (Hegias?), Zenodotus, Damascius.

for reading and not, like most of the school's output, for delivery as lectures.

A continuing succession at Alexandria cannot be traced as early as at Athens; still less is there any evidence of a continuous tradition of Neoplatonic teaching going back to Ammonius Saccas. In the late fourth and early fifth centuries we find Neoplatonism represented there by a mathematician named Theon and his daughter Hypatia, martyred in 415 by a Christian mob, with or without the instigation of the infamous patriarch Cyril (cf. *V. Is.* fr. 104, Socrates *Eccl. Hist.* VII. 14. 5). Yet it was a paradox of the Alexandrian School that, while relations between its pagan members and the Christian authorities frequently assumed a more violent form than anything recorded at Athens, their attitude was less uncompromisingly pagan than that of the Athenians and their relations with individual Christians were often of the friendliest. Our first sign of this is the presence among Hypatia's pupils of the gentleman-farmer-cum-amateur-philosopher, later to turn Christian bishop, Synesius of Cyrene (cf. p. 101). A similarly equivocal position regarding Christianity characterised Alexandria's next major Neoplatonic teacher, Hierocles, a pupil of Plutarch of Athens. Hierocles' own paganism brought him into conflict with the authorities at Constantinople, who had him flogged (*V. Is.* fr. 106); yet his pupils included Aeneas, founder of the Christian philosophical school of Gaza, and his own doctrine strikes a more 'monotheistic' note than that of any other pagan Neoplatonist (cf. pp. 142–3). But it is not until Hermeias (a pupil of Syrianus, to whom he was related by marriage) and his son Ammonius (who in his turn had studied at Athens under Proclus) that a definite succession can be traced at Alexandria.[1] It was under Ammonius in the late fifth and early sixth centuries that the school attained its high point, which coincided with the Athenian School's decline. Ammonius' pupils included both Damascius and Simplicius; also prominent among them was the Christian John Philoponus, editor of Ammonius' Aristotle lectures and author of two polemical works of his own contesting the world's eternity, one (still extant) directed against Proclus, the other (now lost) against Aristotle. The distinctive feature of the latter work, known to us through Simplicius' reply (*Phys.* 1156–82, *De C.* 25–201), is its questioning of the traditional assumption that the heavens are composed of a purer substance than the sublunary world. But Philoponus does not seem to

---

[1] The probable order of succession runs: Hermeias, Ammonius, (Eutocius?), Olympiodorus, Elias, David, Stephanus.

have succeeded to the headship of the school, which under the Platonic commentator Olympiodorus[1] assumed a more decidedly pagan tone. Olympiodorus was still alive in 565, and it was only with his death that the school finally passed into Christian hands, under the Aristotle commentators Elias and David. Their successor Stephanus moved to Constantinople, where in 610 he became head of the newly founded Imperial Academy, while other philosophers were still active at Alexandria at the time of its capture in 641 by the Arabs. The school thus played a major part in the preservation of Neoplatonic influence in both Byzantine and Moslem worlds.

Of the writings of the Athenian and Alexandrian Schools a reasonable number have come down to us, at least if their surviving works are contrasted with those of Porphyry and Iamblichus. But their study presents great, and almost insuperable, difficulties. For, first, their literary form is that of the school treatise and their resulting approach dry and pedantic in the extreme. Secondly, the complexity of their conceptual scheme, by developing the principles explained in our last chapter, has by the last members of the Athenian School assumed nightmare proportions. Thirdly, the vast majority of them consist of commentaries on the Classical philosophers and therefore lack even the advantage of presenting Neoplatonic doctrine in systematic form. To the last rule Proclus' systematic treatises (and perhaps Damascius' *De Principiis*) constitute our only important exceptions. And most of the Alexandrians' extant commentaries have the further disadvantage of dealing not with Plato, but with Aristotle. The picture of Aristotle they present is naturally highly Neoplatonised, but none the less commentary on his works usually raised less controversial metaphysical points than did commentary on Plato. As we shall see, this was one of the very reasons why the Alexandrians preferred to concentrate on Aristotle. They were indeed far from ignoring Plato entirely. Ammonius lectured on both philosophers, but Aristotle was his speciality (*V. Is.* 79), and only his Aristotle commentaries have been preserved; in addition to the commentaries on Aristotle's logic preserved under Ammonius' own name, we have Asclepius' edition of his *Metaphysics* lectures, while Philoponus' commentaries are largely composed of notes of Ammonius' lectures, with some additions by Philoponus himself.[2]

---

[1] Commentaries by him on Aristotle's *Categories* and *Meteorology* are also extant, but he should not be confused with the Olympiodorus under whom Proclus studied Aristotle (*V. Pr.* 9).

[2] The commentary on *De Anima* III, traditionally ascribed to Philoponus, is, however, now regarded as Stephanus' work.

The inferiority of the school's Platonic scholarship can be seen from Olympiodorus' commentaries, which are in any case heavily dependent on the Athenians, while Hermeias' *Phaedrus* commentary consists of notes of Syrianus' lectures taken during Hermeias' Athenian period. The Athenians' contribution to Aristotelian studies seems indeed to have been more notable than the Alexandrians' work on Plato; yet apart from Simplicius' commentaries, which owe as much to his early Alexandrian days as to his Athenian period, nothing survives of their work in this field except four books of Syrianus' *Metaphysics* lectures. And our evidence suggests that this is not a matter of chance survivals, but indicates a basic difference of emphasis between the schools.

The divergences between them have admittedly often been over-estimated. Relations between the two schools were always close and intermarriage between their members common; for instance Hermeias' wife Aedesia was a relative of Syrianus, whose hand Proclus had previously declined (*V. Is.* fr. 124). Moreover many Neoplatonists taught in both cities, or at least studied in one before going on to teach in the other. That Hierocles, Hermeias and Ammonius all sat at the feet of Athenian masters has already been noted. By contrast Syrianus and Isidorus were Alexandrian by birth, and Proclus, Damascius and Simplicius all studied in that city. But the difference of tone is clear from the schools' references to one another. The Athenians, for their part, regarded the Alexandrians, as Plotinus regarded Longinus (cf. p. 38), as scholars rather than philosophers. Damascius' reference to Isidorus as superior to Hypatia 'not merely as a man to a woman, but as a philosopher to a mathematician' (*V. Is.* 164) is well known, and Proclus seems to have had even less respect for the Alexandrians who taught him Aristotle (*V. Pr.* 10; cf. *V. Is.* 34–6). Synesius' comments on contemporary Athens are equally disparaging (*Ep.* 136). For whereas the Athenians shared Iamblichus' enthusiasm both for speculative metaphysics and for the traditional religion, the Alexandrians chose instead to concentrate on pure scholarship and tended, in particular, to be much more lukewarm than their rivals towards theurgy. Hence the tension expressed in remarks like the above.

A tradition of disinterested research had, of course, characterised Alexandria's literary and scientific schools since Hellenistic times. But the Alexandrian School's distinctive tone was no less the result of contemporary pressures. For whereas the Academy had inherited abundant financial resources of its own (*V. Is.* 158, fr. 265, Olympiodorus

In Alc. 141. 1–3), and was situated in a university town which had long since lost its political importance and was now one of the strongholds of the declining paganism, the Alexandrians were not merely dependent for their fees on the municipal authorities, but continually menaced by the presence in their city of the Christian patriarch and his mob of fanatical monks. The lynching of Hypatia was therefore an ever-to-be remembered warning to moderate their paganism. The Athenians indeed tended to judge discretion the better part of valour; for instance Proclus chose to leave Athens for a year rather than risk prosecution for impiety (*V. Pr.* 15). But they were not disposed either to refrain from pagan worship or to moderate their theological teaching. Ammonius, by contrast, was forced by financial pressures to conclude an agreement with the patriarch Athanasius, whose terms are unknown, but for which Damascius reproves him bitterly (*V. Is.* fr. 316). While he did not apparently have to give up lecturing on Plato, there were clearly powerful incentives for the Alexandrians to concentrate on the theologically more neutral Aristotle. Olympiodorus remarks on the need to tone his teaching down (*In Alc.* 22. 14 ff.), and it is significant that even he confines his attention to Plato's ethical dialogues (the *Alcibiades*, *Gorgias* and *Phaedo*), ignoring controversial metaphysical works like the *Parmenides*. On the other side the school's Christian members generally refrain from introducing their own theological views into their commentaries; indeed the contrast between Philoponus' Aristotle commentaries and his polemic against Proclus (significantly composed in 529, the year of the Academy's closure) is striking. Compromises like these account for the school's smooth transition into Christian hands and enabled it to outlast its Athenian rival.

Whether the above points are indicative of more profound doctrinal differences is a vexed question. There can be no doubt that the Neoplatonism of Syrianus and Proclus is basically a development of Iamblichus' teaching, and there is little to support suggestions that Plutarch differed from them in returning from Iamblichus to a more Porphyrian system. The Alexandrians' views are much more elusive. We know little of the teaching of Theon and Hypatia and, while Porphyrian influence predominates in the essays and hymns of Synesius, this could represent Synesius' personal preferences rather than those of Hypatia. But Hierocles' system, as represented in his extant commentary on the Pythagorean *Golden Verses* and the fragments of his work *On Providence* (preserved by Photius *Bibl.* codd. 213 and 251), are a puzzle on any hypothesis. The lower levels of his universe, indeed, are not unlike those of other late Neoplatonists, with their mean terms and their rigidly demarcated ontological levels; what is singular is that its highest member is not the Neoplatonic One, but an Intelligence (*In Carm. Aur.* ed. Mullach 28. 12, Photius *Bibl.* 462B 18), identified with Plato's Craftsman (Photius ibid. 172A 42), who is described as having created both Intelligible and sensible worlds out of nothing—a doctrine unique in all pagan Greek philosophy, but one which Hierocles ascribes not merely to both Plato and Aristotle, but (apparently) to Ammonius Saccas, Origen the pagan, Plotinus and all important Neoplatonists down to Plutarch of Athens (Photius 171–3, 461A–B). One can only conclude with Damascius that Hierocles' moral nobility was not matched by equal intellectual merits (*V. Is.* fr. 106). But in comparing the Athenians and Alexandrians what is most important, and in view of the form of their work particularly difficult, is to determine the views of Ammonius and his successors. Recent research on the whole suggests that the pagan Alexandrians, though preferring to avoid theological controversy, tacitly accepted the Athenian system; in particular, the dependence of their Platonic exegesis on Syrianus and Proclus should be borne in mind. But there was at least one point of some importance on which Ammonius differed from the Athenians, the question of how far Aristotle agreed with Plato.

As we have seen (cf. pp. 24–5), the tendency since Porphyry and Iamblichus had been to maintain the two masters' agreement as far as possible. A good example of the blending of their ideas in later Neoplatonism comes in Proclus' treatment of motion (*ET* 14, *PT* 1. 14). Aristotle's argument that motion must be referred back to a Mover that is itself unmoved Proclus fully endorses; and this Mover he, like Aristotle, identifies with Intelligence. But in addition to a Prime Mover we must also postulate a First Moved, and this, Proclus argues (following *Phaedrus* 245C ff. and *Laws* 894–6), can only be a Self-moved Soul. Since Aristotle had failed to explain how the love inspired by his God in the celestial spheres could set them in motion, this interpolation in his system is not illegitimate, though Proclus also characteristically argues that a mean term is required between wholly unmoved beings and those which require an external mover. Conversely, Plato's reference to the World-soul as endowed with 'divine intelligence' (*Laws* x. 897B 1–2) is taken as recognising its dependence on the two higher Neoplatonic Hypostases (since for the Athenians, as we shall see, the 'divine' level is that of the First Hypostasis). And this, the school

argued, demonstrated Plato's superiority to Aristotle, who had postulated nothing higher than Intelligence (Proclus *PT* I. 3 p. 12. 23 ff., *In
Parm.* 1214. 7–15, *De Prov.* 31. 171). So did Aristotle's view of Intelligence as only a final cause (that is, as responsible only for Reversion
and not also for Procession.)[1] As we have seen, these were not the only
points (though they were the most important ones) on which the
Athenians took issue with Aristotle (cf. Proclus *In Parm.* VII. 73. 10 ff.
and above p. 25). And that they went further in this respect than
Ammonius is shown by the latter's attempt to prove that Aristotle's
God was after all an efficient cause (Simplicius *De C.* 271. 11–27, *Phys.*
1360–3, Asclepius *In Met.* 103. 3–4, 151. 15–32). Elias similarly
ascribes to him the doctrine of a One above Intelligence (In *Cat.* 120.
24 ff.). The latter point was not, however, likely to bulk large in the
Alexandrians' works, since, apart from Olympiodorus, they preferred
to avoid discussing anything higher than Intelligence.[2]

It is therefore exceptionally difficult to form an overall picture of the
Alexandrians' metaphysical views and, until further studies of their
writings are produced, the above comments must be treated as pro-
visional. It is clear, however, that their major achievement lay in continuing the assimilation of Aristotelian doctrine, especially in the field
of logic, that had been begun by Porphyry and Iamblichus, and thereby
assisting in its transmission to the Medieval world. And, though they
tended to keep their feet more firmly planted on the ground than the
Athenians, the latter were no less justified in accusing them of a lack of
metaphysical creativity. For this reason they must fall outside our
present study. Our main concern must be with the Athenian School,
and especially with its best-known representative, Proclus. Of the
works of Plutarch and Syrianus there survive only four books of the
latter's *Metaphysics* commentary and Hermeias' notes of his lectures on
the *Phaedrus*. But it appears, both from these works and from Proclus' own admission, that most of the Athenian School's characteristic
doctrines were already formulated by Syrianus and that Proclus' role
was less that of an original thinker than of a systematiser of other men's

[1] Proclus *In Tim.* I. 266–7, *In Parm.* 922. 1 ff.; cf. *ET* 34, Syrianus *In Met.* 10.
32 ff.
[2] For the Henads in Olympiodorus cf. *In Alc.* 4. 49, 51. 16, *In Phd.* 230, 13
That Simplicius sides with Ammonius shows that the contrast is not simply one
between Athenians and Alexandrians; cf. also *In Cat.* 7. 29–32, *De C.* 640. 27–32,
Phys. 1249. 12–17 for his view that the two masters' disagreements are largely
verbal. Conversely, the Alexandrian author of *Anon. Prol.* 9. 24 ff. follows
Proclus' view. Elias *In Cat.* 122. 27–32 suggests that the same commentators were
liable to take different attitudes to the question in different works.

ideas.[1] As such he has few if any equals in the history of thought. The most important innovation specifically ascribed to Plutarch concerns the interpretation of the second part of the *Parmenides* (cf. p. 22). The basis of his solution was that nine hypotheses must be distinguished, the first five being affirmative, the last four negative. Hypotheses I–V, dealing with the consequences of postulating an absolute Unity, were concerned respectively with the One itself, Intelligence, Soul, Embodied Form and Matter; hypotheses VI–IX constituted a *reductio ad absurdum* demonstrating that without such a unity nothing can exist (Proclus *In Parm.* 1058–61, *PT* I. 10 p. 41. 7 ff., I. 12 pp. 56–8). Further precision was added by Syrianus regarding the second hypothesis, whose fourteen conclusions he regarded as corresponding one for one to the various orders within the Intelligible world, whereas previous interpreters had referred them indiscriminately to the whole of that world (*In Parm.* 1061–4, *PT* I. 10–11). Its object, however, was not the members of the Intelligible world themselves, but the corresponding orders of gods (cf. below p. 147 n. 2 and pp. 150–1). Syrianus thus overcame the objection that the Platonic corpus lacked a systematic treatise on theology and provided a standard to which the theology of other works, both Platonic and non-Platonic, could be referred (*PT* I. 6–7). So understood, the *Parmenides* provided the plan on which Proclus composed his most elaborate work, the *Platonic Theology*.

Despite its importance and its systematic form, however, the *Platonic Theology* has been little studied in modern times. This is due partly to the prolixity and abstruseness of its later books, but also to the absence of a modern edition, a defect only now being rectified. Like Proclus' Platonic commentaries it is incomplete, though it is disputed whether this is due to Proclus himself or the result of later mutilation, perhaps even deliberate mutilation by Proclus' Christian opponents. Of the commentaries themselves those on the *Alcibiades I*, *Timaeus*, and *Parmenides* (as well as one on the first book of Euclid's *Elements*) survive, together with fragments of the *Cratylus* commentary and a collection of essays on topics from the *Republic*, the best known being a defence of Homer against Plato's criticisms and a commentary on the Myth of Er. Of Proclus' other surviving works (which represent only a fraction of his enormous output) only those dealing with metaphysical or religious subjects can be mentioned. First, we may note three short treatises on theological topics, two (the *Decem Dubitationes circa*

[1] Cf. Dodds, *Elements*, pp. xxi–xxv.

Providentiam and the *De Providentia et Fato*) dealing with providence
and fate, and one (the *De Malorum Subsistentia*) with evil. These were
formerly known only in the Medieval Latin translation of William of
Moerbeke, but in recent years most of their Greek text has been
recovered. Theurgy is dealt with in a fragment *On the Hieratic Art*
(also known as the *De Sacrificio et Magia*) and in a few surviving
extracts from Proclus' commentary on the *Chaldaean Oracles*; short
as they are, both these are of great importance for the school's religious
views. But the best known and most influential of Proclus' works
is, of course, his *Elements of Theology*, a remarkable work which,
anticipating the method of Spinoza's *Ethics*, presents the whole of
Neoplatonic metaphysics as a series of 211 propositions, each of which
is reached by logical deduction from its predecessors following the
procedure of Euclidean geometry. A further work, the *Elements of
Physics*, treats Aristotle's natural philosophy in the same way. Its concise and orderly method of exposition have secured the *Elements of
Theology* a just fame. But, taken by itself, it gives a distorted picture
of Proclus' work, representing as it does only its metaphysical, as
opposed to its religious and exegetic sides. Proclus' importance as a
Platonic commentator needs no emphasising; and both his writings
(which include a number of hymns) and Marinus' biography show him
as a deeply religious man. Indeed he believed himself to have been
called to philosophy by Athena in a dream (*V. Pr.* 6) and was a
scrupulous observer of the pagan rituals (ibid. 19) and an adept in
theurgic practice, being vouchsafed luminous visions by Hecate and
possessing powers of healing and rain-making (ibid. 28–9). Hence an
overall picture can be obtained only by study of a representative selection of his works. But to summarise even one of them is impossible in
the space available here, and readers should therefore be reminded that
they deal not just with the doctrines discussed in the present chapter,
but with the principles already considered in connection with Iamblichus. And, as we have noted, many of the details of those principles
must be the work of the Athenian School. But here we must confine
ourselves to those doctrines which there is reason to regard as either
peculiar to, or at least especially characteristic of that school.

II. SOME BASIC DOCTRINES OF THE ATHENIAN SCHOOL

The only important Iamblichean doctrine rejected by Proclus (though
it was later accepted by Damascius, *De Princ.* 1. 4 ff.) was his postula-

tion of an Ineffable Principle above the One (cf. p. 118). For the rest the Athenians saw their task as that of carrying through Iamblichus' principles to their logical conclusion and filling any gaps in the metaphysical hierarchy that he seemed to have left. With one instance, their Introduction of the Intelligible and Intellectual gods, we have already dealt (pp. 133–4). But the most conspicuous example is that of the divine Henads.[1]

The requirements fulfilled by the doctrine in question, which recognises within the First Hypostasis a series of Unities ('Henads') in addition to the One itself, are at least three. First, it establishes complete symmetry between that Hypostasis and lower orders by extending to it Iamblichus' distinction of Unparticipated and Participated Terms (*ET* 21, 113, cf. pp. 126–7). The Henads thus constitute the Participated intermediaries linking lower realities to the One, which now becomes the First Hypostasis' Unparticipated Monad (*ET* 116). And while relations between members of that Hypostasis are declared to be closer even than those between members of the Intelligible order (*In Parm.* 1048. 11–21), it must be emphasised that the Henads are not simply aspects or attributes of the First Cause, but substantial, self-subsistent entities derived from the One and dependent on it (cf. *ET* 114). Hence arise their other functions, one metaphysical, the other religious. The former function, that of bridging the gulf between Unity and Plurality, will be considered shortly; in particular we shall see how, whereas the One is absolutely unknowable, the Henads, though unknowable in themselves, can be known by analogy from their products. First, however, we must examine their religious function, that of providing a place in the Neoplatonic system for the traditional gods.

As we have seen, the Athenians were by no means the first Greek philosophers to raise the latter problem. What is new about their solution is their distinction between the gods (identified with the Henads) and the 'divine' principles on lower levels which participate in the former's divinity by sharing in their unity.[2] Proclus has indeed to admit that such a distinction between gods and principles which are

---

[1] *ET* 113–65; cf. Syrianus *In Met.* 141. 1 ff., 183. 24. Professor J. Dillon, however, has now provided strong arguments for the doctrine's Iamblichean origin.

[2] Cf. *ET* 129, *PT* I. 26 pp. 114–16, etc. It is this equation of divinity with unity that explains the Athenians' reference of the *Parmenides'* second hypothesis (dealing with Participated Unity) to the Henads (*PT* I. 12 p. 56. 11 ff. and above p. 145).

merely 'divine by participation' is one to which Plato, like other Greek thinkers, fails to adhere; nor does he himself always succeed in keeping to it. And (even apart from the polytheistic complications posed by the Henads) the distinction between the Neoplatonists' First and lower Hypostases is evidently much less sharp than that between God and his creation in the Semitic religions. None the less, the idea of 'divinity by participation' has obvious affinities with the Eastern Orthodox Church's teaching that man can be deified by divine grace,[1] and Boethius was therefore by no means unorthodox in introducing it to the West (*Cons.* III. 10). A similar principle governs Proclus' treatment of two major religious topics, Providence and the divine attributes.

Fundamental to Proclus' account of the divine attributes is the basic Neoplatonic doctrine that the same attribute (and even the same god, cf. p. 137) can exist under an appropriate mode on successive levels. Proclus' contribution is merely to emphasise, consistently with his general position, that such attributes are present perfectly and un-equivocally only on the level of the Henads. For instance, while Intelligence possesses self-sufficiency 'by participation', Soul 'by illumination' and the sensible cosmos 'by its likeness to the divine', the gods are self-sufficient by their very nature (*PT* I. 19 p. 91. 16–21).[2] Of particular interest is the later Neoplatonists' claim that each order of reality —apparently, and rather surprisingly, including even the Henads (*ET* 159)—represents an appropriate combination of Limit and Infinity.[3] The cosmogonic role of these two principles in early Pythagoreanism and in Plato's *Philebus* is well known, and their application had been extended to the Intelligible world by Plato's derivation of the Forms from the related principles of Unity and the Indefinite Dyad. Building on such hints, the later Neoplatonists proceeded to discover in every-thing that exists a triad of Limit, Unlimited and the Mixture of the two, which they further equated with the three phases of Abiding in one's cause, Procession and Reversion.[4] The reasons for this correlation should be fairly clear if we recall Plotinus' account of the generation of Intelligence, in which the Formless Infinitude of Intelligible Matter had

---

[1] Cf. V. Lossky, *The Mystical Theology of the Eastern Church*, pp. 133–4.

[2] As in some passages of Plotinus, (cf. p. 59 n. 1), the One is regarded as trans-cending self-sufficiency (*ET* 10).

[3] Cf. *ET* 89–92, *PT* III. 7–9. 131 ff., esp. 133–4, *In Tim.* I. 175 ff., 384 ff., *In Parm.* 1119 ff., Syrianus *In Met.* 112. 14 ff.; for Iamblichus cf. Damascius *De Princ.* I. 101. 11 ff., 103. 6 ff. The details are summarised by Dodds, *Elements*, p. 247 and Beutler, *RE* article 'Proklos', col. 223.

[4] Cf. *PT* III. pp. 135, 141, 144, 157, etc., Damascius *De Princ.* I 86. 10 ff., etc.

received Form and Limit through reversion upon the One (above pp. 66–7). Proclus' only quarrel with Plotinus is in declining to apply the term 'Intelligible Matter' to the phase of Procession (*PT* III. 138); instead he regards the Intelligible world's infinity as consisting in its power, since, though like most other Neoplatonists he denies the existence of numerical infinity (*ET* 86), for him, as for them, the power of all everlasting principles is inexhaustible and therefore boundless (*ET* 84; cf. *Enn.* VI. 5. 11 and above pp. 56–7). But this seems to contradict their other basic principle that the power of the lower Hypostases is less than that of their producers (cf. p. 49). The Athenians' solution was to make infinity, like other divine attributes, a relative term (*ET* 93, *Dec. Dub.* 11. 88–9, Syrianus *In Met.* 147. 13–22). And this further enabled them to counter Alexander's objection that infinity must be unknowable even to God (cf. above pp. 29–30) by maintaining that the infinite power of each level is indeed unlimited (and hence unknowable) for its products, but (since it is self-contained) limited (and therefore knowable) for itself and its priors. A similar concern with Alexander's critique of divine knowledge characterises Proclus' treatment of providence (*ET* 120–2).

That the exercise of providence should form an important part of the Henads' religious function is not surprising. And like all Neoplatonists Proclus takes as his starting-point Plotinus' doctrine that divine providence operates automatically and without deliberate exertion—or, in the Athenian School's terminology, 'in virtue of (the gods') very existence' (*autōi tōi einai*) (e.g. *ET* 122, *PT* I. 15 pp. 74–6). By this means, Proclus claims, Platonists avoid both Aristotle's denial of providence and the Stoics' abolition of divine transcendence (*PT* ibid. p. 76. 10 ff., *In Parm.* 921). Where Proclus goes beyond Plotinus is in regarding providence as the specific function of the Henads, in which other beings share only in virtue of their participation in the Henads' divinity; divine souls, for instance, have a threefold activity, exercising providence *qua* divine, possessing knowledge *qua* endowed with Intelligence and originating motion *qua* souls (*ET* 201; cf. ibid. 134). This association of providence with the Henads Proclus justifies on the grounds, first, that providence involves bestowal of good and that Goodness is the distinctive characteristic of the First Hypostasis (*ET* 119–20, *PT* I. 15. p. 74. 2 ff.) and, secondly, by an etymological derivation of the Greek word *pronoia* (providence) from *pro nou* (pre-intellectual). For, like the One, the Henads transcend Being, Life and Intelligence (*ET* 115), though they prefigure these by their own

triad of Existence-Power-Knowledge (which Proclus further corre-
lates with the three fundamental theological doctrines of *Laws* x; cf.
ET 121, *PT* I. 13–16 and 17 p. 80. 14–23); hence his reference of the
term *pronoia* to the triad's third member, the Henads' super-intellec-
tual cognition (*ET* 120; cf. *Enn.* v. 3. 10. 43). The content of such a
mode of knowledge, it will be recalled, had been a traditional subject
of debate (cf. pp. 59, 115). Proclus' main contribution is his argument, against Alexander, that divine omniscience extends to both
singulars and contingent events.[1] His starting-point is the principle,
formulated by Iamblichus (cf. Ammonius *De Int.* 135. 14–15), that
the nature of knowledge depends not on the object known, but on the
knowing subject; for instance, sensation and reason deal with the same
objects, but the former with their individual, the latter with their
universal aspects. Similarly, divine knowledge must be conditioned not
by the imperfections of its objects, but by the gods' own excellence.
Hence, first, divine knowledge is an indivisible unity, which, being
free from the restrictions of lower levels and extending as far as divine
causality (cf. pp. 155–7), embraces both individuals and universals.
Secondly, the gods grasp temporal events in a single timeless vision
and know contingent events without being affected by contingency
themselves. The logical implications of the latter claim were further
analysed in Ammonius' commentary on Aristotle's discussion of future
contingents (*De Int.* ch. 9. 18a. 28 ff., Ammonius *De Int.* 132–7), and
the resulting theory is presented in Boethius' *Consolation* (v. 4–6). It
thus became the basis of Medieval attempts to reconcile free will with
divine foreknowledge.

We must now turn to the Henads' third function, of mediating
between the One's unknowable unity and lower realities. The view of
some Neoplatonists that the Supreme Principle contains the causes of
those realities—an idea which, as we have seen, could claim Plotinian
and Porphyrian support (cf. pp. 60, 114)—Proclus rejects as inconsistent with the One's absolute unity (*In Parm.* 1107–8). Instead he
introduces plurality into the First Hypostasis by means of the Henads.
A necessary corollary was his rejection of the doctrine, associated with
the opposing view, that the One could be known by analogy from its
products. In consequence Proclus judged it unnecessary to follow
Iamblichus' postulation of an Ineffable principle above the One (*ET*
20. p. 22. 30–1 Dodds). Instead he lays continual stress, particularly in

[1] *ET* 124, *PT* I. 21, *In Tim.* I. 351. 20 ff., *In Parm.* 956. 30 ff., *Dec. Dub.* 2 ff.
(78 ff.), *De Prov.* 62–5 (193–5).

the second book of the *Platonic Theology* and the last part of the *Parmenides* commentary, on the One's own ineffability, emphasising, for instance, that even the *Parmenides*' negations must finally be negated (*In Parm.* VII. 68–76; cf. *PT* II. 109).[1] An even more important consequence is his distinction between the One, which, being Unparticipated, must be wholly unknowable, and the Henads; for though the latter are unknowable in themselves, some conception can none the less be formed of their nature from the beings that participate them (*ET* 123). As Dodds observes,[2] Proclus is thereby enabled to devote more than 400 pages of his *Platonic Theology* to his 'unknowable' gods. For, like other realities, the Henads are arranged in a hierarchical order prefiguring the structure of the lower orders of the universe. There are thus Intelligible Henads (corresponding to Unparticipated Being), Intelligible and Intellectual Henads (to Unparticipated Life), Intellectual Henads (to Unparticipated Intelligence), Supercosmic Henads (to Unparticipated Soul) and Intracosmic Henads (to Divine Participated Souls and the bodies they animate) (*ET* 162–5). In each case the Henads in question are not members of the order whose name they bear (though Proclus himself appears at times to confuse the two), but the transcendent source of that order's distinctive characteristics (in each case, of course, as the diagram overleaf shows, through the appropriate intermediaries). It is this that enables us, by the Way of Analogy, to infer something of the Henads' nature from their effects.

The result is a universe in which the structural principles of Iamblichean Neoplatonism are carried to their logical conclusion and in which, more than ever before, each individual entity has its own fixed place. It will be simplest, and avoid recapitulation of earlier chapters, to exhibit the structure of the upper levels of that universe in the form of a diagram.[3] Above all it can be seen how each individual principle has a twofold origin, deriving its generic characteristics from its own order's Unparticipated Monad and its specific characteristics from the corresponding principle in the order immediately above it; for instance, individual souls are the joint product of Unparticipated Soul

---

[1] Hence the Law of Contradiction does not apply to the One; for, though contraries are nowhere both true, on the level of the One they are both false (*In Parm.* VII. 72. 2–22).

[2] *Elements of Theology*, p. 266.

[3] Based on the diagram on p. 282 of Dodds' edition of the *Elements*, and following the scheme of that work, which omits the Intelligible and Intellectual gods.

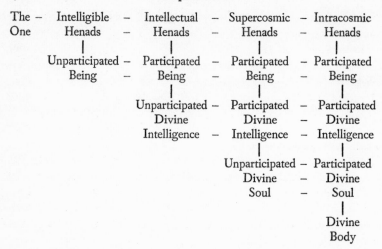

The –	Intelligible	–	Intellectual	–	Supercosmic	–	Intracosmic
One	Henads	–	Henads	–	Henads	–	Henads
	│		│		│		│
	Unparticipated –		Participated	–	Participated	–	Participated
	Being	–	Being	–	Being	–	Being
			│		│		│
			Unparticipated –		Participated	–	Participated
			Divine		Divine	–	Divine
			Intelligence	–	Intelligence	–	Intelligence
					│		│
					Unparticipated	–	Participated
					Divine	–	Divine
					Soul	–	Soul
							│
							Divine
							Body

and of their own transcendent Intelligence. Hence, by the law that effects revert upon their causes, an entity may make contact with higher levels of reality through the intermediary of either of these principles (*ET* 108–9). But this law is drastically qualified by the further axiom that the members of the higher Hypostases, being closer to the One, must be fewer in number, though greater in power, than those of lower levels (*ET* 61–2). Hence, as we have seen, not all souls have their own transcendent Intelligence (cf. above p. 120), just as not all Intelligences have their own divine Henad (*ET* 110–11), though by a confusing exception the members of the Intelligible order (i.e. the Forms) are declared to be equal in number to the Henads on which they depend (*ET* 135). From this arises the division of souls into three classes, divine souls, dependent on an individual divine Intelligence, human souls, which lack a transcendent Intelligence of their own, and daemonic souls, which constitute a mean between the two, since, though they possess their own Intelligence, and are therefore able to exercise thought continually, their Intelligence is not divine, since it lacks a Henad of its own (*ET* 184–5, 202). Hence their identification with the souls perpetually attendant on the gods described at *Phaedrus* 248A (cf. Iamblichus *Myst.* I. 10. 36. 6–13), a passage whose description of souls as following the procession of the gods now assumes considerable importance, since it is only through the intermediary of a superhuman soul that the human soul can now make contact with the Intelligible world (*ET* 204). Still less can union with the One be within man's own powers, or attainable through philosophy (*PT* II. 96); it requires the operation of a transcendent force, with which theurgy puts us in contact.

The foundation of this possibility is the consideration that the term 'Henad', like 'Soul' and 'Intelligence', can be used in either of two ways (cf. pp. 127–8), denoting either the self-subsistent gods themselves or their 'irradiations' (or 'images'), the unities present in lower beings (*ET* 64; cf. *In Parm.* 1062. 22 ff.). As we have seen, without unity nothing could exist (*ET* 1; cf. above p. 48); and, on the principle that like is known by like, it is through the unity (or 'henad') present within the human soul that mystical union with the One can be attained. For this unity the later Neoplatonists have various terms, their favourite being the 'summit' or 'flower' (*anthos*) of Intelligence (i.e. Intelligence's finest part, a term derived from the *Chaldaean Oracles*);[1] elsewhere a yet higher principle, 'the flower of the whole soul', is distinguished (*Ph. Ch.* fr. 4 Jahn). It is this principle, at the core of our being, that we attain by unifying our mind and through which we contact the divine. This, of course, recalls Plotinus' doctrine of the two states of Intelligence (cf. p. 88), but with the important difference that the Intelligence referred to is no longer for Proclus the transcendent Second Hypostasis, but merely an 'irradiation' therefrom.[2] Similarly while repeating Plotinus' metaphor of the 'centre' of the soul (cf. p. 89), Proclus agrees with Iamblichus against Plotinus in denying that any part of our soul remains unfallen (*ET* 211, *In Tim.* III. 333. 29 ff.; cf. p. 120). Hence for him, as for Iamblichus, theurgy provides the only way of salvation.[3]

It had always been a problem to distinguish theurgy from vulgar magic. Since the external operations of the two were often identical, it was plausible to see their distinction as lying in the respective states of mind of their practitioners. Hence the importance assigned in later

[1] *Or. Ch.* p. 11 Kr.; cf. *PT* I. 3. pp. 14–17, *In Alc.* 247–8, *De Prov.* 31–2 (171–2), *In Parm.* 1044. 27–8, 1047. 16–24, 1071. 9 ff., *In Tim.* I. 211. 24ff., *In Crat.* CXIII. 66. 11–13.
[2] This is why Proclus sometimes seems to affirm (*Ph. Ch.* fr. 4), what he elsewhere emphatically denies, that we are an 'intelligible cosmos' (*In Parm.* 948). All things are indeed within us, but only 'in a manner appropriate to the soul' (*PT* I. 3 p. 16. 16–18).
[3] Readers should be warned that the relation of the above ideas, and those which follow, to ritual theurgy is far from clear. Some scholars see in the former a higher type of theurgy, having little but the name in common with the latter. That ritual theurgy has limitations is suggested by *In Crat.* LXXI. 32. 18 ff. and CXIII. 65. 23–6 (references I owe to Mr. Andrew Smith).

Neoplatonism to a triad (needless to say) of virtues, faith (*pistis*), truth (*alētheia*) and love (*erōs*), to which hope (*elpis*) is often conjoined as a fourth.[1] Concerning the origin and significance of this remarkable triad there is agreement on only one point, that it was taken by the Neoplatonists not from Christianity, but from the *Chaldaean Oracles* (p. 26 *Kr.*); whether its appearance there has any connection with the Pauline triad of faith, hope and *agapē* (1 Cor. XIII) is something we are unlikely ever to be able to decide. The triad is mentioned by both Porphyry (*Ad Marc.* XXIV) and Iamblichus (*Myst.* v. 26. p. 239); but since the only detailed discussions we possess are in connection with the Athenian School's religious views, consideration of it has been postponed until now. The *Oracles* had treated the three principles as cosmic forces; and Proclus similarly ascribes them the metaphysical role of linking the various orders one with another, and in particular of linking lower principles to the divine triad of Goodness, Wisdom and Beauty (*PT* I. 25, *In Alc.* 51–3; cf. *In Tim.* I. 212. 20–5). The correlation of Truth with Wisdom and Love with Beauty is Platonic and self-explanatory. But Proclus' account of love strikes a disconcerting note for those who would draw a neat opposition between Platonic *erōs* and Christian *agapē*, since it distinguishes two forms of love, the normal Platonic, 'ascending' form, motivating lower principles to aspire towards their superiors, and a 'descending' or 'providential' form (*erōs pronoētikos*), prompting those superiors to care for their products (*In Alc.* 54–6). As presented by Proclus, the latter marks a transposition to the cosmic plane of the Platonic philosopher's care for his beloved. But though such a transposition could claim justification from the *Timaeus*' account of the Divine Craftsman's motives (29E), Plato had not specifically described him as motivated by love and Plotinus, as we have seen, had in effect rejected any notion of a 'descending' love on the part either of the philosopher or of God (cf. pp. 64, 86). We have thus one more sign of the later Neoplatonists' increased stress on divine grace. And it is this light that we should consider their new, and wholly un-Platonic, doctrine of faith as superior to rational cognition and as leading to union with the Good.

Proclus was well aware, needless to say, that the *Republic* had used 'faith' as a technical term for belief about the sensible world and thereby

[1] For recent discussions of the triad cf. H. Lewy, *Chaldaean Oracles and Theurgy*, pp. 144–8, A. H. Armstrong, 'Platonic Eros and Christian Agape', *Downside Review* 79 (1961) 105–21, E. R. Dodds, *Pagan and Christian in an Age of Anxiety*, pp. 122–3, J. M. Rist, *Plotinus: the Road to Reality*, ch. 17 (pp. 231–46).

ranked it *below* reason (*Rep.* VI. 511D–E), and his own account is careful to distinguish such faith from what he has in mind (*PT* I. 25 p. 110. 17–22). His use of 'faith' may thus be in large part a paradox similar to the Medievals' recognition of a 'learned ignorance' transcending knowledge. But his association of faith with the Good shows the influence of the Chaldaean tradition's view of theurgy as the way to the supreme principle and of faith as the theurgic virtue par excellence (cf. *PT* ibid. p. 113. 4–10, *In Alc.* 53. 1–2). As we have seen, the final goal of theurgy is mystical experience (p. 108), and for Proclus, as for Gregory of Nyssa and St. John of the Cross, faith seems to have the function of emboldening the mystic to leave the solidity of conceptual thought and launch himself into the divine darkness. Its use probably reflects not so much a lack of confidence on Proclus' part about the individual soul's capacities (since faith is described at *PT* ibid. 110. 2–16, as the force linking the gods themselves to the One; cf. *PT* IV. 194), but rather the new attitude of trusting dependence necessitated by the later Neoplatonists' stress on divine transcendence. It thus links up with the saying of Theodorus of Asine, which Proclus more than once quotes, that 'all things pray except the First' (*In Tim.* I. 213. 2–3, *CMAG* VI. 148. 12–18), an expression in religious language of the principle that everything reverts upon its cause, and so indirectly upon the cause of all. That even inanimate objects aspire to imitate the Good had been implicit both in the *Phaedo* (74D ff.) and in Aristotle, and it is the likeness to the gods that they acquire by this reversion that for the later Neoplatonists justifies their use in theurgy.[1] And it is natural to see Proclus' references to 'divine faith' as recognising a similar force on the superhuman level. At all events, while positive Christian influence on Proclus must remain unproven, it seems clear that the need to construct a religion rivalling Christianity is a major force behind his use of the terms just considered.

A similar combination of metaphysical, religious and exegetic aims is visible in the Athenians' other main doctrinal innovation,[2] concerning the relative causal efficacy of higher and lower principles, and involving two closely related doctrines. The first is that, since a being's power derives from the same source as does its existence, the higher principles must be responsible not merely for their own immediate products, but for all the latter's effects (*ET* 56). The second, more

[1] Cf. *ET* 39, *PT* II. 104–5, *In Tim.* I. 210. 2 ff., *In Crat.* LXXI. 30. 19 ff.
[2] Professor J. Dillon observes that Olympiodorus *In Alc.* 110. 13 ff. implies that the doctrine was not Iamblichean.

radical, innovation, is that the causal efficacy of higher principles extends further down the scale of being than that of lower ones (*ET* 57, 71–2). It was basic to Neoplatonism that the higher members of the metaphysical hierarchy have greater power and must therefore be the causes of more effects than their products; it was this, as we have seen, that had led the later Neoplatonists to rank Being above Life and Life above Intelligence (*ET* 101, cf. above p. 125). But, this being so, it is clear that the power of Being extends the furthest of the three, since all material objects must possess form and therefore being, whereas only plants have life and only animals a rudimentary intelligence (cf. *PT* III. 127–9). Similarly an individual man or animal exists as a body before it exhibits life and exhibits life before it acquires intelligence; whereas in old age and death the disappearance of the three principles takes place in reverse order (*ET* 70; cf. Syrianus *In Met.* 29. 2–8). But that not even the power of Being (i.e. of Form) extends as far as Matter is clear from the latter's formlessness;[1] and it is this that explains the paradoxical resemblance between Matter's formlessness and that of the One, or, in the Athenians' terminology, their 'similarity of dissimilarity' (*PT* I. 12. p. 57. 18–20, Syrianus *In Met.* 153. 2–7, etc.). It was this similarity that had enabled the later Neoplatonists to refer the negations of the *Parmenides'* fifth hypothesis to Matter, and so to contrast them with the first hypothesis' negative account of the One. And it now becomes explicable on the grounds that Matter is the product of the One alone, the influence of all higher principles having previously given out. More generally, it is clear why complication increases towards the centre of the metaphysical hierarchy, reaching its maximum in the rational soul (cf. p. 91), since principles at the centre of that hierarchy are the product of more causes than those towards either extreme (*ET* 58–9).

The principle equally served the school's exegetic and religious purposes. In the former sphere it explained why the *Timaeus'* Craftsman (whose exact status within the spiritual hierarchy was disputed, but whom the Neoplatonists never identified with the One),[2] had been confronted with a pre-existing Matter (*In Tim.* 1. 387. 5 ff.). On the religious side it would appear to provide a justification of theurgy; for since Matter is now regarded as produced directly by the One, whereas Soul is separated from the latter by numerous intervening terms, it

---

[1] *ET* 72; cf. *PT* I. 3. p. 13. 23 ff., *In Parm.* VII. 56. 3–6, Syrianus *In Met.* 59. 16–18, etc.

[2] For Neoplatonic views on the Craftsman cf. *In Tim.* 1. 299–319.

would seem obviously easier to contact the divine power in material objects.[1] This does not, however, seem to be explicitly stated in any extant text. What the new account of causality does achieve—and thus far it certainly serves to justify theurgy—is to secure the equal presence of divine power on every level (cf. *In Tim.* 1. 209. 13 ff.)—a defence of divine immanence which it is interesting to contrast with that of Plotinus. Such a view of divine causality was clearly more congenial to Christians than those of earlier Neoplatonists and it was to find its way, through the Arabic *Liber de Causis*, into Medieval Scholasticism.

It was evidently impossible on such a view to retain Plotinus' identification of Matter with Evil. Plotinus had found it difficult either to reconcile this identification with his monism or to attribute all the soul's evil to Matter (cf. p. 78), and on these and other grounds it is rejected by Proclus (*Mal. Subs.* 30–7. 229–39). But Plotinus' equation of evil with non-being could not be jettisoned if divine omnipotence was to be reconciled with the *Republic*'s insistence that evil is never due to God (*Rep.* II. 379–80, cf. *Mal. Subs.* 2–3. 197–9, Boethius *Cons.* III. 12). Proclus' solution is to make evil a mere absence of good; more precisely it is a *parhypostasis*, a term denoting, first, that evil is a mere *by-product* or perversion of the universal aspiration towards the good, and, secondly, that evil *has no genuine existence*. For, first, even the material world's evil is so only for its parts, not for the whole; secondly, since there is no absolute principle of evil, the latter is never unmixed, and is always turned by providence to good. Finally, evil is present only on the lower metaphysical levels, as a result of their inability to receive the good bestowed by their priors in its original purity; hence, needless to say, it has no place in the divine Hypostases. Except for the denial of an absolute principle of evil, all this is merely a more systematic restatement of long-established doctrine.[2]

Proclus' view of the soul adds little to that of Iamblichus. One interesting innovation is his mediation between Porphyry and Iamblichus in recognising two subtle 'vehicles' of the soul, one immortal, the other perishable.[3] With this goes a compromise on the irrational soul's immortality, for according to Proclus the immortal vehicle is the seat of certain 'roots of irrational life', which the soul always retains,

---

[1] Cf. Dodds, *Elements of Theology*, p. 233 (commenting props. 58 and 59).

[2] Cf. *Mal. Subs.* 50–4 (252–9), *PT* I. 18, *In Tim.* 1. 373 ff., Simplicius *In Ench.* 69–81 Dübner.

[3] *In Tim.* III. 236. 31 ff., 297. 16 ff.; cf. *ET* 196, 205, 207–10 and above pp. 108–9.

and which provide the initial stimulus behind her descent into this world. By this means he resolves the awkward problem how irrational movements can arise in a discarnate soul (cf. p. 78). On the whole the 'positive' view of the soul's descent predominates in Proclus—necessarily, since he maintains (probably following Iamblichus) that she is required to descend at least once during each cosmic cycle (*ET* 206, *In Tim.* III. 278. 9 ff.; cf. Sallustius *DM* xx. 2–3). Indeed he even maintains that her descent imitates divine providential love (*In Alc.* 32. 9 ff.). But his attitude elsewhere is more pessimistic (e.g. *Mal. Subs.* 12. 210); nor is this surprising, since we have seen (p. 20) that the conflict in question was too deeply engrained in Platonism for simple removal.

III. DAMASCIUS AND THE END OF THE ACADEMY

From Damascius, the last head of the Academy, we possess some lecture-notes on the *Philebus* and an important and abstruse treatise on First Principles (*De Principiis*) cast—appropriately in view of the Athenians' interpretation of that dialogue—in the form of a commentary on the *Parmenides*. Much of Damascius' treatise is taken up with polemic against Proclus' interpretation of the work; in particular Damascius follows Iamblichus in placing an Ineffable principle above the One (*De Princ.* I. 4. 6 ff.). Somewhat after the manner of the anonymous *Parmenides* commentator, but even more decidedly, he emphasises the Supreme Principle's inaccessibility to conceptual thought (cf. e.g. *De Princ.* I. 15. 13 ff.), while laying continual stress, on every level, on the relativity of all concepts and the inadequacy of human language (e.g. *De Princ.* I. 109. 10 ff.); a good example is his exposure of the inadequacy of the traditional emanation imagery (cf. ibid. I. 273. 1 ff.). A full account of Damascius' thought will have to await a reliable edition of his work; in the meantime we may simply observe that, while he was doing no more than bring out some of the traditional teaching's implications, yet with him, as with the anonymous commentator, the consequences were little less than annihilation of the whole Neoplatonic hierarchy. Most probably such centrifugal tendencies would have been successfully resisted, had the school continued, as they had been in the past; it is significant that Philoponus' contemporary attempt to abolish the dichotomy between celestial and sublunary spheres (cf. 139) met little success even among Christians, who might have been expected to welcome such an attack on pagan religion. But for the Athenian School there was no more time. Platonic doctrines had already come under sharp attack in the Christian Aristotelian School of Gaza, and Justinian's closure of the Academy was symptomatic of a general reaction against Platonism, particularly in its pagan Athenian form. Stephanus is recorded as having taught both Plato and Aristotle at Constantinople in the seventh century; but in the main the Byzantine schools concentrated on the latter philosopher. That the Athenians' influence on Byzantine thought was none the less profound was the result of the remarkable forgery of the Dionysian corpus, one of the main sources of Neoplatonism's later influence, with which our final chapter will deal.

CHAPTER SIX

The Influence of Neoplatonism

As this chapter will show, a survey of Neoplatonism's influence threatens to become little less than a cultural history of Europe and the Near East down to the Renaissance, and on some points far beyond. The reason this has not always been recognised is that that influence was often indirect. That the Middle Ages and Renaissance saw Plato through Middle Platonic and Neoplatonic spectacles is indeed vaguely acknowledged; what may be less appreciated is the extent to which Neoplatonic ideas affected Medieval interpretations of Aristotle. This is important, since it means that the dominant trend of Christian theology, in both its Platonic and Aristotelian forms, has always been Neoplatonic. Here we can concentrate only on a few of the more important episodes in this history; we shall, for instance, be able to say little of Neoplatonic influence on the development of science or on Renaissance and modern occultism. Nor, it must be emphasised, is our aim to give a complete or balanced account of the philosophers we shall discuss, or to claim that all of them could without qualification be described as 'Neoplatonists', but to bring out, first, the extent of Neoplatonism's later influence and, secondly, the variety of forms it could assume. In particular we shall see how later debates frequently echo those we have seen within pagan Neoplatonism and how Neo-platonically-minded thinkers dealt with the new problem of recon-ciling pagan philosophy with the demands of revealed religion. To this problem the Byzantine, Moslem and Medieval Western worlds responded each in their separate ways, until their several streams came together in the cultural life of the Renaissance.

One way—and, as it proved, an astonishingly effective way—of preserving Neoplatonic influence in the face of official hostility was taken within the Byzantine world by the late fifth- or early sixth-cen-tury author of the writings which have come down to us under the name of St. Paul's first Athenian convert, Dionysius the Areopagite, in which the doctrines of Athenian Neoplatonism are presented in Christian dress. Apart from some letters, the Dionysian corpus comprises four works: the brief but immensely influential *Mystical Theology*, dealing with 'apophatic' or negative theology and with the practical discipline of the mystic; the *Divine Names*, dealing with affirmative or 'cataphatic' theology; and the *Celestial Hierarchy* and *Ecclesiastical Hierarchy*, which consider the mediation of divinity to terrestrial beings through the heavenly orders of angels and the terrestrial orders of the church. The author's identity and date, his relation to the Athenian School's known members and the sincerity or otherwise of his Christianity are still matters of keen debate. What must be stressed is that his was far from the first attempt to integrate Neoplatonism and Orthodox theology. Negative theology had been firmly established in the Eastern tradition since Clement of Alexandria in the second century, while the thought and mysticism of the fourth-century Cappadocian Fathers, Gregory Nazianzen (*c.* 330–*c.* 390), Basil of Caesarea (*c.* 330–379) and especially Gregory of Nyssa (died 394) was under strong Plotinian influence. The problem posed by the Dionysian corpus, despite its supposed Apostolic authority, was that its Neoplatonism was that of the more avowedly pagan Athenian School; in particular Dionysius' angelology seemed too reminiscent of the Athenian School's orders of gods. Hence his God tended to become merely the supreme term in the metaphysical hierarchy, and as such to be conceived as operating on the material world only through intermediaries. In this Dionysius echoed the ambivalent tendencies of pagan Neoplatonism and, what was perhaps even more serious, he seemed equally equivocal on the fundamental point separating Neoplatonic and Christian world-views, whether creation is a result of the divine nature or of a gratuitous act of grace (cf. pp. 102 ff.). Hence his sacramentalism tended to lose its supernatural element and become hard to distinguish from pagan theurgy (pp. 105, 108). Finally Dionysius seemed to pay too little attention to the Incarnation. The justice of these charges cannot be assessed here; we must simply note that they were made, and that it was therefore only after its orthodoxy had been vindicated by the commentaries of John of Scythopolis (*c.* 530) and Maximus the Confessor (580–662) that the Dionysian corpus gained full acceptance. Its influence on Medieval Western theology and mysticism, dating from the Latin translation made in 858 by the Irish philosopher John Scotus Eriugena (*c.* 810–*c.* 877), which was soon followed by others, was no less considerable. Greater controversy was caused by Eriugena's own thought, a development of Byzantine Neoplatonist ideas which will repay brief consideration.

A major tension within Neoplatonism, as we have seen, was its ambivalent attitude to the material world. Hence it is not surprising that both sides in the eighth-century Iconoclast debate, over the veneration of divine images, and the fourteenth-century Hesychast controversy, in which Gregory Palamas (1296–1357) defended the mysticism of the divine light against the monk Baarlaam's purely apophatic theology, should have expressed themselves in Neoplatonic terms. But it was characteristic of the Eastern Church's attitude to the material order that the positive evaluation of that order triumphed on both occasions. The reason was Byzantine Neoplatonism's view of creation as a 'theophany', or manifestation of the divine, a development of the Platonic view of the sensible world as an image of the Intelligible which gave the former a more positive value; of this the theory of icons was simply a particular application. Where Eriugena went wrong in ecclesiastical eyes in attempting to introduce the doctrine to the West was in treating creation as a *natural* unfolding of the divine unity, and in declaring in consequence that in creating other things God is equally creating himself (*Div. Nat.* III. 23). Hence the condemnation for pantheism of his treatise *On the Division of Nature*.

So far all the Neoplatonic influences on the Byzantine world which we have considered were indirect. Study of the pagan Neoplatonists themselves was resumed only during the eleventh-century Byzantine Renaissance, centred on the school of Michael Psellus (1018–79). A well-known passage of Psellus' *Chronographia* (VI. 37–8) recounts his Neoplatonic studies and his especial enthusiasm for Proclus. But though it is to Psellus that we owe much of our information about the theurgic side of Proclus' work, Psellus' attitude to theurgy was by no means uncritical; indeed he attacked the contemporary patriarch Cerularius for allegedly introducing theurgic rites into the Church. But Psellus' own orthodoxy did not pass unquestioned and his pupil John Italus was excommunicated in 1082 for teaching pagan doctrines, including, it was alleged, transmigration. Psellus' own attitude seems ambiguous. On the one hand, there is no reason to doubt his professions of loyalty to the Church; on the other, he did not succeed in reconciling his philosophy with revealed religion and was clearly far more devoted to the former than to the latter. We shall find a similar attitude among the Arab philosophers, with their famous doctrine of the 'double truth', and perhaps in Boethius among the Latins. Similar apprehensions were aroused concerning the fifteenth-century

Platonic school established at Mistra in the Peloponnese by George Gemistus Pletho (c. 1360–c. 1450)—not unjustly if his enemies' reports of his doctrine are accurate. He was none the less sent as a delegate to the Council of Florence in 1438 to negotiate the reunion of the Eastern and Western Churches, and there inspired Cosimo de' Medici to found his own Platonic Academy, while his pupil Bessarion actually changed from the Greek to the Latin Church, where he became a cardinal. The result of all these factors was the transmission to the West of the basic writings of Plato and the pagan Neoplatonists, most of them for the first time. The results we shall presently see.

The Moslem world had meanwhile received an utterly different version of Neoplatonism. Its basic component, a Neoplatonised Aristotelianism, was a continuation of the philosophical tradition of the Alexandrian School. The latter, as we have noted, survived into Arab times, until about 720 it removed to Antioch and about 900 to Baghdad. But it was far from the only channel by which Neoplatonic thought reached the Arabs, another major source being Near Eastern Syriac translations of Greek texts. And while many Neoplatonic works reached the Moslems through one or other of these routes, the major role was played by another remarkable forgery, the so-called *Theology of Aristotle*, which in fact consists of extracts from Enneads IV–VI padded out with supplementary or explanatory material perhaps derived from Porphyry's lost commentary. That in its present form the work is a deliberate forgery is proved by its preface, in which 'Aristotle' describes it as the culmination at which all his other works have been aiming. Two other Plotinian paraphrases, the *Epistle of Divine Science* and the *Sayings of the Greek Sage* are known, but, lacking Aristotelian authority, had much less influence. Also less important for the Arab world, but fundamental for Medieval European Scholasticism, was another pseudo-Aristotelian apocryphon, the *Book Concerning the Pure Good*, known to the Medieval West under the title 'Liber de Causis', a work in fact based on Proclus' *Elements of Theology*. The confusion caused by such works can be imagined; for instance chapter III (paras. 67–76) of the so-called *Theology* (based on *Enn.* IV. 7. 8[5]) refutes Aristotle's own doctrine of the soul, which it ascribes to 'the materialists'. And the result was that the Arabs' interpretation of Aristotle was at least as Neoplatonic as their interpretation of Plato— perhaps more so, since the latter was seen through the eyes of pre-Plotinian interpreters, notably of Galen; for instance most of the Arabs agreed with Galen and Philoponus, another major influence on their thought, in taking the *Timaeus*' temporal creation literally. Another departure from Neoplatonism was their revival of Plato's political philosophy. Yet some of the Moslems maintained the agreement of Plato and Aristotle, notably al-Farabi, who wrote a work to demonstrate it.

Nor should the influence of pre-Neoplatonic sources, notably Alexander of Aphrodisias, on Arabic interpretations of Aristotle be minimised. Yet the Neoplatonic apocrypha none the less provided the minimum addition necessary to make Aristotelianism acceptable to a religious mind, notably in making God an efficient as well as a final cause, through the doctrine of emanation. Hence the *Theology*'s influence was as important as that of Aristotle's own *Metaphysics* and not even Averroes, despite his desire to return from Avicenna's Neoplatonism to a stricter Aristotelianism, could wholly reject its ideas.[1] For the Arabic philosophers, albeit in somewhat different ways, were all sincerely religious men, though their religion was not such as to commend itself to Moslem orthodoxy. For in contrast to its situation within Christianity, Neoplatonism formed only a minor component within orthodox Moslem theology until the time of al-Ghazzali (1058–1111). And while the first of the major Moslem Peripatetics, the ninth-century philosopher al-Kindi, attempted to reconcile his philosophy with revelation, notably by abandoning the world's eternity, among his successors, the Turk al-Farabi (died 950), the Persian Ibn Sina (Avicenna, 980–1037) and the Spanish Moor Ibn Rushd (Averroes, 1126–98), the opposite attitude prevailed. No account can be given here of the differences between the various philosophers, which are as important as their similarities. All that concerns us here is their basic standpoint vis-à-vis orthodoxy, summarised in the notorious doctrine of the 'double truth'; whether or not this was explicitly taught by the philosophers, it certainly expresses their position. Its basis was the rejection of any rational reconciliation of reason and revelation, which were both allowed to be true in their own sphere. Hence if it did not actually treat revealed religion (as Averroes seemed to), as merely a symbolic presentation of philosophical teaching for the masses, it at least secured philosophy's autonomy from theological interference. Hence, for instance, the philosophers' rejection of creation out of nothing in favour of emanation. Hence too their naturalistic explanations of miracles and prophecy, the former by cosmic sympathy (cf.

---

[1] Emanation is in fact criticised in Averroes' *Incoherence of the Incoherence* (III. 186), but appears to be accepted by him elsewhere.

pp. 70-1), the latter as the result of the prophet's union with Aristotle's Active Intelligence; the resemblance between Avicenna's teaching on the latter point, with its combination of Stoic and Neoplatonic ideas, and that of Iamblichus (cf. Averroes *Tahafut-al-Tahafut* XVI. 496-7, and above pp. 122-3) is particularly striking. The philosophers' attitude to personal immortality varied; where they agreed was in rejecting the orthodox doctrine of bodily resurrection. The latter was one of three fundamental points levelled against them in Ghazzali's orthodox manifesto, the *Incoherence of the Philosophers*, the others being their affirmation of the world's eternity and their denial that God knows individuals. It is interesting to compare these three points with Synesius of Cyrene's three reservations (cf. pp. 101 ff.); the problem of divine knowledge, of course, bulked large within Aristotelianism and had been particularly stressed by Alexander (cf. pp. 29-30), while the Arabs' abandonment of pre-existence similarly resulted from their desire to combine Neoplatonic with Aristotelian psychology. Ghazzali's criticisms were answered in Averroes' *Incoherence of the Incoherence* (*Tahafut-al-Tahafut*) in one of the most far-reaching and absorbing debates in the history of religious thought. Ghazzali was successful and the Aristotelian school's influence on Moslem thought came to an end. Its future lay rather in Western European Scholasticism, whose translation of Arabic texts began in the twelfth century. Thus another stream of Neoplatonic thought reached the West.

Ghazzali's triumph did not, however, mark the end of Neoplatonic influence upon Islam. We have noted the Neoplatonic tendency of Ghazzali's own theology; indeed Averroes charges him with some justice of maintaining some of the doctrines he criticises in the philosophers. Even more important was his contribution to Islamic mysticism (or Sufism); in fact Neoplatonic ideas are unlikely to have been absent from Sufism before (though the movement's origins have been the subject of much dispute), but with Ghazzali they become predominant. Among earlier Sufis the Egyptian Dhu'l-Nūn (died 859) is credited with the introduction of Hellenic ideas, though these may have been Hermetic rather than Neoplatonic; at all events, he is unlikely to have known the *Theology*, which was not translated until near the end of his life. Yet another version of Islamic Neoplatonism was to emerge in the theosophical school of the Persian Suhrawardi (1155-91), based on ideas derived from the *Theology* and already present in Avicenna; yet, in contrast to the Moslem Peripatetics, Suhrawardi considered himself a Platonist and stressed Aristotle's inferiority. All the above traditions, philosophical, mystical and theosophical unite in the work of the Spanish-born Ibn 'Arabi (1165–1240), who combines the theophanic view of the universe with a monism, which in its conception of God as attaining self-awareness in man departs from the main stream of Neoplatonism in the direction of Numenius and the anonymous *Parmenides* commentator (cf. pp. 116–18), whom Arabi also resembles in his paradoxical resolution of the immanence-transcendence dilemma.

Neoplatonic influences on Medieval Jewish thought and mysticism must be treated more briefly. Their presence in the Cabala is proved by a quotation from the *Theology of Aristotle* in Moses de Leon, the supposed author of the *Zohar*;[1] in philosophy, Neoplatonic influence is strongest in the avowedly Platonising teaching of Ibn Gebirol (Avicebron, *c.* 1021–*c.* 1058), best known for his development of Plotinus' views on Intelligible Matter. To this school Maimonides' (1135–1204) combination of a stricter Aristotelianism with a radically negative theology stands rather in the position of Averroes vis-à-vis Avicenna. A major importance of this Jewish philosophical tradition was in transmitting Neoplatonic ideas to Spinoza.

In comparison with the Arabs' knowledge of Neoplatonism, as of Greek philosophical texts in general, that of the early Medieval West was meagre. Indeed much Medieval Platonism, the dominant force in Western thought until the Scholastic period, was not Neoplatonism at all, but Middle Platonism. This applies particularly to Chalcidius' (fourth-century?) commentary on the *Timaeus*, the only Platonic dialogue known to the West until Aristippus' twelfth-century translations of the *Meno* and *Phaedo*; for despite Chalcidius' probable post-Plotinian date it is Numenius' influence that dominates his work. Other important sources were the second-century Latin Platonist Apuleius and the translation of the Hermetic *Asclepius* erroneously ascribed to him. But even those Latin authors whose Neoplatonism is unquestioned generally teach a system considerably more simplified, and so closer to Middle Platonism, than that of Plotinus himself. For this we have seen two inter-related reasons (above p. 96), the Westerners' impatience with metaphysical subtleties and their consequent enthusiasm for Porphyry's popularising version of his master's thought. Hence even those Latin authors, like Augustine (354–430), who had certainly read Plotinus himself, tended to see him through Porphyrian

---

[1] Scholem, *Major Trends in Jewish Mysticism*, p. 203.

eyes. Among the pagans this is true of Macrobius (*fl. c.* 400), author of a commentary on Cicero's *Somnium Scipionis* presenting Neoplatonic doctrine in a form assimilable by the educated upper-class Romans of his day. Augustine's inability to see the full contrast between Plotinus' Hypostases and the Christian trinity is similarly explicable by Porphyry's 'telescoping' of the former. None the less Augustine's knowledge of Plotinus, particularly of his psychology, was far from superficial, examples being his analysis of the respective roles of body and soul in sensation[1] and the famous 'subjectivist' view of time presented in *Confessions* XI. And even later in his life, after his *Retractations* had criticised many of his earlier Platonic doctrines, their influence on him remained profound; unfortunately we cannot analyse this here nor consider the many radical changes which they underwent in the light of Augustine's personal experience.

Two Latin writers stand apart from the main stream, not least in virtue of the superiority of their philosophical training to that of most of their Latin contemporaries. One is the fourth-century theologian Marius Victorinus, whose translation of Plotinus was used by Augustine, and who in his later years became converted to Christianity and produced several treatises attacking the Arian heresy and reflecting the anonymous *Parmenides* commentator's view of the Hypostases; if the commentary is in fact Porphyry's, it represents a side of his work otherwise without later influence. The other author, Boethius (480–524), represents the Alexandrian tradition of later Neoplatonism. This emerges particularly in his logical emphasis, which amply justifies his claim to the title 'First of the Schoolmen', and in his view of the agreement of Plato and Aristotle. To demonstrate this he intended to translate the whole of the two authors' works into Latin, but had translated only Aristotle's logical treatises and Porphyry's *Isagoge*, when he was arrested by the Gothic king Theodoric on a charge of treason. It was while awaiting execution that he composed his most Platonic work, the *Consolation of Philosophy*. It has aroused comment that while Boethius' trinitarian tractates, composed earlier in his life, demonstrate his theological orthodoxy, it was to Platonism that he turned in time of crisis; a possible explanation was suggested above (p. 162). However, the undogmatic and 'undenominational' character of Alexandrian Neoplatonism made it easy for Boethius to avoid most doctrines incompatible with Christianity, though like other Platonists

[1] Cf. Gilson, *Christian Philosophy of St. Augustine*, pp. 56–65, 276–82.

he maintains the soul's pre-existence and the world's everlastingness. As we have noted, the former doctrine was not yet fully unorthodox (cf. pp. 103–4), while even Aquinas was to admit that the latter could be justified from the standpoint of natural reason, though not of revelation. However, Boethius stresses the contrast between the world's temporal everlastingness and God's timeless eternity, producing in the process the standard Scholastic definition of eternity as 'the complete, simultaneous and perfect possession of endless life' (*'interminabilis vitae tota simul et perfecta possessio'*, *Cons*. v. 6). The dependence of his account on the Athenian and Alexandrian masters we have already noted (cf. p. 150).

Eriugena's translation of Dionysius and the twelfth-century and later translations of philosophical treatises from the Arabic marked important stages in the West's recovery of Neoplatonism and ensured that the establishment of Aristotle as *the* philosopher marked no decline in Neoplatonic influence; indeed, it may well have strengthened it. Translations of Aristotle and his Neoplatonic commentators were soon being made from the original Greek. To their influence was added that of the translations produced between 1268 and 1281 by Aquinas' friend William of Moerbeke, Archbishop of Corinth, of Proclus' *Elements of Theology*, his *Parmenides* and *Timaeus* commentaries and his three short religious treatises. These translations enabled Aquinas to detect the spuriousness of the *Liber de Causis* and so to free Aristotle from many of the Neoplatonic accretions he had acquired under the Arabs.[1] Another factor contributing to the same end was the need to reconcile Aristotle with Catholic orthodoxy, which led Aquinas, as it had earlier led the so-called Avicennising Augustinians, such as William of Auvergne (*c*. 1180–1249), to reject emanation in favour of creation out of nothing and to tone down the transcendentalist implications of the Active Intelligence doctrine. But Aquinas was far from abandoning the *De Causis* itself; indeed along with Dionysius (on whose *Divine Names* he composed a commentary), Augustine, Boethius and now Proclus it left so substantial a Neoplatonic imprint on his work that Dean Inge was able to declare him closer to Plotinus than to the real Aristotle.[2] Only one example of the interaction of these forces can here be given, Aquinas' claim that Aristotle's God, by understanding

---

[1] The pseudo-Aristotelian *Theology* had been translated at the end of the twelfth century, but never acquired the same influence among the Latins that it had among the Arabs.

[2] *Philosophy of Plotinus I*, p. 15 n. 1.

himself, must understand everything else (*Met.* XII. 11). In the *Contra Gentiles* (1. 49. 6) he invokes Dionysius' authority (*DN* VII. 2) for this doctrine, but the Arabs had found it stated by 'Aristotle' himself at *Theology* II. 24, a paraphrase of *Enn.* IV. 4. 2. 10–14.

With other Neoplatonic influences on Aquinas, and on the other great Scholastics, we cannot here deal. We can only note two directions in which Neoplatonic influence exerted itself subsequent to, and dependent on him. One is Dante's *Divine Comedy*, whose concluding vision, like much else in the poem, is wholly Neoplatonic. The other is the Rhineland school of mysticism, represented by the Dominican Meister Eckhart (*c.* 1260–1327) and his pupils Tauler (*c.* 1300–61) and Suso (*c.* 1295–1366). Like Dionysius and Plotinus himself Eckhart has often been lifted out of context by mystical enthusiasts, and it has been a contribution of modern research to situate him firmly within the Scholastic tradition. It is none the less noteworthy that the Rhineland mystics' advocacy of certain Neoplatonic themes, notably the negative theology, is more wholehearted than that of Aquinas himself. Hence Eckhart's advocacy of doctrines, notably his distinction between God and the Unknowable Godhead and his admission of an uncreated element in the soul, which went further in Plotinus' direction than the Church could tolerate, and led in 1329 to his posthumous condemnation.

The thought of Nicholas Cusanus (Nicholas of Cusa or Cues, 1401–64) is to a great extent a synthesis of the Dionysian tradition, as presented by the Rhineland school. But it was Proclus' works that formed Cusanus' favourite reading, now including the *Platonic Theology*, of which he had a special translation made; for as a cardinal he was involved in the negotiations for reunion with the East, and so enabled to play his part in the transmission of ancient wisdom to the West. The strength of Proclus' influence on his thought modern studies have confirmed; an important example is the dependence of Cusanus' basic principle that in God opposites coincide on the last part of Proclus' *Parmenides* commentary.[1] The most original features of Cusanus' philosophy stem from the influence of Ockhamite nominalism; for though his denial of the separate existence of universals is not inconsistent with the Neoplatonists' attitude to the Forms (cf. p. 18), Cusanus, rather than follow Medieval Neoplatonism in placing the Forms within the Divine Mind, prefers instead to speak of God

---

[1] Cf. R. Klibansky, *Ein Proklos-Fund und seine Bedeutung*, p. 28, *Plato's Parmenides in the Middle Ages and Renaissance*, pp. 304–6; also above, p. 151 n. 1.

Himself as the one Ideal Standard and hence as the Supreme Universal (*Doct. Ign.* II. 6). In similar vein he abandons the Neoplatonists' compromise between classical and mystical views on the evaluation of finitude and infinity; in Cusanus' thought infinity reigns supreme. Hence his stress, summarised in the title of his most famous treatise, *On Learned Ignorance* (*De Docta Ignorantia*), on the inadequacy of conceptual knowledge; for within the conditioned world knowledge can only be approximate, and between that world and the divine Infinity there can be no common measure. Finally, Cusanus' rejection of the traditional finite universe precludes any absolute distinction between higher and lower regions; hence no grounds remain for regarding the heavens as superior to the earth (*Doct. Ign.* II. 12). Thus Philoponus' revolution is carried through (cf. p. 139) and Neoplatonism takes a decided step beyond its ancient and Medieval limitations into the world of the Renaissance.

In fact Cusanus' ideas were no less in advance of those of most of the Italian Renaissance Neoplatonists, to whom we must now turn. Here again we must confine ourselves to a few general observations on some of the movement's leading figures. Of Renaissance Platonism's cultural and intellectual influence ,which has probably been greater on art, literature and science than on philosophy proper, little can here be said; how dominant that influence was in the artistic field Wind's *Pagan Mysteries in the Renaissance* has shown. A few misconceptions about Renaissance Platonism must, however, be removed. First, and most important, it was *not* a return from Neoplatonism to the 'genuine Plato'; separation between the two was scarcely begun before Leibniz and was not fully achieved until the nineteenth century. Nor does the mathematical emphasis of some Renaissance Platonists, including Cusanus, necessarily imply their abandonment of Neoplatonism; it may mean simply a preference for its Iamblichean-Procline over its Plotinian form (cf. p. 18). Secondly, Renaissance enthusiasm did not confine itself to the least fantastic aspects of Neoplatonism; a taste for the occult was characteristic of the time, not least among many of the pioneers of modern science, Paracelsus and Kepler being notable examples. Thirdly, and linked with the last-mentioned point, until Casaubon's dating of the *Hermetica* in 1614 the Platonic tradition was regarded as a later development of the pristine Egyptian wisdom of Hermes Trismegistus, the supposed original source of the *philosophia perennis*. And finally, and in contrast to literary humanists like Petrarch, Renaissance Neoplatonism was by no means invariably hostile either to Aristotle or to Medieval Scholasticism. As we shall see, the exact relation of Plato and Aristotle remained (as always) a matter of keen debate.

But Florentine Platonism's major contribution was, of course, its making available to the West of those ancient philosophers whose works had been previously known only indirectly. The inspiration of Gemistus Pletho bore fruit, as we have seen (p. 163), in Marsilio Ficino's (1433–99) Platonic Academy and his editions and translations, notably of Hermes Trismegistus (1463), Plato (1464–9) and (with commentary) of Plotinus (1484–92). Ficino's own major work, the *Platonic Theology on the Immortality of the Soul* appeared in 1474, while his commentary on the *Symposium* (1469) was a major source, along with Giordano Bruno's *Eroici Furori*, of Renaissance, especially Elizabethan, ideas on love. Ficino's dominant aim, the demonstration of the harmony between the Platonic and Chaldaean traditions and Christianity, was carried a stage further by his younger contemporary, Giovanni Pico della Mirandola (1463–94), who added Jewish Cabalism to the list of authorities. From these varied sources Pico produced a list of 900 theses (including 55 Platonic Conclusions drawn from Proclus), whose harmony he proposed to demonstrate in public debate. However, several of the theses were condemned by the Church, and Pico's premature death put an end to the project. Pico's most famous work, his *Oration on the Dignity of Man*, an exposition of the Neoplatonic view, fundamental to Renaissance humanism, of man as microcosm, was to have formed the prologue to his defence of his ideas.

No more than the ancient Neoplatonists were their Renaissance successors mere carbon copies either of their ancient sources or of one another. An example of their transformation of the ancients' ideas is their tacit substitution, to accord with Christian doctrine, of the triad Procession-Rapture-Reversion for the traditional Neoplatonic scheme (cf. pp. 132–3). It was this triad which they saw expressed in the traditional iconography of the three Graces, an interpretation which explains the group's popularity in Renaissance art.[1] The differences between Ficino and Pico were no less important. First, there is the more mystical tone of Pico's thought; for whereas Ficino, who stood closer to the literary humanist tradition, regarded contemplation as the fulfilment of man's natural powers, Pico's aim was mystical self-extinction. Secondly, Ficino, as a priest, showed more concern for theological orthodoxy than Pico, a difference visible in their respective

[1] Cf. Wind op. cit., pp. 36 ff.

attitudes to the occult; for though Pico was more critical of astrology
than Ficino, the latter treated magic simply as a means of psycho-
therapy, whereas Pico, in accordance with his Cabalistic leanings,
extended its application into the religious sphere. Their major philosophical dispute concerned the perennial question whether Aristotle
agreed with Plato, Ficino taking the negative, Pico the affirmative side
in his treatise *On Being and Unity*. The key to Pico's solution is his
Thomistic interpretation of 'Being', which enables him to argue that
the Aristotelian view of God as the Supreme Being means the same as
Plato's location of the One beyond Being, and hence that both philosophers make Unity and Being coextensive; a necessary corollary was
Pico's abandonment of the Neoplatonic interpretation of the *Parmenides*. The debate had been initiated by a treatise of Pletho arguing
Aristotle's inferiority, a view repeated during the next century by
Francesco Patrizzi (1529–97), representative of the occult scientific
trends within Renaissance Neoplatonism and editor and translator of
ancient texts; among his editions was one of the Latin version of the
pseudo-Aristotelian *Theology*, whose authenticity Patrizzi accepted
and which, not surprisingly, he preferred to Aristotle's genuine
works.

While Pico and Patrizzi might differ on Aristotle, their philosophies
incurred the common fate of condemnation by the Church. Yet neither
was intentionally unorthodox, and in this they differed from the most
notorious of the Renaissance Platonists, Giordano Bruno (1548–1600),
who, not content with 'telescoping' Plotinus' three Hypostases into
one another, took the further step, which all ancient Neoplatonists
had resisted, of identifying the infinity of Matter with that of the One.
Of particular interest are Bruno's arguments, in the fourth chapter of
his *Cause, Principle and Unity*, for the identification of Plotinus' sensible matter with his intelligible matter. More generally, Bruno's
thought marks a more rigorous application of Cusanus' principle of
the coincidence of opposites (and particularly of potentiality and
actuality) in God than Cusanus himself had dared. And it was this,
along with his advocacy of an avowedly anti-Christian Hermetic
religion, that brought him to the stake.

Scholastic (including Neoplatonic) ideas make up a large part of the
philosophy of Descartes; they are influential, for example, on his
theology, but most important of all is the concept of consciousness on
which his psychology rests, and which, though alien to Classical Greek
thought, constitutes one of Descartes' many borrowings from the

Augustinian tradition, and thereby from Neoplatonism. But on two crucial points he breaks with the Neoplatonic tradition. One is his famous dichotomy between mind and matter, which is much sharper than that of any ancient philosopher and wholly alien to Aristotelianism (where the soul is the form of the body) and Neoplatonism (where the body is an image of the soul). It is admittedly easier to bewail the unfortunate results of this divorce than to show how it should be rectified; and certainly it was necessary if science was to progress. The same cannot be said of Descartes' other innovation, his simplistic identification of mental activity with consciousness, which led him to ignore all the unconscious psychological processes to which Plotinus had drawn attention (cf. p. 5). It was one of the aims of Platonically-inclined thinkers during the next two centuries to correct this omission, prominent examples being Leibniz and the Cambridge Platonists (whereas Locke was to side with Descartes).[1]

With Neoplatonism's post-Cartesian influence we must deal even more briefly. Its most notable feature is the contrast between the situation in Britain and that on the Continent. In the former its philosophical influence has largely been confined to second- or third-rank figures, such as the Cambridge Platonists, led by Henry More (1614–87) and Ralph Cudworth (1617–88), in the seventeenth century, and Coleridge in the nineteenth, though mention must also be made of Berkeley's curious late work *Siris*, which passes from a meditation on the occult medicinal properties of tar-water to a mystical vision of the divine unity. By contrast, post-Cartesian Continental thought has retained a substantial Neoplatonic component. Thus in the seventeenth century Spinoza's monism and Leibniz' monadism represent different developments of a common Neoplatonic substratum, while in the nineteenth century Schelling's Plotinian-influenced thought counterpoints Hegel's more Procline system. A few of the more important correspondences with ancient Neoplatonism have been touched on in our study (cf. pp. 70, 130–1). The common feature of the nineteenth-century German Idealists is their application of an in many ways Neoplatonic scheme to the world's *historical* evolution, a process carried yet further during the present century by Henri Bergson. Bergson's thought can be viewed as an attempt to restate Plotinus' philosophy of Soul (significantly ignoring his eternal Intelligible world) in terms of modern scientific ideas, and it was Plotinus' fourth Ennead, on which Bergson lectured during 1897–8 at the Collège de France, that supplied him

[1] Cf. L. L. Whyte, *The Unconscious Before Freud*, pp. 86 ff.

with some of his most fruitful ideas, for instance his distinction, in *Matière et Mémoire*, between conscious and habitual memory (cf. pp. 80–1).

In England, on the other hand, Neoplatonism's main influence has been in the field of literature, especially during the Elizabethan period and among the Romantics, who felt the school's appeal no less than their German contemporaries. The Platonic tradition's influence on William Blake has recently been illuminated by Kathleen Raine; a good example is his painting *The Sea of Time and Space*, based on Porphyry's *De Antro Nympharum* (reproduced as frontispiece).[1] As an example of the Elizabethans' use of Neoplatonic texts we may quote Spenser's adaptation of the opening of Plotinus' treatise I. 6 on Beauty:

> How vainely then doe ydle wits inuent,
>> That beautie is nought else, but mixture made
>> Of colours faire, and goodly temp'rament
>> Of pure complexions, that shall quickly fade
>> And passe away, like to a sommers shade;
>> Or that it is but comely composition
>> Of parts well measurd, with meet disposition!
>> ... can proportion of the outward part,
>> Moue such affection in the inward mynd,
>> That it can rob both sense and reason blynd[2]
>
> *(Fowre hymns: of Beautie)*

In the present century Neoplatonic influence is particularly strong on Yeats, ranging from such isolated phrases as 'honey of generation', an echo of the *De Antro Nympharum*,[2] to his paraphrase of the Delphic Oracle on Plotinus (1931).

The case of Yeats shows that Neoplatonism's appeal has by no means been exhausted in modern times. Modern scholarly examination of the movement, on the other hand, has been slow compared with that of most branches of the Classics; indeed until very recent years it had attracted relatively few first-class scholars. The reasons for this neglect are three. First, the Neoplatonists' style was not such as to attract those trained in philology and literature, while their difficulty obscured (and

---

[1] Discussed by Raine, *Blake and Tradition*, ch. 3, pp. 69–98.

[2] *Among School Children* (1928); cf. Porphyry *AN* chs. 16–17; I owe these parallels to my friend and former pupil, Mr. David Esterly, whose unpublished thesis shows the vast improvement in Yeats' previously very superficial knowledge of Plotinus that resulted from his reading of MacKenna's translation.

still tends to obscure) their intellectual merits. Secondly, they lay out-side the chronological limits within which a Classical writer could claim respectability, while they came too early to fall within the pro-vince of the Medievalist. Thirdly, when in the nineteenth century Neo-platonism was finally distinguished from Plato's own teaching, the school was not seen as a natural and interesting development of Classical Greek thought, but as a regrettable deviation therefrom; nor outside Romantic and Hegelian circles were the movement's basic ideas attractive to the nineteenth- and early twentieth-century philoso-phical climate. Hence the preponderance among the Neoplatonists' early nineteenth-century editors and translators of those whose interest was devotional rather than scholarly, notably Creuzer in Germany, Cousin in France, and in England the remarkable figure of Thomas Taylor (1758–1835), whose translations of many later Neo-platonic texts are still the only ones available. Though stylistically even less attractive than their Greek originals, these were remarkably accurate for their time and made Plato and many Neoplatonic writings available to the English Romantics, of whom only Coleridge and Shelley could read them in the original Greek. But the general level of nineteenth-century Neoplatonic scholarship was unsatisfactory; though editions were produced of most Neoplatonic texts (with the important exception of Proclus' *Platonic Theology*), most of the work has had, or will have, to be re-done. Perhaps the most satisfactory were the Ber-lin editions of the Aristotle commentators, which did not, however, lead to detailed study of the commentators themselves. General understanding of the Neoplatonists was advanced by the pioneer studies of Simon (1845) and Vacherot (1846), though the error of their basic perspective, summarised in the phrase 'School of Alexandria', has been noted (cf. pp. 11–12). The tendency of these scholars to see Neoplatonism simply as Oriental mysticism was contested in Zeller's *History of Greek Philosophy* and in Whittaker's English study, first published in 1901, but the school's internal development was not fully clarified until 1910, with Praechter's *Richtungen und Schulen im Neu-platonismus*. Praechter's article was particularly important in bringing out Iamblichus' influence, while Bidez' *Vie de Porphyre* (1913) laid the ground-work for subsequent study of Porphyry. The most notable contribution to later Neoplatonic studies to appear in the present century was, however, Dodds' edition of Proclus' *Elements*, published in 1936. Dodds' 1928 article on the Neoplatonic interpretation of the *Parmenides* had similarly served to illuminate Plotinus' background, while other notable contributions in this field included W. Theiler's *Vorbereitung des Neuplatonismus* (1930), R. E. Witt's book on Albinus (1937) and E. A. Leemans' (1937) edition of Numenius' fragments.

The results of this research into Plotinus' background were summarised in A. H. Armstrong's *Architecture of the Intelligible Universe in the Philosophy of Plotinus* (1940). And it was Plotinus himself who, not surprisingly, attracted most interwar attention. In England MacKenna's translation (1917–30) and Inge's Gifford Lectures (1917–18) proved effective publicists, while translations were made into French by E. Bréhier (1924–38) and German by R. Harder (1930–7). The latter was, and remains, the most accurate version yet produced; by contrast, the value of Bréhier's Budé edition lay rather in his admirable introductions to the various treatises than in his translation or his text, which exemplified the rule, noted by Henry and Schwyzer, that each edition of the *Enneads* produced during the nineteenth and the first half of the twentieth century marked a deterioration by comparison with its predecessors.[1] This situation began to be rectified only in 1951, with the first volume of Henry and Schwyzer's critical edition, which for the first time took account of the whole manuscript tradition. Unfortunately this has not yet reached Ennead VI, but in the the meantime a complete text, more adventurous than Henry and Schwyzer's, but taking account of their work, both published and unpublished, has appeared in Theiler and Beutler's revision of Harder's translation, to which notes have been added. Armstrong's Loeb edition has similarly taken Henry and Schwyzer as its basis. Understanding of Plotinus has been further advanced by numerous general and specialised studies—relatively few of them, alas, available in English—and a lexicon of his vocabulary should soon appear, but lack of a philosophical commentary still hinders detailed investigation.

Later Neoplatonism has only much more recently begun to be considered intellectually respectable, but the last few years have seen a flood of editions and studies of many of its basic texts, the most recent examples being Hadot's important *Porphyre et Victorinus* and the first volume of Saffrey and Westerink's Budé *Platonic Theology*, which should at last secure for this basic work the study it deserves. Iamblichus has so far received much less attention than Porphyry or Proclus, but his *De Mysteriis* has appeared in the Budé series, and an edition of his fragments is in preparation, as are reliable editions of the *Chaldaean Oracles* and Damascius' *De Principiis*. In general, Anglo-

---

[1] *Plotini Enneades* I., p. xxix.

Saxon scholars have been slower to turn to the Neoplatonists than their Continental colleagues, though Dodds, Armstrong, A. C. Lloyd, J. M. Rist and others form notable exceptions. By contrast English study of the school's later influence has been far from negligible, and the work of the Warburg Institute and those associated with it deserves special mention.

That Neoplatonism's cultural influence entitles it to very serious study can hardly be contested. Opinions may be more divided as to whether it has anything to say to us today. In considering this we may first of all observe that, like other movements, Neoplatonism contains good and bad; it would obviously be silly to place Hierocles or Olympiodorus on a level with Plotinus, or to claim that everything even in Plotinus has permanent value. If we confine ourselves to the school's main trends, its religious and experiential side seems to have more to offer than its deductive metaphysics. It may be rash in the light of past experience to conclude with certainty that such metaphysics has been buried for good, but all present appearances point in that direction. However, this by no means destroys Neoplatonism's philosophical importance, since, as should be clear from our study, much of the school's best and most original philosophising comes in its *analyses* of theological and psychological concepts and of conscious experience. Plotinus, of course, provides the most conspicuous examples (cf. p. 44), but we should not forget the numerous points, such as the implications of the One's role as the Absolute, on which his followers clarified his ideas. And on its empirical side the school constitutes the leading Western representative of the project mooted in modern times by William James[1] and others, of constructing a theology on the basis of religious experience. Hence it should have much to teach those who now essay a similar task. No less important are the religious divergences between its members, notably between Plotinus and Iamblichus, whom we have seen to stand for opposing ways, both perpetually attractive, of solving the problem of divine immanence versus transcendence.

The school's specific contemporary relevance would seem to be twofold. Philosophically it offers an antidote to the view, widespread among modern Anglo-Saxon philosophers, that philosophy must accord with the dictates of 'common sense'. And here Neoplatonism's empirical basis assumes especial importance; for it shows that the paradoxicality of its conclusions cannot be avoided simply by rejecting

[1] *Varieties of Religious Experience*, pp. 436–8.

its metaphysics as nonsensical, since paradoxicality is inherent in the nature of conscious experience itself, whatever conclusions may be built on it. This is, of course, most evident on the deeper, mystical levels but it is also true to a lesser extent of everyday conscious experience; hence the failure of recent attempts to deal with consciousness in terms of 'ordinary language'.

The second point, Neoplatonism's relevance to the contemporary religious scene, will be clear from the briefest perusal of Plotinus' treatise *Against the Gnostics*. It is true that not all the Neoplatonists' religious attitudes can still be accepted; in particular, even at their best they give too little importance to the body and the material world. Yet, as Hadot rightly observes, our reaction to such excesses must be a *purification* of the spiritual life, not the wholesale abolition of an important part of human experience.[1] That religious experience must be given its due the contemporary mystical revival makes clear; yet in their turn our present-day prophets, notably those of the psychedelic cults, too often ignore the necessity to the religious life of discrimination and self-discipline, and in this differ from the best mystics of all traditions, including the Orientals they profess to follow. The dilemma of reason's place in the spiritual life is, as we have seen, an acute and ultimately an insoluble one; too rigid a conceptual system leads to ossification, too little rationality to chaos, both in theology and in the individual mind. This dilemma was posed with particular force by the Neoplatonists' historical situation; and, whatever criticisms may be made on individual points, their basic reaction was unquestionably a sound one, and a sign of the general sanity and Hellenic moderation of their approach. Their successes and failures have therefore much to teach us in our own spiritual search; for it is on our own success or failure in attaining a due balance that the future of our civilisation depends.

[1] *Plotin*, p. 159.

Abbreviations

CH Corpus Hermeticum
CMAG Catalogue des manuscrits al-
 chimiques grecques
CQ Classical Quarterly
Or Ch=Oracula Chaldaica
 (*Kr.* = ed. Kroll)
PG Patrologia Graeca, ed. Migne
RE Pauly's Realencyclopädie der
 classischen Altertumswissenschaft
Ep. Epistle
Hist. History
Or. Oration
T. testimonium
fr. fragment
prop. proposition

ALBINUS
 Epit. Epitome
 Isag. Isagoge

ALEXANDER OF APHRODISIAS
 De An. De Anima
 Mant. De Anima Mantissa
 Met. In Aristotelis Metaphysica
 Quaest. Quaestiones

AMMONIUS, son of Hermeias, *see*
 ARISTOTLE
Anon. Prol. Anonymous
 Prolegomena to Platonic Philosophy

AQUINAS
 Met. In Aristotelis Metaphysica
 ST Summa Theologiae

ARISTOTLE
 Cat. Categories
 De An. De Anima
 De C. De Caelo
 De Int. De Interpretatione
 De Phil. De Philosophia

EN Ethica Nicomachea
Met. Metaphysics
Phys. Physics

ARNOBIUS
 Adv. Nat. Adversus Nationes

ASCLEPIUS
 In Nic. Arithm. In Nicomachi
 Arithmeticam Introductionem
 In Met. In Aristotelis Metaphy-
 sica

AUGUSTINE
 C. Acad. Contra Academicos
 CD De Civitate Dei
 Conf. Confessions

BOETHIUS
 Cons. Consolation of Philosophy

CHALCIDIUS
 In Tim. In Platonis Timaeum

CICERO
 Ac. Post. Academica Posteriora
 Ac. Pr. Academica Priora (Lu-
 cullus)
 ND De Natura Deorum
 Tusc. Tusculan Disputations

CLEMENT OF ALEXANDRIA
 (Clem. Alex.)
 Strom. Stromateis

DAMASCIUS
 De Princ. De Principiis (Dubi-
 tationes et Solutiones in Platonis
 Parmenidem)
 V.Is. Vita Isidori

DAVID
 In Isag. In Porphyrii Isagogen

DIONYSIUS AREOPAGITA
 DN De Divinis Nominibus

ELIAS see ARISTOTLE and DAVID

ERIUGENA, JOANNES SCOTUS
 Div. Nat. De Divisione Naturae

EUNAPIUS
 VS Vitae Sophistarum

EUSEBIUS
 DE Demonstratio Evangelica
 EH Ecclesiastical History
 PE Praeparatio Evangelica

HERMEIAS
 In Phdr. In Platonis Phaedrum

HIEROCLES
 De Prov. De Providentia
 In Carm Aur. In Carmen Aur-
 eum

IAMBLICHUS
 De An. De Anima
 Myst. De Mysteriis

MACARIUS MAGNES
 Apocr. Apocriticus

MACROBIUS
 In Somn. Sc. In Ciceronis Somnium Scipionis

MARINUS
 V.Pr. Vita Procli

NEMESIUS OF EMESA
 Nat. Hom. De Natura Hominis

NICHOLAS CUSANUS
 Doct. Ign. De Docta Ignorantia

OLYMPIODORUS
 In Alc. In Platonis Primum
 Alcibiadem
 In Phd. In Platonis Phaedonem

ORIGEN
 C. Cels. Contra Celsum
 De Princ. De Principiis

PHILO OF ALEXANDRIA
 Aet. M. De Aeternitate Mundi
 Op. M. De Opificio Mundi

PHILOPONUS, JOANNES see also
 ARISTOTLE
 Aet. M. De Aeternitate Mundi

PHOTIUS
 Bibl. Bibliotheca

PLATO
 Alc. Alcibiades I
 Crat. Cratylus

Ep. Epistle
Epin. Epinomis
Parm. Parmenides
Phd. Phaedo
Phdr. Phaedrus
Phil. Philebus
Rep. Republic
Soph. Sophist
Symp. Symposium
Theaet. Theaetetus
Tim. Timaeus

PLOTINUS
 Enn. Enneads

PLUTARCH OF CHAERONEA
 De Lib. De Libidine et Aegri-
 tudine
 Procr. An. De Procreatione Animae

PORPHYRY
 Ad Marc. Ad Marcellam
 AN De Antro Nympharum
 C. Chr. Contra Christianos
 Ep. Letter to Anebo
 Hist. Phil. History of Philosophy
 Isag. Isagoge
 Sent. Sentences
 V.Pl. Vita Plotini

PROCLUS
 Dec. Dub. Decem Dubitationes
 circa Providentiam
 De Prov. De Providentia et Fato
 ET Elements of Theology
 In Alc. In Platonis Primum Alci-
 biadem
 In Crat. In Platonis Cratylum
 In Parm. In Platonis Parmeni-
 dem
 In Remp. In Platonis Rempubli-
 cam
 In Tim. In Platonis Timaeum
 Mal. Subs. De Malorum Subsis-
 tentia
 Ph. Ch. Eclogae de Philosophia
 Chaldaica
 PT Platonic Theology

SALLUSTIUS
 DM De Dis et Mundo

SEXTUS EMPIRICUS
   Math.   *Adversus Mathematicos*
   PH   *Pyrrhoneae Hypotyposes*
SIMPLICIUS *see* also ARISTOTLE
   In Ench.   *In Epicteti Enchiridion*

STOBAEUS
   Ecl.   *Eclogae*
SYRIANUS
   In Met.   *In Aristotelis Metaphysica*

Citations of Ancient Sources

Dates and places of publication are given, for the most part, only of editions not mentioned in the Bibliography.

GREEK COMMENTATORS ON ARISTOTLE: cited by pages and lines of the Berlin edition (*Commentaria in Aristotelem Graeca*, 1882–1907).

CHRISTIAN FATHERS: unless otherwise stated, cited by volumes and pages of Migne's *Patrologia*.

ALEXANDER OF APHRODISIAS, *De Anima* and other works preserved in Greek: cited by pages and lines of the Berlin *Supplementum Aristotelicum*.

ALBINUS, *Epitome*: chapter subdivisions follow Louis' edition.

NUMENIUS: numbering of fragments and testimonia follows Leemans; source references are added for the most important of them.

PLOTINUS, and PORPHYRY'S *Vita Plotini*: cited by traditional chapters and Bréhier's lines, reproduced by Henry and Schwyzer. Numbers in square brackets are those of treatises according to Porphyry's chronological order.

PORPHYRY, *Sentences*: numbering follows Mommert's Teubner edition (Leipzig 1907).

Letter to Anebo: cited by Sodano's paragraphs and subdivisions. Source references are generally added.

Contra Christianos: numbering of fragments follows Harnack.

Miscellaneous Inquiries (Symmikta Zētēmata): see NEMESIUS.

CHALDAEAN ORACLES: cited by pages of Kroll's edition (Breslau 1894, repr. Hildesheim 1962).

IAMBLICHUS, *De Mysteriis*: cited by pages and lines of Parthey's edition (Berlin 1857), reproduced in des Places' Budé edition.

De Anima: see STOBAEUS.

SALLUSTIUS, *De Dis et Mundo*: chapter subdivisions follow Rochefort's Budé edition.

PROCLUS, *Elements of Theology*: citations of propositions follow traditional numbering. References have sometimes been added to Dodds' pages and lines.

Platonic Theology, Book I: page and line references to Saffrey and Westerink's Budé edition; Books II–VI: page references to Portus' edition (Hamburg 1618, repr. Frankfurt 1960).

Decem Dubitationes circa Providentiam, De Providentia et Fato, De Malorum Subsistentia: cited by paragraphs and Cousin's pages, reproduced in Boese's edition.

In Parmenidem: cited by pages and lines of Cousin's edition (Paris 1864, repr. Hildesheim 1961), except for last part of Book VII, where references are to Klibansky, Labowsky and Anscombe's edition of Moerbeke's Latin version.

PROCLUS and OLYMPIODORUS, *In Alcibiadem:* cited by Creuzer's pages and lines, reproduced in Westerink's editions (Pr. Amsterdam 1954, Ol. ibid. 1956).

PROCLUS, *In Timaeum, In Rempublicam, In Cratylum;* OLYMPIODORUS, *In Phaedonem;* PHILOPONUS, *De Aeternitate Mundi:* cited by pages and lines of the Teubner editions.

HIEROCLES, *De Providentia:* see PHOTIUS.

HERMEIAS, *In Phaedrum:* cited by pages and lines of Couvreur's edition (Paris 1901).

DAMASCIUS, *De Principiis (Dubitationes et Solutiones in Platonis Parmenidem)* cited by pages and lines of Ruelle's edition (Paris 1889, repr. Amsterdam 1966).

Vita Isidori: numbering of extracts and fragments follows Zintzen's edition.

NEMESIUS, *De Natura Hominis:* cited by pages of the 1565 Antwerp edition and by those of Matthaei (Halle 1810). *Patrologia* references have been frequently added.

STOBAEUS, *Eclogae:* cited by pages and lines of Wachsmuth and Hense's edition (Berlin 1884–1923).

PHOTIUS, *Bibliotheca:* cited by pages and lines of Bekker's edition (Berlin 1825).

In all other cases references are to traditional pages or subdivisions, except where a particular edition is named.

Bibliography

I. GENERAL

Modern editions of Neoplatonic texts are listed in the bibliography to the *Cambridge History of Later Greek and Early Medieval Philosophy* (ed. A. H. Armstrong, Cambridge 1967). The list below is largely confined to annotated editions and translations; cf. also my note on 'Citations of Ancient Sources' (pp. 182–3). Many late Neoplatonic texts are still untranslated; in other cases the translations of Thomas Taylor, though cumbersome and often hard to procure, may be used in the absence of anything better. For a complete list of the latter see the bibliography to Kathleen Raine and G. M. Harper (ed.), *Thomas Taylor, the Platonist: Selected Writings*, pp. 523–33. The Loeb series (text with English translation) includes, among other authors: Plotinus (3 volumes published out of 6, covering *Enn.* I–III), Philo of Alexandria, Plutarch of Chaeronea, Eunapius' *Lives of the Sophists*, the Emperor Julian, Augustine's *Confessions, City of God* and *Letters*, and Boethius' theological tractates and *Consolation*. The Budé series (introduction, text and French translation) includes Plotinus, the *Hermetica*, Iamblichus' *De Mysteriis*, Julian and Sallustius. Budé editions are also in progress of Proclus' *Platonic Theology* (vol. 1=Book 1 so far published), Damascius' *De Principiis*, and the *Chaldaean Oracles*. For a selection of important passages in the original Greek see C. J. de Vogel, *Greek Philosophy*: vol. III, *the Hellenistic-Roman Period* (Leiden 1959). For a collection of passages in translation (mostly from Plotinus) see E. R. Dodds, *Select Passages Illustrating Neoplatonism* (London 1923).

The most complete accounts of our factual information about individual Neoplatonists are generally those (in German) in Pauly's *Realencyclopädie der Classischen Altertumswissenschaft*; the articles of H.-R. Schwyzer (on Plotinus), R. Beutler (on Numenius, Porphyry, Plutarch of Athens, Proclus and Olympiodorus) and K. Praechter (on Syrianus, Hierocles, Simplicius and others) deserve special mention.

The only general survey of Neoplatonism in English by a single author is T. Whittaker's *The Neoplatonists* (4th ed. 1928, repr.

Hildesheim 1961). A more recent survey, by several hands, is provided in the *Cambridge History of Later Greek and Early Medieval Philosophy*, on which cf. also the bibliographies to our several chapters below. Cf. also the account of J. Trouillard in *Histoire de la philosophie I: orient, antiquité, moyen âge*, pp. 886–935 (*Encyclopédie de la Pleiade*, Paris 1969). The accounts in Ueberweg's *Die Philosophie des Altertums*, revised by K. Praechter (13th ed., Basel 1953), and Zeller's *Die Philosophie der Griechen* (vol. III, 2, 5th ed., Leipzig 1923, repr. Hildesheim 1963) are still of considerable use. For good short surveys cf. A. H. Armstrong, *An Introduction to Ancient Philosophy* (repr., with critical introduction, London 1968) and E. Bréhier, *History of Ancient Philosophy: the Hellenistic and Roman Age* (English trans., Chicago 1965).

On Neoplatonism's historical and social background cf. the relevant volumes of the *Cambridge Ancient History* and, for the later period, A. H. M. Jones' monumental *Later Roman Empire* (3 vols., Oxford 1964) and his shorter *Decline of the Ancient World* (London 1966). Michael Grant's *The Climax of Rome* (London 1968) is an attractive popular survey of late second- and early third-century civilisation, with a chapter on Marcus Aurelius and Plotinus. On the religious background cf. J. Ferguson, *The Religions of the Roman Empire* (London 1970); M. P. Nilsson, *Geschichte der Griechischen Religion*, zweiter band (Munich 1961) and his shorter *Greek Piety* (Oxford 1948); E. R. Dodds, *Pagan and Christian in an Age of Anxiety* (Cambridge 1965); A.-J. Festugière, *La Révélation d'Hermès Trismégiste* (4 vols., Paris 1944–54): vol. I, *L'Astrologie et les sciences Occultes*, vol. II, *Le Dieu cosmique*, vol. III, *Les Doctrines de l'âme*, vol. IV, *Le Dieu inconnu et la Gnose*; and the various works of F. Cumont, especially his *Lux Perpetua* (Paris 1949), dealing with ideas of the soul.

The best introduction to Gnosticism is H. Jonas, *The Gnostic Religion* (2nd ed., Boston 1963, including chapters comparing the Gnostic and Neoplatonic world-views); translations of some important Gnostic texts will be found in R. M. Grant's *Gnosticism: an Anthology* (London 1961). The identity of Plotinus' Gnostics is discussed by H.-Ch. Puech, 'Plotin et les Gnostiques', *Entretiens Hardt V*, pp. 161–90. Cf. also Zandee's monograph mentioned p. 13 n. 1.

2. NEOPLATONISM'S PHILOSOPHICAL SOURCES

The best discussions of Plotinus' debt to earlier thought are the papers in *Entretiens Hardt V*, 'Les Sources de Plotin' (Vandoeuvres-Geneva 1960), by E. R. Dodds, W. Theiler, P. Hadot, H.-Ch. Puech, H. Dörrie, V. Cilento, R. Harder, H.-R. Schwyzer, A. H. Armstrong and P. Henry. Their conclusions are summarised in Henry's introduction (pp. xxxv–lxiv) to the third and later editions of MacKenna's translation of the *Enneads*. A recent discussion is that of J. M. Rist, *Plotinus: the Road to Reality*, ch. 13, pp. 169–87 (who argues, however, in my view mistakenly, that Plotinus was aware of differing from Plato). On Neoplatonic interpretations of the *Parmenides*, cf. E. R. Dodds, 'The *Parmenides* of Plato and the Origin of the Neoplatonic One', *CQ* 22 (1928) 129–42, and pp. lxxv–lxxxix of Saffrey and Westerink's introduction to Book I of Proclus' *Platonic Theology*.

Other useful works include W. Theiler, *Die Vorbereitung des Neuplatonismus* (Berlin 1930, repr. Berlin/Zurich 1964); R. E. Witt, 'Plotinus and Posidonius', *CQ* 24 (1930) 198–207, and 'The Plotinian Logos and its Stoic Basis', *CQ* 25 (1931) 103–11; P. Merlan, *From Platonism to Neoplatonism* (2nd ed., The Hague 1960), *Monopsychism, Mysticism, Metaconsciousness: Problems of the Soul in the Neo-Aristotelian and Neoplatonic Tradition* (The Hague 1963). Cf. also Merlan's survey in the first part (pp. 13–132) of the *Cambridge History of Later Greek and Early Medieval Philosophy*, especially chs. 4–6, dealing respectively with Middle Platonism, Neopythagoreanism and the later Peripatetics.

The best introduction to Middle Platonism is R. E. Witt, *Albinus and the History of Middle Platonism* (Cambridge 1937). For a view of Albinus as a more coherent thinker cf. J. H. Loenen, 'Albinus' metaphysics: an attempt at rehabilitation', *Mnemosyne* Series IV, vol. IX (1956) 296–319, vol. X (1957) 35–56. Albinus' *Epitome* is edited, with French translation, by P. Louis (Paris 1945). A new general survey of Middle Platonism, including Philo of Alexandria, Alexandrian Christian Platonism and the *Chaldaean Oracles*, is being prepared by J. M. Dillon for the present Classical Life and Letters series; discussions of important aspects of the movement will be found in the third and fourth volumes of Festugière's *La Révélation d'Hermès Trismégiste*.

On Alexander of Aphrodisias cf. P. Moraux, *Alexandre d'Aphrodise, exégète de la noétique d'Aristote* (Paris 1942); P. Thillet, 'Un Traité inconnu d'Alexandre d'Aphrodise sur la providence dans une version arabe inédite,' *Actes du premier congrès international de philosophie mediévale: L'Homme et son destin* (Louvain 1960) 313–24; F. P. Hager, 'Die Aristotelesinterpretation des Alexander von Aphrodisias und die Aristoteleskritik Plotins bezüglich der Lehre vom Geist', *Archiv für Geschichte der Philosophie* 46 (1964) 174–87.

Numenius' fragments are collected and edited by E. A. Leemans, 'Studie over den Wijsgeer Numenius van Apamea met Uitgave der Fragmenten', *Mém. de l'acad. royale de Belgique, classe des lettres*, XXXVII, 2 (Brussels 1937). The best discussion of his thought is that of E. R. Dodds, 'Numenius and Ammonius', *Entretiens Hardt V*, pp. 3–61. Among earlier studies cf. H.-Ch. Puech, 'Numénius d'Apamée et les théologies orientales au second siècle', *Mélanges Bidez* (*Ann. de l'Institut de Philologie et d'Histoire orientales et slaves*, Brussels 1934) 745–78; and R. Beutler, *RE* article, 'Numenios', supp.-Band VII (1940) cols. 664–78.

3. PLOTINUS

Porphyry's biography is printed in all modern editions and translations of the *Enneads*; cf. especially the notes to R. Harder's edition (*Plotins Schriften V^c*), completed after Harder's death by W. Marg (Hamburg 1958). Recent English accounts of Plotinus' life are those of A. H. Armstrong, *Cambridge History*, chs. 12–13, pp. 195–221, and J. M. Rist, *Plotinus: the Road to Reality*, ch. 2, pp. 2–20.

The *Enneads*: Text, ed. P. Henry and H.-R. Schwyzer; vol. I (*Enn.* I–III) Paris-Brussels 1951; vol. II (*Enn.* IV–V) 1959; smaller, revised edition in the Oxford Classical Texts series, vol. I, 1964. Text, translation and notes: French, E. Bréhier (Budé series), 7 vols., Paris 1924–38 (cf. above p. 176); German (with extensive notes), R. Harder, 5 vols. in 11 (vols. II–V completed by W. Theiler and R. Beutler), Hamburg 1956–67; English, A. H. Armstrong (Loeb Classical Library), 3 vols. (*Enn.* I–III) so far appeared (London and Harvard 1966–). The treatise III. 7 on Time and Eternity has recently been edited, with German translation, introduction and commentary by W. Beierwaltes, *Plotin über Ewigkeit und Zeit* (Frankfurt 1967).

The only complete English translation of the *Enneads* is that of Stephen MacKenna (4th, revised, ed., London 1969), a more literary version than Armstrong's, but misleading on many points of detail. Cf. also the excellent Italian translation of V. Cilento (3 vols. in 4), to which is appended a very full bibliography of earlier works on Plotinus by B. Marien (Bari 1947–9), and the explanatory material (especially the parallel passages) assembled in M. N. Bouillet's nineteenth-century French version (3 vols., Paris 1857–61). A. H. Armstrong's *Plotinus* (Ethical and Religious Classics of East and West, London 1953) is a useful volume of select passages in translation. For translations of selected treatises cf. Grace Turnbull, *The Essence of Plotinus* (abridged treatises in a revision of MacKenna, New York 1948); Joseph Katz, *The Philosophy of Plotinus* (New York 1950); Elmer O'Brien, *The Essential Plotinus* (Mentor Books, New York 1964). On the style of the *Enneads* cf. Bréhier's introduction to his Budé edition, vol. 1 pp. xiv–xxxix, and Schwyzer, *RE* article, 'Plotinos', cols. 512–30. On Plotinus' images cf. Bréhier's *Images plotiniennes, images bergsoniennes*, repr. in his posthumously published *Etudes de philosophie antique* (Paris 1955) pp. 292–307; R. Ferwerda, *La Signification des images et des métaphores dans la pensée de Plotin* (Groningen 1965).

The best introduction to Plotinus in English is that of A. H. Armstrong, *Cambridge History of Later Greek and Early Medieval Philosophy*, part III, pp. 195–268; cf. also the introduction to his Loeb edition, vol. 1 pp. vii–xxxiii. Other good introductory surveys include E. Bréhier, *The Philosophy of Plotinus* (English trans., Chicago 1958); M. de Gandillac, *La Sagesse de Plotin* (2nd ed., Paris 1966); P. Hadot, *Plotin, ou la simplicité du regard* (Paris 1963); N. Baladi, *La Pensée de Plotin* (Paris 1970). Cf. also W. R. Inge, *The Philosophy of Plotinus* (2 vols., 3rd ed., London 1929, repr. 1948); A. H. Armstrong, *The Architecture of the Intelligible Universe in the Philosophy of Plotinus* (Cambridge 1940, repr. Amsterdam 1967); J. M. Rist, *Plotinus: the Road to Reality* (Cambridge 1967); H.-R. Schwyzer, *RE* article, 'Plotinos', Band XXI.1 (1951) cols. 471–592; J. Trouillard, *La Purification plotinienne* (Paris 1955), and *La Procession plotinienne* (Paris 1955).

The standard work on Plotinus' mysticism is R. Arnou, *Le Désir de Dieu dans la philosophie de Plotin* (Paris 1921, 2nd ed., Rome 1968). Cf. also the more recent discussions of P. Henry (introduction to MacKenna pp. lxiv–lxx), E. R. Dodds, *Pagan and Christian in an Age of Anxiety*, ch. 3, pp. 69–101, and J. M. Rist, *Plotinus: the Road to Reality*, ch. 16, pp. 213–30.

4. PORPHYRY AND IAMBLICHUS

Editions and translations

PORPHYRY: *Sentences*, English translation by T. Davidson, *Journal of Speculative Philosophy III* (1869) 46–73; *De Antro Nympharum*, trans. Thomas Taylor, repr. in Kathleen Raine and G. M. Harper (ed.), *Thomas Taylor, the Platonist: Selected Writings*, pp. 295–342; *Ad Marcellam*, ed. with German translation and commentary, W. Pötscher (Leiden 1969); *Letter to Anebo*, ed. with Italian translation, A. R. Sodano (Naples 1958); *De Regressu Animae*, fragments assembled from Augustine's *City of God* in Bidez, *Vie de Porphyre*, pp. 27*–44*; *Miscellaneous Inquiries*, ed. with commentary, H. Dörrie, *Porphyrios' 'Symmikta Zetemata'* (Zetemata 20, Munich 1959). Nemesius, *On the Nature of Man*, our main source for the *Miscellaneous Inquiries*, is translated into English by W. Telfer (Library of Christian Classics, London 1955).

Anonymous *Parmenides* commentary, ed. with French translation and notes by P. Hadot, *Porphyre et Victorinus*, vol. II.

IAMBLICHUS: *De Mysteriis*, ed. with French translation, E. des Places (Budé, Paris 1966); English translation (with Porphyry's *Letter to Anebo*), A. Wilder (New York 1911); *On the Soul* (fragments preserved by Stobaeus), French translation with notes, A.-J. Festugière, *Révélation d'Hermès Trismégiste*, vol. III, appendix I, pp. 171–264. A complete edition, with translation and commentary, of all Iamblichus' fragments, by Professors J. Dillon and C. Zintzen, is in preparation.

SALLUSTIUS: English translation, with introduction and commentary, A. D. Nock (Cambridge 1926, repr. 1966); text and French translation, G. Rochefort (Budé, Paris 1960).

General

The best account of later Neoplatonism is that of A. C. Lloyd, *Cambridge History of Later Greek and Early Medieval Philosophy*, part IV, chs. 17–19 (pp. 271–325), chapter 18 (pp. 283–301) being devoted to Porphyry and Iamblichus.

On Porphyry cf. J. Bidez, *Vie de Porphyre* (Ghent 1913, repr. Hildesheim 1964), discussed above p. 99 n. 1; R. Beutler, *RE* article, 'Porphyrios', Band XXII. 1 (1953) cols. 175–313; *Entretiens Hardt XII*, 'Porphyre', containing papers by H. Dörrie, J.-H. Waszink, W.

Theiler, P. Hadot, A. R. Sodano, J. Pépin and R. Walzer (Van-doeuvres-Geneva 1966); P. Hadot, *Porphyre et Victorinus* (2 vols., Paris 1968).

No full-length account of Iamblichus exists in any language; on his thought cf. K. Praechter, *Richtungen und Schulen im Neuplatonismus*, Genethliakon C. Robert (Berlin 1910) pp. 105–56, J. Bidez, 'Le Philosophe Jamblique et son école', *Revue des études grecques* 32 (1919) 29–40, and pp. xix–xxiii of Dodds' introduction to his edition of Proclus' *Elements*, as well as many pages of his commentary.

On the conflict between Neoplatonism and Christianity cf. E. R. Dodds, *Pagan and Christian in an Age of Anxiety*, ch. 4 (pp. 102–38); P. de Labriolle, *La Réaction paienne* (Paris 1934); R. Walzer, *Galen on Jews and Christians* (Oxford 1949); *Origen: Contra Celsum*, trans. H. Chadwick (Cambridge 1953); A. Momigliano (ed.), *The Conflict between Paganism and Christianity in the Fourth Century* (Oxford 1963); J. Pépin, *Théologie cosmique et théologie chrétienne* (Paris 1964). The fragments of Porphyry's polemic were edited by A. Harnack, 'Abhandlungen der preussischen Akademie der Wissenschaften', *Phil.-hist. Kl.* 1916. 1. The bulk of them derive from the *Apocriticus* of the Christian apologist Macarius Magnes, trans. by T. W. Crafer (London 1919).

On the *Chaldaean Oracles* cf. H. Lewy, *Chaldaean Oracles and Theurgy* (Cairo 1956, reviewed by E. R. Dodds, *Harvard Theological Review* LIV (1961) 263–73) and W. Theiler, *Die Chaldäischen Orakel und die Hymnen des Synesios* (Halle 1942), repr. in his *Forschungen zum Neuplatonismus* (Berlin 1966), pp. 252–301. A new edition of their fragments by E. des Places has just appeared in the Budé series; (cf. Addenda below).

On theurgy cf. E. R. Dodds, 'Theurgy and its Relation to Neo-platonism', *Journal of Roman Studies* 37 (1947) 55–69, repr. as appendix 2 to *The Greeks and the Irrational* (Berkeley 1956), pp. 283–311; C. Zintzen, 'Die Wertung von Mystik und Magie in der Neuplatonischen Philosophie', *Rheinisches Museum NF.* 108 (1965) 71–100.

On Neoplatonic exegesis cf. Praechter's *Richtungen und Schulen* and J. Pépin, 'Porphyre, exégète d'Homère', *Entretiens Hardt XII*, pp. 231–72.

5. THE ATHENIAN AND ALEXANDRIAN
SCHOOLS

General

Recent discussions of the history of these schools and the relations between them include H. D. Saffrey, 'Le Chrétien Jean Philopon et la survivance de l'école d'Alexandrie au VIᵉ siècle', *Revue des études grecques* 72 (1954) 396–400; H. I. Marrou, 'Synesius of Cyrene and Alexandrian Neoplatonism', in A. Momigliano (ed.), *The Conflict between Paganism and Christianity in the Fourth Century* (Oxford 1963) pp. 126–50; A. Cameron, 'The last days of the Academy at Athens', *Proceedings of the Cambridge Philological Society* 195 (n. s. 15, 1969) 7–29; and, especially, the introductions to Westerink's edition (with English translation) of the *Anonymous Prolegomena to Platonic Philosophy* (Amsterdam 1962) and vol. 1 of Saffrey and Westerink's Budé *Platonic Theology* (pp. ix–lxxxix).

The most important work on later Neoplatonism is Dodds' edition of Proclus' *Elements* (cf. below under 'editions'). On Proclus' thought cf. also L. J. Rosán, *The Philosophy of Proclus* (New York 1949, with important bibliography; R. Beutler, *RE* article, 'Proklos', Band XXIII. 1 (1957) cols. 186–247; W. Beierwaltes, *Proklos: Grundzüge seiner Metaphysik* (Frankfurt 1965); A. C. Lloyd, *Cambridge History*, ch. 19 (pp. 302–25); A. E. Taylor, 'The philosophy of Proclus', *Proc. Aristotelian Society* XVIII (1918), repr. in Taylor's *Philosophical Studies* (London 1934), pp. 151–91; L. H. Grondijs, 'L'Ame, le nous et les hénades dans la théologie de Proclus', *Proc. Royal Netherlands Academy* n. s. 23. 2 (1960) 29–42. For an account of Proclus' commentaries cf. pp. 231–314 of the fourth edition of Whittaker's *Neoplatonists*.

A translation of Marinus' biography of Proclus will be found in Rosán's *Philosophy of Proclus*. Damascius' *Life of Isidorus* has recently been edited by C. Zintzen (Hildesheim 1967); the older edition of R. Asmus (Leipzig 1911) contains a German translation.

Editions and translations

Proclus, *Elements of Theology*, ed. with English translation, introduction and commentary, E. R. Dodds (2nd ed., Oxford 1963); French trans., with introduction and notes, J. Trouillard (Paris 1965). *Platonic Theology*, ed. with French trans., introduction and notes, H. D. Saffrey and L. G. Westerink (Budé series, Book 1, Paris 1968); Italian trans.,

A. Turolla (Bari 1957). *Alcibiades* commentary, English trans., W. O'Neill (The Hague 1965). *Timaeus* commentary, French trans., A.-J. Festugière (5 vols., Paris 1966-8). *Parmenides* commentary, French trans., A. E. Chaignet (3 vols., Paris 1900); the last part of the seventh book, extant only in William of Moerbeke's Latin translation, has been edited, with English translation and notes, by R. Klibansky, C. Labowsky and E. Anscombe (London 1953). The Greek text of the *Decem Dubitationes circa Providentiam*, *De Providentia et Fato* and *De Malorum Subsistentia*, formerly extant only in Latin, has been largely recovered and edited by H. Boese (Berlin 1960). The Greek text of the fragment *On the Hieratic Art* (*De Sacrificio et Magia*) was published by J. Bidez, *CMAG VI* (Brussels 1928) 148-51; Thomas Taylor's English paraphrase of Ficino's Latin version, published in the introduction to his translation of the Orphic hymns, is reprinted on pp. 194-7 of Raine and Harper, *Thomas Taylor, the Platonist*. The *Commentary on Euclid's Elements* is translated by G. R. Morrow (Princeton 1970).

Neither Ruelle's edition (2 vols., Paris 1889, repr. Amsterdam 1966) nor Chaignet's translation (3 vols., Paris 1898) of Damascius' *De Principiis* is satisfactory. A new edition by Mme. C. Galpérine is in preparation for the Budé series. On his thought cf. E. Bréhier, *L'Idée du néant et le problème de l'origine radicale dans le néoplatonisme grec*, reprinted in *Etudes de philosophie antique* pp. 248-83; R. Strömberg, 'Damascius: his Personality and Importance', *Eranos* 44 (1946) 175-92.

On Philoponus cf. S. Sambursky, *The Physical World of Late Antiquity* (London 1962); for a selection of his texts, in German translation, see W. Böhm, *Johannes Philoponus; Ausgewählte Schriften* (Munich 1967).

6. INFLUENCES

(*i*) For general surveys of Neoplatonism's later influence cf R. Klibansky, *The Continuity of the Platonic Tradition during the Middle Ages* (2nd ed., London 1951) and the last chapter of Whittaker's *Neoplatonists* (4th ed. pp. 185-204). For surveys of the earlier period, down to the eleventh century, see parts v–viii of the *Cambridge History of Later Greek and Early Medieval Philosophy*, including contributions by R. A. Markus on Marius Victorinus and Augustine, I. P. Sheldon-Williams on Greek Christian Platonism from the Cappadocians to

Maximus and Eriugena, H. Liebeschütz on Western Christian thought from Boethius to Anselm, and R. Walzer on Early Islamic philosophy (with special emphasis on al-Farabi). Volume 1 of the *Encyclopédie de la Pleiade* History of Philosophy includes sections on Greek Patristic and Byzantine thought by B. Tatakis, Medieval Jewish philosophy by A. Neher, Islamic philosophy to Averroes by H. Corbin, O. Yahia and S. H. Nasr, and Medieval Western philosophy by J. Jolivet.

Both the histories just referred to contain important bibliographies. A list of some important studies on Medieval Platonism will be found in W. Beierwaltes (ed.), *Platonismus in der Philosophie des Mittelalters* (Darmstadt 1969), bibliographical references to works dealing with Greek influence on Arabic thought in F. E. Peters, *Aristotle and the Arabs* (London and New York 1968), and a bibliography of works on Renaissance Neoplatonism in P. O. Kristeller, *Eight Philosophers of the Italian Renaissance* (London 1965). Cf. also the bibliographical references in Gilson's *History of Christian Philosophy in the Middle Ages* (London 1955).

(*ii*) Pseudo-Dionysius' *Divine Names* and *Mystical Theology* are translated by C. E. Rolt (London 1920, repr. 1966). On his works and their sources cf. H. Koch, *Ps.-Dionysius Areopagita in seinen Beziehungen zum Neuplatonismus und Mysterienwesen (Forschungen zur Christlichen Literatur und Dogmengeschichte* I. 2–3, Mainz 1900); R. Roques, *L'Univers Dionysien* (Paris 1954); E. Corsini, *Il trattato De divinis nominibus dello Pseudo-Dionigi e i commenti neoplatonici al Parmenide* (Turin 1962).

On Byzantine thought cf. also J. Daniélou, *Platonisme et Théologie Mystique* (Paris 1963, on Gregory of Nyssa); B. Tatakis, *La Philosophie Byzantine* (Paris 1949); V. Lossky, *The Mystical Theology of the Eastern Church* (English trans., London 1957); E. von Ivánka, *Plato Christianus: Übernahme und Umgestaltung des Platonismus durch die Väter* (Einsiedeln 1964); J. M. Hussey, *Church and Learning in the Byzantine Empire 867–1185* (New York 1937); C. Zervos, *Un Philosophe néoplatonicien du XIᵉ siècle: Michel Psellos* (Paris 1920); F. Masai, *Pléthon et le platonisme de Mistra* (Paris 1956); S. Runciman, *The Last Byzantine Renaissance* (Cambridge 1970); K. Setton, The Byzantine Background to the Italian Renaissance', *Proc. American Philosophical Society* vol. c (1956) 1–76.

(*iii*) English translations by G. Lewis of the Arabic paraphrases of Plotinus will be found in the second volume of Henry and Schwyzer's larger edition of the *Enneads*. On Neoplatonic influence on the Medieval Arabic tradition cf. also R. Walzer, *Greek into Arabic: Essays on Islamic Philosophy* (Oxford 1962); F. E. Peters, *Aristotle and the Arabs* (London and New York 1968); Averroes, *Incoherence of the Incoherence*, trans. with notes by S. van den Bergh (2 vols., London 1954); S. H. Nasr, *Three Moslem Sages: Avicenna, Suhrawardi, Ibn 'Arabi* (Harvard 1964); S. M. Afnan, *Avicenna* (London 1958); L. Gardet, *La Pensée réligieuse d'Avicenne* (Paris 1951); F. Rahman, *Prophecy in Islam* (London 1958); A. E. Affifi, *The Mystical Philosophy of Ibn al-'Arabi* (Cambridge 1939); H. Corbin, *Avicenna and the Visionary Recital* (English trans., London and New York 1960), and *Creative Imagination in the Sufism of Ibn 'Arabi* (English trans., London 1969).

(*iv*) On Neoplatonic influences on Augustine and other late Latin writers cf. P. Henry, *Plotin et l'occident* (Louvain 1934); P. Courcelle, *Les Lettres grecques en occident de Macrobe à Cassiodore* (2nd ed., Paris 1948), English trans., *Late Latin Writers and their Greek Sources* (Harvard 1969); J. Guitton, *Le Temps et l'eternité chez Plotin et Saint Augustin* (3rd ed., Paris 1959); W. Theiler, *Porphyrios und Augustin* (Halle 1933), repr. in *Forschungen zum Neuplatonismus* (Berlin 1966) pp. 160–251; E. Gilson, *The Christian Philosophy of Saint Augustine* (English trans., London 1961); R. J. O'Connell, *St. Augustine's Early Theory of Man*, A.D. 386–391 (Harvard 1968), and *St. Augustine's Confessions* (Harvard 1969).

On Neoplatonism and Medieval thought cf. also E. Gilson, *History of Christian Philosophy in the Middle Ages* (London 1955); E. von Ivánka, *Plato Christianus* (Einsiedeln 1964); W. Beierwaltes (ed.), *Platonismus in der Philosophie des Mittelalters* (Darmstadt 1969); C. S. Lewis, *The Discarded Image* (Cambridge 1964); M. Cappuyns, *Jean Scot Érigène: sa vie, son oeuvre, sa pensée* (Louvain /Paris 1933, repr. 1964); H. D. Saffrey, 'L'État actuel des recherches sur le livre des causes comme source de la métaphysique au moyen age', *Miscellanea Medievalia II* (*Die Metaphysik im Mittelalter*, Berlin 1963) 267–81; W. Beierwaltes, 'Der Kommentar zum *liber de causis* als neuplatonisches Element in der Philosophie des Thomas von Aquin', *Philos. Rundschau* 11 (1963) 192–215; J. Péghaire, 'L'Axiome, *'Bonum est diffusivum sui*' dans le néoplatonisme et le thomisme', *Revue de l'Université d'Ottawa*, section spéciale, vol. 1 (1932) 5–30; K. Kremer, *Die Neu-platonische Seinsphilosophie und ihre Wirkung auf Thomas von Aquin* (Leiden 1966); R. Klibansky, 'Ein Proklos-Fund und seine Bedeutung', *Sitzungsberichte der Akademie der Wissenschaften Heidelberg, philos.-hist. Klasse*, 1928–9, abh. 5; 'Plato's *Parmenides* in the Middle Ages and Renaissance', *Medieval and Renaissance Studies I.* 2 (London 1943), 281–333.

(*v*) English translations of Renaissance Neoplatonic texts include NICHOLAS CUSANUS, *Of Learned Ignorance*, trans. Fr. G. Heron (London 1954); PICO DELLA MIRANDOLA, *On the Dignity of Man, On Being and Unity* and *Heptaplus* (Library of Liberal Arts, Indianapolis/New York 1965); BRUNO, *Cause, Principle and Unity*, trans. J. Lindsay (London 1964), *Heroic Frenzies*, trans. P. E. Memmo Jr. (Chapel Hill, N.C. 1966). FICINO's *Theologia Platonica* is being translated into French (3 vols. published, Paris 1964–) by R. Marcel, who has also translated his commentary on Plato's *Symposium* (Paris 1956). Cf. also P. O. Kristeller, *Renaissance Thought* (New York 1961), *Eight Philosophers of the Italian Renaissance* (including, among the Platonists, FICINO, PICO, PATRIZZI and BRUNO, London 1965), and *The Philosophy of Marsilio Ficino* (New York 1943); Nesca C. Robb, *Neoplatonism of the Italian Renaissance* (London 1935); Edgar Wind, *Pagan Mysteries in the Renaissance* (2nd ed., London 1967); D. P. Walker, *Spiritual and Demonic Magic from Ficino to Campanella* (London 1958); L. Miles, *John Colet and the Platonic Tradition* (La Salle, Ill., 1961); Frances A. Yates, *Giordano Bruno and the Hermetic Tradition* (London 1964).

(*vi*) On post-Renaissance influences cf. A. Lovejoy, *The Great Chain of Being* (Harvard 1936); H. A. Wolfson, *The Philosophy of Spinoza* (2 vols., Harvard 1934); E. Bréhier, *Néoplatonisme et spinozisme*, repr. in *Etudes de philosophie antique*, pp. 289–91; C. A. Patrides (ed.), *The Cambridge Platonists* (London 1969); G. W. F. Hegel, *Lectures on the History of Philosophy*, vol. II (trans. E. S. Haldane and F. H. Simson, London 1894); R. M. Mossé-Bastide, *Bergson et Plotin* (Paris 1959); Kathleen Raine, *Blake and Tradition* (2 vols., London 1969); Kathleen Raine and G. M. Harper (ed.), *Thomas Taylor, the Platonist: Selected Writings* (London and New York 1969).

ADDENDA

The following works have appeared since the first draft of this book.

Section 3

D. Roloff (ed.), *Plotin: Die Gross-schrift*, III, 8–v, 8–v, 5–II, 9 (running commentary on the treatises in question) Berlin 1970.

Section 4

Oracles Chaldaiques, ed. E. des Places (Budé, Paris 1971). Text and French translation of the fragments of the *Chaldaean Oracles* and Psellus' commentary, together with other relevant texts from Psellus and Proclus' *Eclogae de Philosophia Chaldaica*. Porphyry, *De Antro Nympharum*. Text and English translation, Arethusa Monographs 1 (Buffalo, N.Y. 1970).

Section 5

Proclus, *Republic* commentary, French trans., A.-J. Festugière (3 vols, Paris 1970).

Index